PRINCIPLES OF INTERNATIONAL FINANCE

Principles of
INTERNATIONAL
FINANCE

Daniel R. Kane

CROOM HELM
London • New York • Sydney

© 1988 Daniel R. Kane
Croom Helm Ltd, Provident House,
Burrell Row, Beckenham, Kent BR3 1AT

Croom Helm Australia, 44–50 Waterloo Road,
North Ryde, 2113, New South Wales

Published in the USA by
Croom Helm
in association with Routledge, Chapman & Hall, Inc.
29 West 35th Street, New York, NY 10001

British Library Cataloguing in Publication Data

Kane, Daniel R.
    Principles of international finance.
    1. International finance
    I. Title
    332'.042   HG3881

    ISBN 0-7099-1584-5
    ISBN 0-7099-3134-4 Pbk

Library of Congress Cataloging-in-Publication Data

Kane, Daniel R., 1949–
    Principles of international finance.

    Bibliography: p.
    Includes index.
    1. International finance. I. Title.
HG3881.K263 1987   332.042   87-24388
ISBN 0-7099-1584-5
ISBN 0-7099-3134-4 (pbk.)

Filmset by Mayhew Typesetting, Bristol, England
Printed and bound in Great Britain by Mackays of Chatham Ltd, Kent

Contents

Figures

Tables

Preface

In recent years, the growing interest in international finance has created demand for a textbook which is able to present the subject to a wider audience of economics and business undergraduates. At the same time, the trend towards separate courses in international trade and finance has given rise to the need for a text specifically written for finance courses, without the extra material — and hence extra cost — of trade theory. *Principles of International Finance* has been written specifically to fulfil these needs and is aimed at the undergraduate studying international finance for the first time.

The structure of the book has been designed so that it may be adopted as a complete one-semester course in international finance. It is divided into four parts, each representing one of the major divisions of the topic, and each chapter has a summary and questions for discussion which can be used with the concepts for review as revision aids and tests of understanding as the course proceeds.

The contents of the book have been 'fine-tuned' in use over the years in courses the author has given at various levels and in different countries. Experience in these courses has also shown that a text which is to be accessible to a wide range of students should be non-mathematical, presume no more than a general background in macroeconomics, and be written in a clear and straightforward style. All of these factors were taken into account in the writing of this book.

I wish to thank the following friends and colleagues for their perceptive comments and suggested improvements to various chapters: Michael Davenport, Ho Soo Hang, Basant Kapur, Colin Kirkpatrick, Linda Low, Ow Chwee Huay, Roger Sandilands, Colin Simkin, Tan Hock and Fred Thoele.

Above all, however, I wish to thank my wife, June Kane, who read and re-read the text, editing and brainstorming with me at each stage, and who ultimately contributed almost as much to the work as I did.

Daniel R. Kane

To June
Even more of all you never wanted to know about
economics . . .

Part One

The Foreign Exchange Market and the Balance of Payments

The foreign exchange market (Chapter 1) is the market in which foreign currencies are bought and sold. As such, it is an integral component of international finance.

Currencies are transacted to finance international trade and to facilitate international capital flows, but their conversion involves uncertainty. This creates risk which can either be eliminated (to minimise losses) or exploited (to maximise profits). The extent to which this risk is averted or accepted determines the use to which different types of foreign exchange rates and trading techniques are put. These are examined in Chapter 2.

Both trade and capital flows are recorded in the balance of payments, which is a systematic record of a country's international transactions. The balance of payments, which is the subject of Chapter 3, indicates whether a country is in external equilibrium or disequilibrium and the extent to which corrective policies, if any, should be implemented.

1

The Foreign Exchange Market

The **foreign exchange market** is:

A market for the purchase and sale of foreign currencies (foreign exchange).

It has no single physical location, but exists where and when there is a need to transact foreign currencies. Markets are principally found in leading financial centres such as London and New York and consist of market-makers, who are prepared to deal in foreign currencies. These market-makers comprise banks and brokers who are prepared to buy and sell foreign currencies from other banks, brokers, corporations, the general public and even governments.

The price at which currencies are transacted is the **foreign exchange rate**, which is:

The price of one currency expressed in terms of another.

It indicates the number of units of foreign currency which buyers and sellers are prepared to exchange for units of domestic or other foreign currency. More specifically, the exchange rate can be expressed as the number of units of domestic currency which buyers and sellers are prepared to exchange for one unit of foreign currency. For example, if one pound sterling trades for two US dollars, the exchange rate from a UK perspective would be 50 pence per dollar (£0.50/$) and from a US perspective, two dollars per pound ($2/£).

The exchange rate will be transmitted via telecommunications to markets throughout the world and will prevail for as long as buyers and sellers are willing to transact dollars and sterling at this particular rate. More specifically, it will prevail until there is a change in one or more of the variables underlying the demand for or supply of either dollars or sterling.

DEMAND FOR FOREIGN EXCHANGE

The demand for foreign exchange arises from the need to convert domestic currency into foreign currencies. These conversions are generally undertaken to pay for:

(i) Goods and services purchased overseas. A US resident, for example, buying a car from the UK, will need sterling to pay for this import. Similarly, a US tourist in England will need sterling to pay for services consumed whilst in that country.

(ii) Overseas assets, which may take the form of direct investment, such as the construction by a US corporation of a plant in the UK, or portfolio investment, which might arise, for example, when US residents purchase UK government bonds or open sterling bank accounts.

Foreign demand for sterling is determined by a variety of factors consisting of (but not confined to):

1. The price of sterling (exchange rate) $P_£$
2. The sterling price of UK products P_{UK}
3. The price of competing products P_C
4. Foreign incomes Y
5. UK interest rates i_{UK}

(Other, less quantifiable factors include preferences, expectations and the weather.)

The relationship between the demand for sterling and these variables can be expressed notationally:

$$Q_{D£} = f(P_£, P_{UK}, P_C, Y, i_{UK}). \tag{1-1}$$

This relationship can also be expressed in the form of a simple demand curve (Figure 1.1), which relates the demand for sterling (horizontal axis) to the price of sterling expressed in US dollars — the exchange rate (vertical axis). (The vertical axis always depicts the price of whichever currency appears on the horizontal axis.)

Changes in the sterling exchange rate, other variables held constant, change the quantity of sterling demanded (movement along the demand curve). In notational form, the relationship between changes

Figure 1.1: The demand for sterling (non-exchange rate variables held constant). Changes in the exchange rate lead to changes in the quantity of sterling demanded (movements along the demand curve).

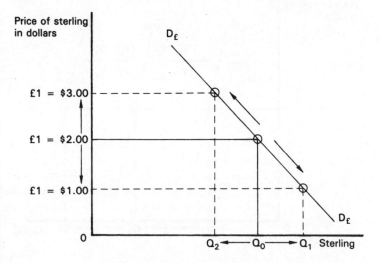

in this exchange rate and quantity demanded is expressed as:

$$\Delta P_£ \rightarrow \Delta Q_{D£} (\bar{P}_{UK}, \bar{P}_C, \bar{Y}, \bar{i}_{UK})$$

where the bars indicate that the variables remain unchanged. This relationship is also illustrated in Figure 1.1, which shows, for example, that a decrease in the price of sterling (**depreciation**) from £1 = \$2.00 to £1 = \$1.00 increases the quantity of sterling demanded from Q_0 to Q_1 since each dollar now buys more sterling. Similarly, an increase in the price of sterling (**appreciation**) from £1 = \$2.00 to £1 = \$3.00 decreases the quantity of sterling demanded from Q_0 to Q_2, since each dollar now buys less sterling. Consequently, an exchange rate depreciation increases the quantity of currency demanded, while an exchange rate appreciation decreases the quantity of currency demanded. This can be summarised as:

Changes in exchange rates, all other variables held constant, result in changes in the quantity of foreign exchange demanded which are shown as movements *along* the demand curve.

Changes in variables other than the sterling exchange rate change

5

Figure 1.2: The demand for sterling (exchange rate held constant). Changes in non-exchange rate variables lead to changes in the demand for sterling (shifts of the demand curve).

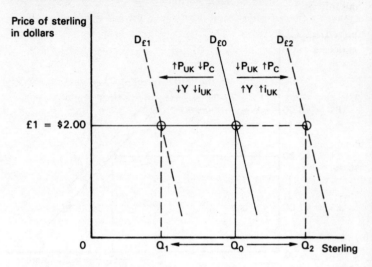

the demand for sterling (shift of the demand curve). This relationship can be expressed as:

$$\Delta P_{UK}, \Delta P_C, \Delta Y, \Delta i_{UK} \rightarrow \Delta Q_{D£} \ (\overline{P_£}).$$

It is illustrated in Figure 1.2 which shows, for example, that a decrease in UK interest rates, which reduces foreign demand for UK investments, shifts the demand curve for sterling to the left from $D_{£0}$ to $D_{£1}$, and reduces the demand for sterling from Q_0 to Q_1 even though the price of sterling remains unchanged. Correspondingly, an increase in foreign incomes, which increases foreign demand for UK products, shifts the demand curve for sterling to the right from $D_{£0}$ to $D_{£2}$ and increases the demand for sterling from Q_0 to Q_2, even though the price of sterling again remains unchanged. These changes can be summarised as:

Changes in variables other than the exchange rate result in changes in the demand for foreign exchange which are shown as *shifts* of the demand curve.

ELASTICITY AND THE DEMAND FOR FOREIGN EXCHANGE

Price elasticity of demand determines the extent to which price changes influence changes in the demand for and hence expenditure on individual products. This is illustrated in Figure 1.3, which shows variations in elasticity along a linear demand curve.[1]

Figure 1.3: Demand and the price elasticity of demand. Price elasticity of demand determines the extent to which price changes influence changes in demand and product expenditure.

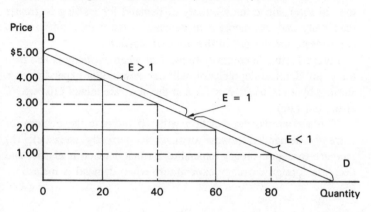

A fall in price from $4 to $3 along the *elastic* segment of the demand curve (E > 1) causes quantity demanded to increase from 20 to 40 units, while a fall in price from $2 to $1 along the *inelastic* segment of the demand curve (E < 1) causes quantity demanded to increase from 60 to 80 units. Expenditure has *increased* from $80 to $120 in the former case and *decreased* from $120 to $80 in the latter. In other words, a fall in price will cause total expenditure to increase when demand is elastic but decrease when demand is inelastic (*ceteris paribus*). A rise in price will have the opposite effect.

Changes in foreign exchange rates exert a similar impact on the demand for foreign exchange (since the foreign exchange rate is the price of one currency expressed in terms of another). The impact of such changes will depend on the elasticity of demand for foreign exchange.

Exchange rate depreciation

The depreciation of a currency (fall in price) will always increase the quantity of currency demanded (assuming a downward sloping demand curve). Whether or not foreign currency expenditure on the currency also increases, however, will depend on the currency's price (exchange rate) elasticity of demand.

Figure 1.4(a) shows the effect of a depreciation in sterling from £1 = $3.00 to £1 = $2.00. Dollar expenditure on sterling *increases* by a net £170 (£100 × $2/£ at the new rate minus £10 × $3/£ at the old rate), since the elasticity of demand for sterling is greater than unity and the increase in demand is more than sufficient to compensate for the fall in the price of sterling.

Figure 1.4(b), in contrast, shows that when elasticity is less than unity, an identical depreciation will *decrease* dollar expenditure on sterling by a net $6 (£12 × $2/£ at the new rate minus £10 × $3/£ at the old rate).

In other words, depreciation will: (i) increase the quantity of currency demanded (unless demand is perfectly inelastic); (ii) increase foreign currency expenditure when demand is elastic, and decrease foreign currency expenditure when demand is inelastic.

Exchange rate appreciation

The effect of appreciation is essentially the converse of currency depreciation, and will: (i) decrease the quantity of currency demanded (unless demand is perfectly inelastic); (ii) decrease foreign currency expenditure when demand is elastic, and increase foreign currency expenditure when demand is inelastic.

The relationship between elasticity and the demand for foreign exchange also influences the supply of foreign exchange.

SUPPLY OF FOREIGN EXCHANGE

> *The supply of one currency is simultaneously determined by the demand for another currency in the foreign exchange market.*

For example, overseas demand for UK goods, services and assets will generate demand for sterling. This has to be purchased in the foreign exchange market with foreign currencies such as the dollar.

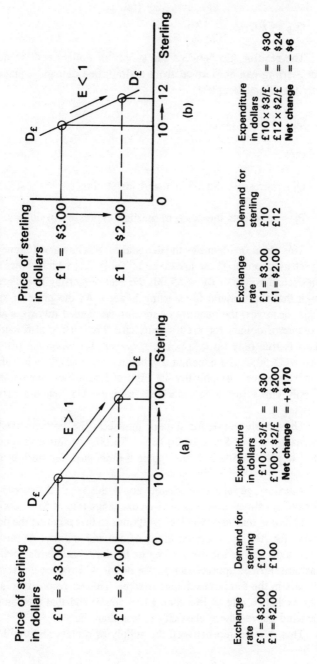

Figure 1.4: Sterling depreciation and the elasticity of demand for sterling. Changes in foreign currency expenditure on sterling resulting from a sterling depreciation depend on the elasticity of demand for sterling.

(a)

Exchange rate	Demand for sterling	Expenditure in dollars	
£1 = $3.00	£10	£10 × $3/£	= $30
£1 = $2.00	£100	£100 × $2/£	= $200
		Net change	**= +$170**

(b)

Exchange rate	Demand for sterling	Expenditure in dollars	
£1 = $3.00	£10	£10 × $3/£	= $30
£1 = $2.00	£12	£12 × $2/£	= $24
		Net change	**= −$6**

The supply of dollars is consequently determined by the demand for sterling. This can be expressed as:

$$Q_{S\$} = f(Q_{D£}). \tag{1-2}$$

The relationship between the supply of dollars and the demand for sterling can be derived from a simplified demand equation for sterling. For example:

$$Q_{D£} = 10 - 2P_£$$

where:

$Q_{D£}$ represents the US demand for sterling

$P_£$ represents the price of sterling expressed in dollars.

This equation identifies the demand for sterling at different prices (exchange rates). These are given in Table 1.1, which shows that at an exchange rate of £1 = $5.00, the cost of sterling in dollars is so high that the demand for sterling is zero. As the price of sterling falls, however, the quantity of sterling demanded increases and the volume of dollars required to purchase this sterling also increases. This is true only up to a point, however, for when the price falls below $2.50, dollar expenditures begin to decline. Data in Table 1.1 are reproduced graphically in Figure 1.5, which shows the US supply curve for dollars derived from the US demand curve for sterling.

The supply curve for dollars intersects the vertical axis at an exchange rate of $1 = £0.20 (£1 = $5.00). At this exchange rate, the supply of dollars is zero since the demand for sterling is also zero.

At exchange rates immediately above this level, the supply curve for dollars slopes upwards until an exchange rate of $1 = £0.40 (£1 = $2.50) is reached, which corresponds to that point on the demand curve for sterling where elasticity of demand is unity. At this level, the supply curve for dollars begins to slope backwards, indicating that any further appreciation in the dollar will reduce the supply of dollars in the foreign exchange market. This corresponds to a sterling exchange rate of less than £1 = $2.50 and that portion of the demand curve where elasticity is less than unity.

This relationship between the supply of dollars and the demand

Figure 1.5: US supply of dollars and US demand for sterling. The US supply curve for dollars represents dollar expenditure on sterling and is derived from the US demand curve for sterling.

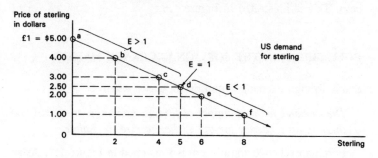

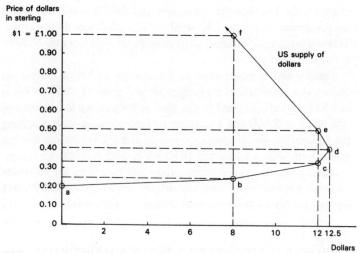

Table 1.1: Dollar expenditures and the demand for sterling. Dollar expenditures on sterling vary with the price of sterling (the exchange rate).

$P_£$	$Q_{D£}$	Dollar Expenditures
$5.00	0	$0
$4.00	2	$8.00
$3.00	4	$12.00
$2.50	5	$12.50
$2.00	6	$12.00
$1.00	8	$8.00

for sterling illustrates that the supply of one currency is derived from the demand for another and that the supply of and demand for foreign exchange are little more than opposite sides of the same coin. This is illustrated in Figure 1.6.[2]

EQUILIBRIUM IN THE FOREIGN EXCHANGE MARKET

Stable foreign exchange equilibrium arises when:

The demand for and supply of foreign exchange are equal and there is no tendency for the exchange rate to change.

Foreign exchange equilibrium is illustrated in Figure 1.7. As an example, the UK demand for dollars and the US supply of dollars are combined, as are the UK supply of and US demand for sterling. This produces equilibrium quantities and exchange rates for both the dollar and sterling.

Equilibrium is established in the foreign exchange market for dollars at a hypothetical exchange rate and quantity of $1 = £0.33 and $30 respectively, and in the market for sterling at a reciprocal rate of £1 = $3.00 and a quantity of £10, obtained by multiplying the equilibrium dollar exchange rate in sterling by the equilibrium quantity of dollars transacted (£0.33/$ × $30 = £10).

Equilibrium foreign exchange rates and quantities for all traded currencies are similarly mutually determined by the market demand for and supply of the individual currencies concerned.

EQUILIBRIUM DISTURBANCES IN THE FOREIGN EXCHANGE MARKET

The foreign exchange market is affected by disturbances which, for individual currencies, may be of either domestic or foreign origin.

Domestic disturbances

Consider the potential foreign exchange impact on the US dollar and the Deutsche Mark of a domestic (German) disturbance resulting from an increase in German demand for US cars, caused by an increase in German incomes.

The increase in German incomes prompts a non-exchange rate

Figure 1.6: US demand for sterling and the US supply of dollars and UK demand for dollars and the UK supply of sterling. The US demand for sterling determines the US supply of dollars and the UK demand for dollars determines the UK supply of sterling.

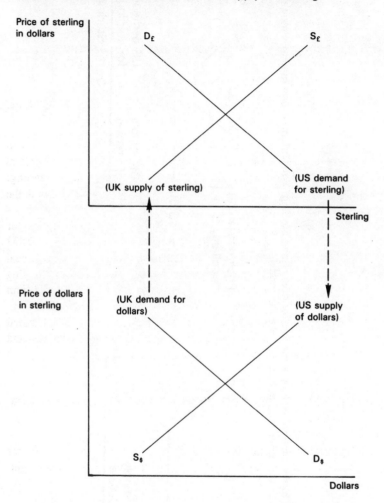

Figure 1.7: Equilibrium in the foreign exchange market for dollars and sterling. Equilibrium in one market simultaneously determines equilibrium in the other market in a two-market model.

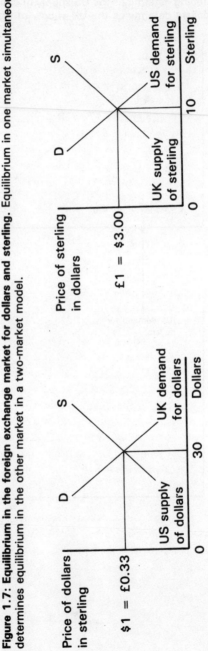

related increase in German demand for US cars, which leads to an increase in German demand for dollars and an increase in the German supply of Deutsche Marks with which to purchase the dollars. These increases result in an upward shift to the right of the demand curve for dollars (D_1) (Figure 1.8(a)) and in a downward shift to the right of the supply curve for Deutsche Marks (S_1) (Figure 1.8(b)). The impact of these disturbances will depend on the extent of government/central bank intervention (if any) in the foreign exchange market.

In the absence of official intervention, the increase in the demand for dollars from a hypothetical $10 to $15 and the increase in the supply of Deutsche Marks from a hypothetical DM 20 to DM 45 will result, *ceteris paribus*, in the appreciation of the dollar and the depreciation of the Deutsche Mark from a hypothetical equilibrium exchange rate of $1 = DM 2.00 (DM 1 = $0.50) to a new equilibrium exchange rate of $1 = DM 3.00 (DM 1 = $0.33).

The prospect of an appreciating dollar/depreciating Deutsche Mark might conflict with a policy of exchange rate stability, however, and prompt official intervention in the foreign exchange market to stabilise exchange rates. This might take two forms:

The extra demand for dollars/supply of Deutsche Marks might be channelled away from the foreign exchange market to avoid disturbing the equilibrium exchange rate of $1 = DM 2.00 (DM 1 = $0.50). This could be done in two ways: The US authorities in the form of the US central bank (Federal Reserve Board) could buy/sell the extra Deutsche Marks/dollars directly (adding to US reserve holdings of Deutsche Marks) or, more likely, the German authorities in the form of the German central bank (Bundesbank) could purchase the extra Deutsche Marks with dollars held as part of Germany's **foreign exchange reserves**. These consist of foreign currencies (principally dollars) and constitute the receipts from and payments for overseas transactions. This latter option would deplete German reserve holdings and would be sustained only for as long as reserves were available, or for as long as additional dollars could be borrowed from other countries or from official institutions, such as the International Monetary Fund (IMF). Either way, the extra demand for dollars is satisfied with central bank supplies amounting to $Q^* - 10$. The extra supply of Deutsche Marks is absorbed through central bank purchases amounting to $Q^{**} - 20$ (Figures 1.9(a) and (b) respectively).

Both the extra demand for dollars and the extra supply of Deutsche Marks are greater than they would be in the absence of

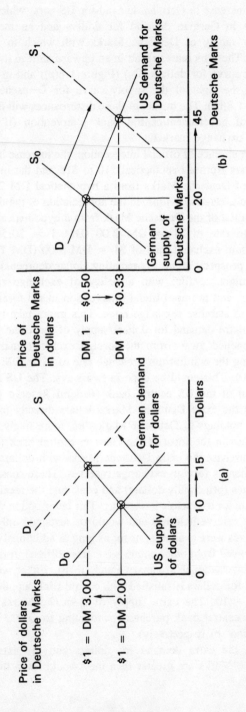

Figure 1.8: Demand for and supply of dollars and Deutsche Marks. Increased German demand for dollars shifts the demand curve for dollars up to the right (D_1) and the supply curve for Deutsche Marks down to right (S_1).

official intervention. Since the dollar has not been allowed to appreciate nor the Deutsche Mark to depreciate, dollar demand/ Deutsche Mark supply have risen above free market levels of $15 and DM 45 respectively. Official intervention has thus perpetuated and also magnified the effect of exchange rate disequilibria.

Official intervention to stabilise exchange rates could also take the form of attempts to restore the conditions which established the original exchange rate equilibrium of $1 = DM 2.00. This might be accomplished through the introduction of **exchange controls** which would directly restrict German purchases of dollars, or **import controls**, which would indirectly restrict German purchases of dollars through restrictions on the purchase of US automobiles. This would shift the demand curve for dollars back to D_0 (Figure 1.9(a)) and the supply curve for Deutsche Marks back to S_0 (Figure 1.9(b)), so restoring equilibrium at $1 = DM 2.00 and DM 1 = $0.50 respectively. Such controls enable countries to conserve scarce foreign exchange reserves, albeit at the cost of potential resource misallocation, and are frequently resorted to by countries whose economies or political philosophies cannot withstand sustained reserve depletions.

To summarise: the potential effects of a domestic (German) disturbance resulting from increased German demand for US automobiles, might be:

(i) a dollar appreciation and Deutsche Mark depreciation in the absence of official intervention in the foreign exchange market; or

(ii) the accumulation of US Deutsche Mark reserves if there is US intervention in the market to stabilise exchange rates; or, more likely,

(iii) the depletion of German dollar reserves and/or increased international borrowing to secure additional reserves if there is German intervention in the market to stabilise exchange rates; or

(iv) the introduction of exchange or import controls to stabilise exchange rates and conserve foreign exchange reserves.

Foreign disturbances

Consider the potential foreign exchange impact on the US dollar and the Deutsche Mark of a foreign (non-German) disturbance resulting from an increase in the number of US tourists visiting Germany, caused by an increase in US incomes.

17

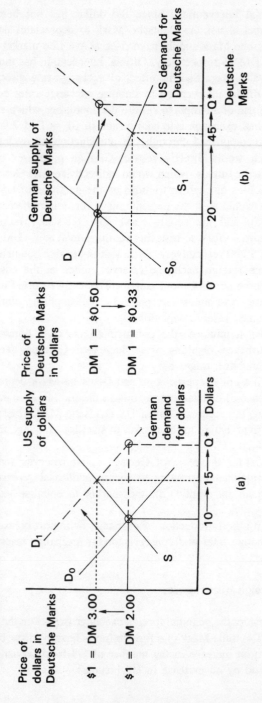

Figure 1.9: Official intervention and the demand for and supply of dollars and Deutsche Marks (increased dollar demand). Official intervention to stabilise the exchange rate at $1 = DM 2 (DM 1 = $0.50) results in a market demand for dollars of Q* and market supply of Deutsche Marks of Q**.

The increase in US incomes prompts a non-exchange rate related increase in US demand for German services, which leads to an increase in US demand for Deutsche Marks and an increase in the US supply of dollars with which to purchase the Deutsche Marks. These increases result in a shift down to the right of the supply curve for dollars (Figure 1.10(a)) and a shift up to the right of the demand curve for Deutsche Marks (Figure 1.10(b)).

In the absence of official intervention, the increased supply of dollars (S_1) (panel a) and the increased demand for Deutsche Marks (D_1) (panel b) will result in a depreciation of the dollar and an appreciation of the Deutsche Mark from a hypothetical equilibrium exchange rate of \$1 = DM 2.00 (DM 1 = \$0.50) to a new equilibrium exchange rate of \$1 = DM 1.50 (DM 1 = \$0.67).

As was the case with the domestic disturbance, a foreign disturbance and its consequences might be dealt with by official intervention. This might take the form of channelling the extra supply of dollars and demand for Deutsche Marks away from the market through central bank purchases of dollars and sales of Deutsche Marks. In this situation the supply of dollars will be Q* (panel a) and the demand for Deutsche Marks will be Q** (panel b), both of which will again be greater than if the market had been allowed to operate freely, since neither the dollar nor the Deutsche Mark has been allowed to depreciate/appreciate to limit the extra supply of and demand for each currency respectively.

Alternatively, the authorities might seek to limit dollar sales and Deutsche Mark purchases through direct controls — for example, quantitative restrictions on exchange transactions or measures to discourage foreign currency conversions. The effect of such controls would be to shift the supply curve for dollars and the demand curve for Deutsche Marks back to S_0 and D_0 respectively (Figure 1.10(a) and (b)).

The potential effects of a foreign (non-German) disturbance resulting from an increase in the number of US tourists visiting Germany may be summarised as:

(i) A dollar depreciation and Deutsche Mark appreciation in the absence of official intervention in the foreign exchange market; or

(ii) The accumulation of German dollar reserves if there is German intervention in the market to stabilise exchange rates; or, less likely,

(iii) The depletion of US Deutsche Mark reserves and/or

19

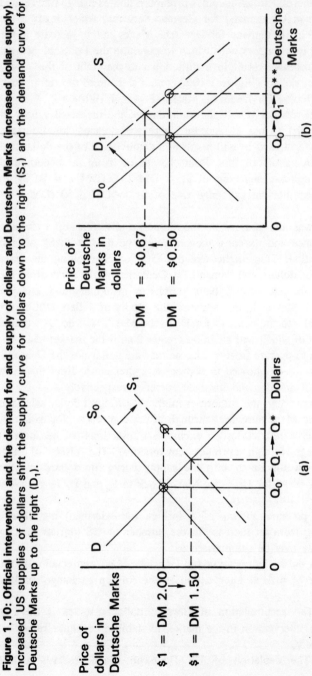

Figure 1.10: Official intervention and the demand for and supply of dollars and Deutsche Marks (increased dollar supply). Increased US supplies of dollars shift the supply curve for dollars down to the right (S_1) and the demand curve for Deutsche Marks up to the right (D_1).

increased international borrowing to secure additional reserves if there is US intervention in the market to stabilise exchange rates; or

(iv) The introduction of exchange controls to stabilise exchange rates and conserve foreign exchange reserves.

DISEQUILIBRIUM IN THE FOREIGN EXCHANGE MARKET

Central monetary authorities frequently intervene in foreign exchange markets to limit or prevent exchange rate adjustments which conflict with economic, social and even political objectives. The effect of this is to maintain currencies at overvalued or under-valued exchange rates. The resulting exchange rate disequilibria, however, can generate exchange rate pressures potentially leading to fundamental realignments of internationally agreed exchange rates. Such realignments became a feature of the post-war international monetary system and contributed to the eventual collapse of the existing order of administered exchange rates.

Overvalued currencies

Currencies are overvalued (relative to their equilibrium exchange rate) when their market supply exceeds their market demand. An increased supply of domestic currency caused, for example, by an increase in imports or foreign (outward) investment will lead to disequilibrium. Similarly, a decrease in the demand for domestic currency caused by a decrease in exports or foreign (inward) investment will also lead to disequilibrium. In both situations, the result will be a tendency for the domestic currency to depreciate relative to one or more foreign currencies. An example is given in Figure 1.11, where an increased supply (S_2) and/or reduced demand (D_2) of sterling causes sterling to depreciate to a new equilibrium exchange rate of less than £1 = \$2.80. Intervention to maintain the domestic currency at its original equilibrium rate, however, will perpetuate the excess supply of currency ($Q_S - Q_D$), and this will persist for as long as the central monetary authority is prepared to support this rate with sales of foreign currency reserves, or for as long as the factors accounting for the excess supply of domestic currency persist. The point will eventually be reached, however (in the absence of other corrective measures), when the exchange rate

Figure 1.11: Disequilibrium in the foreign exchange market for sterling. Official support for sterling at the overvalued exchange rate of £1 = $2.80 perpetuates a situation of excess supply relative to demand in the foreign exchange market.

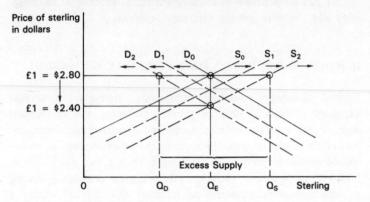

can no longer be supported and an exchange rate realignment becomes inevitable. A **devaluation**, which is an administered depreciation, will be necessary to restore equilibrium and equate market demand for and supply of the currency in foreign exchange markets. The longer corrective action is delayed, the greater the potential cost in terms of economic dislocation and reserve depletion.

One example of an overvalued currency is sterling in the early 1960s. Its exchange rate of £1 = $2.80 had been established in 1949, but it became increasingly apparent that this rate no longer reflected Britain's international trading competitiveness, since repeated attempts to increase exports and decrease imports by conventional measures such as fiscal policy had proved largely unsuccessful. Britain's international trading position continued to deteriorate and still the government resisted the potential solution of a sterling devaluation.

Exchange rate pressures were intensified, moreover, by two factors.

The first was **leads** and **lags**. Conversions out of sterling for foreign currency import payments and conversions into sterling of foreign currency export receipts were leaded (advanced) and lagged (delayed) respectively to benefit from an anticipated sterling realignment.[3] The effect of these leads and lags was to shift the sterling

22

supply and demand curves further to the right and left respectively, thereby intensifying exchange rate pressures.

The second factor was currency speculation. Speculators sold sterling to the Bank of England at $2.80 in the hope of buying back the currency at a new, lower exchange rate. This not only exacerbated exchange rate pressures (indicated by a further shift to the right in the sterling supply curve), but also contributed to a substantial depletion of UK exchange reserves.

Confronted with a misaligned exchange rate, rapidly depleting reserves and extensive overseas borrowing to secure additional reserves, the UK authorities eventually recognised the inevitable and, in November 1967, formally devalued sterling to £1 = $2.40.

Undervalued currencies

Currencies are undervalued (relative to their equilibrium exchange rate) when their market demand exceeds their market supply. Disequilibrium can result, for example, either from an increase in exports or inward investment, or from a decrease in imports or outward investment. In both situations, the result will be a tendency for the domestic currency to appreciate relative to one or more foreign currencies.

An example is given in Figure 1.12, which shows that increased demand (D_2) and reduced supply (S_2) of Deutsche Marks will cause the Deutsche Mark to appreciate to a new equilibrium exchange rate of DM 1 = $0.33. Intervention to maintain the exchange rate at the existing level of DM 1 = $0.25 will perpetuate excess demand for Deutsche Marks $(Q_D - Q_S)$, which will have to be satisfied through central bank sales of Deutsche Marks for whichever foreign currencies are tendered. This will continue for as long as the excess demand for Deutsche Marks persists and support operations continue.

Exchange rate pressures will also be intensified by the leading of export receipts and the lagging of import payments, and by the activities of speculators who will buy undervalued currencies in the hope of subsequently selling them at more favourable exchange rates. The effect of these influences will be to shift the demand and supply curves for the undervalued currency further to the right and the left respectively.

Whereas support operations by the central bank of an overvalued

Figure 1.12: Disequilibrium in the foreign exchange market for Deutsche Marks. Official support for the Deutsche Mark at the undervalued exchange rate of DM 1 = $0.25 perpetuates a situation of excess demand relative to supply in the foreign exchange market.

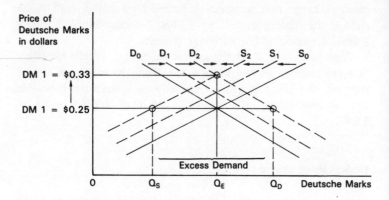

currency are constrained by the availability of foreign exchange reserves or additional borrowings, support operations by the central bank of an undervalued currency are less constrained, since they involve the purchase of foreign currencies with domestic currency which the central bank can create. The problem thus becomes one of excessive reserve augmentation rather than depletion. This is illustrated in Figure 1.12, where domestic currency sales ($Q_D - Q_S$) generate increases in reserves equivalent to ($Q_D - Q_S$) × $0.25.

This fact partly explains the asymmetry in the international exchange rate adjustment process which tends to favour creditor countries with undervalued currencies at the expense of debtor countries with overvalued currencies. The problem of an undervalued currency cannot be ignored indefinitely, however, for in the absence of a currency **revaluation**[4] (administered appreciation), the creation of domestic currency by central banks to finance support operations increases the domestic money supply. This might result in domestic inflation, which in turn will make exports less attractive and imports more attractive. Excess demand for domestic currency will consequently fall but at the expense of new or higher domestic inflation.

Inflation, of course, can be controlled through a successful contractionary open market operations policy which will sterilise any increase in the domestic money supply. (**Sterilisation** is neutralising the expansionary/contractionary impact of increases/ decreases in domestic liquidity.) Such a policy, however, would also neutralise the impact of the increased money supply on the relative prices of exports and imports. This would prevent exports/imports from decreasing/increasing and would consequently perpetuate the undervaluation of the domestic currency.

SUMMARY

The foreign exchange rate is the price of one currency expressed in terms of another. It is determined in the foreign exchange market where currencies are bought and sold.

The demand for foreign exchange arises from the need to pay for foreign goods and services and overseas assets. The demand for one currency simultaneously determines the supply of another in the foreign exchange market.

The demand for and supply of foreign exchange determine the foreign exchange rate. Increases in the demand for and decreases in the supply of foreign exchange result in exchange rate appreciations which increase the value of currencies. Decreases in the demand for and increases in the supply of foreign exchange result in exchange rate depreciations which decrease the value of currencies.

Currencies for which excess supply is artificially maintained are overvalued. Equilibrium is restored through exchange rate devaluations.

Currencies for which excess demand is artificially maintained are undervalued. Equilibrium is restored through exchange rate revaluations.

CONCEPTS FOR REVIEW

Appreciation

Depreciation

Devaluation

Exchange controls

Foreign exchange market

Foreign exchange rate

Foreign exchange reserves

Import controls

Leads and lags

Revaluation

Sterilisation

QUESTIONS FOR DISCUSSION

1. What determines the demand for foreign exchange? How do changes in these determinants affect the demand for foreign exchange?
2. Explain how the supply of foreign exchange is derived from the demand for foreign exchange.
3. Show how a domestic disturbance might result in the appreciation of a domestic currency.
4. What is meant by 'official intervention' in the foreign exchange market? Under what circumstances might such intervention result in the accumulation of foreign exchange reserves?
5. Explain, with the aid of diagrams, how leads and lags and currency speculation might exacerbate exchange rate pressures.

Notes

1. Linear demand curves, although a special case, do not detract from the validity of the analysis and greatly simplify exposition.
2. Analysis is confined to the elastic segment of the demand curve and the corresponding upward sloping portion of the supply curve to simplify exposition.
3. The cost of, or revenue from, a $100 import/export would have increased from £35.71 before devaluation ($100/$2.80/£) to £41.67 after devaluation ($100/$2.40/£).
4. Although the term 'upvaluation' is sometimes used by economic commentators, in general 'revaluation' is more common.

2

Capital Flows and the Foreign Exchange Market

Foreign exchange transactions generate capital flows which carry with them inherent economic risk. This risk may be either eliminated (to minimise losses) or exploited (to maximise profits) through the selective use of different types of foreign exchange rates and trading techniques.

THE SPOT EXCHANGE MARKET

Transactions where foreign currency notes and coins are physically exchanged are of minor economic consequence and tend to be confined to tourism and activities of an illicit nature. The majority of foreign exchange transactions involve the transfer of demand deposits maintained with banks domiciled in the countries of the currencies traded.

Transactions involving the purchase and sale of foreign exchange for delivery within two working days are conducted in the **spot exchange market** and are referred to as **spot transactions**. The exchange rates applying to these transactions are **spot exchange rates**, examples of which are shown in Table 2.1, with rates quoted as units of foreign currency per dollar, except for sterling which is normally quoted in dollars per unit of sterling.

Foreign exchange dealers throughout the world constantly monitor these rates, which immediately reflect changes in demand and supply pressures transmitted to the market by dealers acting either on their own behalf or on behalf of their trading customers. Turnover in the foreign exchange markets of leading financial centres such as London and New York amounts to billions of dollars daily and even hourly at times of international exchange rate crises.

Variations in this turnover, prompted by either demand or supply considerations, account for the constant fluctuations in exchange rate quotations.[1]

Normal trading conditions, however, frequently dictate currency deliveries extending well beyond those available on a spot basis, so recourse is then made to a different kind of foreign exchange market.

THE FORWARD EXCHANGE MARKET

The absence of perfect foresight and the lack of synchronisation between foreign currency receipts and payments creates uncertainty. The economic risk which results from this may be reduced or exploited for profit by channelling foreign exchange transactions through the **forward exchange market**. This is a market in which:

Purchases and sales of currencies are contracted in the present for receipt and delivery in the future,

and the **forward exchange rate** is:

The rate at which future transactions are contracted in the present.

The distinguishing feature of forward exchange transactions is that they represent a contractual obligation to trade currencies at a future date (periods of one, three and six months are common) at an exchange rate agreed upon at the time of the contract. Once agreed, this rate remains in effect until the contract is executed and does not respond to fluctuations in either the spot rate or the forward rate for other contracts.

Forward exchange rates are determined by the forward demand for and forward supply of foreign exchange. For example, a British exporter of computers who expects to receive payment in dollars in three months might seek to reduce the risk of an unfavourable interim movement in the dollar spot exchange rate by contracting to sell dollars forward for delivery in three months. This means that he guarantees in advance the sterling value of the dollars he will receive and then deliver. Increased demand for/reduced supply of a currency for delivery in the future will tend to increase the value of the currency relative to its spot rate, while reduced demand/

Table 2.1: Selected US dollar spot and forward exchange rates, 2 July 1984.

	Spot	Forward One Month	% p.a.	Forward Three Months	% p.a.
UK[†]	1.3505–1.3515	0.33–0.36c dis	−3.06	0.92–0.96c dis	−2.78
Ireland[†]	1.0965–1.0975	0.02cpm–0.03dis	−0.05	0.02–0.12dis	−0.25
Canada	1.3160–1.3165	0.02–0.04c dis	−0.27	0.05–0.08dis	−0.20
NethInd.	3.1485–3.1505	1.66–1.62c pm	6.25	4.78–4.73 pm	6.30
Belgium	56.70–56.75	2½–1c pm	0.37	9–7 pm	0.56
Denmark	10.22½–10.23	1.30–0.80ore pm	1.23	3.60–3.10 pm	1.31
W. Ger.	2.7893–2.7905	1.57–1.52pf pm	6.63	4.45–4.40 pm	6.33
Portugal	145.50–146.00	par–100c dis	−4.09	par–300 dis	−4.09
Spain	158.25–158.35	25–40c dis	−2.46	90–120 dis	−2.65
Italy	1716½–1717½	5–5½ lire dis	−3.66	13¾–14¾ dis	−3.31
Norway	8.01¾–8.02¼	0.10ore pm–0.40d	−0.22	0.20–0.70 dis	−0.22
France	8.5625–8.5675	0.10–0.30c dis	−0.28	0.50–1.00 dis	−0.35
Sweden	8.1875–8.1925	1–1½ore dis	−1.83	2–2½ dis	−1.10
Japan	238.50–238.60	1.27–1.17y pm	6.13	3.60–3.50 pm	5.95
Austria	19.58¼–19.59½	9.20–8.70gro pm	5.48	27.50–25.50 pm	5.41
Switz.	2.3415–2.3425	1.57–1.53c pm	7.94	4.55–4.51 pm	7.74

[†]UK and Ireland are quoted in US currency. Forward premiums and discounts apply to the US dollar and not to the individual currency. Belgian rate is for convertible francs. Financial franc 57.63–57.68.
Source: *Financial Times*, 3 July 1984.

increased supply will decrease the value of the currency relative to its spot rate. A currency is said to be at a **forward premium** when its future value exceeds its present value and at a **forward discount** when its future value is less than its present value. Premiums and discounts therefore represent the difference between a currency's forward and spot exchange rates. Since they represent absolute currency differences which are not readily comparable amongst different currencies, they are expressed as a percentage of the spot rate calculated on an annual percentage basis:

Forward Premium Rate $(+)$ or Discount Rate $(-)$ =

$$\frac{\text{Forward Exchange Rate} - \text{Spot Exchange Rate}}{\text{Spot Exchange Rate}} \times \frac{12 \text{ months}}{\text{Forward Contract Maturity in Months}} \times 100\%$$

If, for example, the sterling spot and three-month forward exchange rates were quoted at £1 = $2.00 and £1 = $2.02 respectively, the forward premium on sterling would be two cents which, expressed on an annual percentage basis, would be:

$$\frac{\$2.02 - \$2.00}{\$2.00} \times \frac{12 \text{ months}}{3 \text{ months}} \times 100\% = 4\% \text{ p.a.}$$

Alternatively, if the forward exchange rate for sterling were £1 = $1.97, the forward discount would be three cents, or:

$$\frac{\$1.97 - \$2.00}{\$2.00} \times \frac{12 \text{ months}}{3 \text{ months}} \times 100\% = -6\% \text{ p.a.}$$

In the former example, market conditions are such that forward demand for sterling for delivery in three months exceeds forward supply, so sellers will receive an extra two cents (premium) for each unit of sterling sold compared to the spot exchange rate. In the latter example, market conditions are reversed and sellers are prepared to accept three cents less for each unit sold compared to the spot exchange rate. Conversely, sterling buyers must be prepared to pay an extra two cents to acquire sterling in three months in the former example, but will expect to pay three cents less for the same transaction in the latter example.[2]

The size of forward premiums and discounts varies with the length of the forward contract and with market conditions. A typical selection of forward dollar exchange rates is illustrated in Table 2.1. These range from a one-month forward discount of −4.09% p.a. against the Portuguese escudo to a one-month forward premium of 7.94% against the Swiss franc.

Changes in forward premiums and discounts reflect changes in the forward demand for and supply of foreign exchange. These in turn partly reflect the extent to which capital flows are channelled from the present to the future in response to changing market conditions. A number of trading techniques are resorted to to take account of these conditions:

HEDGING

The existence of uncertainty creates economic risk. **Hedging** in the foreign exchange market is the:

Elimination or avoidance of foreign exchange risk.

It is achieved by avoiding '**open**' **positions** in foreign exchange. These are:

Imbalances in foreign currency assets and liabilities

and may assume two forms:

'**Long**' **positions** arise when foreign currency assets exceed foreign currency liabilities (net assets).

'**Short**' **positions** arise when foreign currency liabilities exceed foreign currency assets (net liabilities).

Both positions involve economic risk since they expose operators to potential losses resulting from adverse movements in foreign exchange rates. A spot depreciation of the currency in which net assets are held will tend to lower the foreign currency value of these assets and a spot appreciation will raise the foreign currency value of outstanding net liabilities. (Exchange rate movements in the opposite direction will generate gains but these do not normally give cause for concern.) Potential losses may be avoided by hedging in the foreign exchange market, by covering uncovered positions either through the forward sale of those currencies in which net assets are denominated or by the forward purchase of those currencies in which net liabilities are denominated. In both situations the potential cost of adverse currency fluctuations will be limited to the cost of the forward cover determined at the outset of the forward exchange transaction:

Forward cover cost =

Net foreign currency × Foreign currency forward
asset/liability   discount/premium

EXAMPLE 1

Consider the case of a US resident who expects to receive £2,000 in three months.

The anticipated sum is worth $4,000 at a current spot exchange rate of £1 = $2.00, but should sterling depreciate to £1 = $1.50 by the end of this period, the US resident will receive only $3,000 and will incur a foreign exchange loss of $1,000. If, however, the US resident had initially contracted to sell sterling forward at a three-month forward rate of £1 = $1.90, for example,[3] he would have received $3,800 and the 'loss' would have been limited to the $200 cost of the forward transaction. The existence of a long position (net foreign currency asset) and the failure to cover (hedge) this position exposed the US resident to an unfavourable and avoidable movement in the sterling spot exchange rate. (A sterling appreciation, of course, would have yielded more than the anticipated $4,000, but the object of hedging is loss minimisation, not profit maximisation).

Forward cover cost = Net foreign   × Foreign currency
                      currency asset   forward discount

               =   £2,000   × $0.10/£   = $200

EXAMPLE 2

Consider the case of a US resident who must make a £2,000 payment in three months.

The cost of the sterling liability will be $4,000 at a spot exchange rate of £1 = $2.00 but would increase to $5,000 if sterling appreciated to £1 = $2.50. This would involve the resident in a $1,000 loss. By hedging the liability in the forward exchange market by purchasing sterling at a forward rate of £1 = $2.20, for example, he could have limited his loss to the $400 cost of the forward cover.

Forward cover cost =	Net foreign currency liability	×	Foreign currency forward premium	
=	£2,000	×	$0.20/£	= $400

SPECULATION

The opposite of hedging is **speculation**, which is:

The acceptance of foreign exchange risk.

Speculation is a difficult trading technique to identify with certainty, since it is impossible to identify positively the deliberate intention to reap foreign exchange gains. Speculation is consequently considered to be present whenever open foreign exchange positions, be they long or short, are maintained, since these necessarily involve risk and hence the possibility of speculative gains. The stereotyped Swiss banker, whose activities undermine currencies and even economies, may thus well be speculating, but so also are exporters who lag their receipts and importers who lead their payments or traders who neglect to cover their foreign exchange exposure in the forward exchange markets. So is the British tourist returning from a vacation in Germany who delays the reconversion of his Deutsche Marks into sterling!

Speculation may be conducted through either the spot or forward exchange markets and involves the establishment of short positions in weak currencies, which are expected to depreciate or be devalued, and of long positions in strong currencies, which are expected to appreciate or be revalued.

Weak currency speculation

The essence of weak currency speculation is to 'sell dear and buy cheap'. This may be accomplished in the forward market by selling a weak currency forward in the hope of subsequently buying it back in the spot market after it has depreciated or has been devalued to a level below that of the original forward contract. The greater the difference between the forward rate and the new lower spot rate, the greater will be the speculator's profits. The establishment of short positions through the forward exchange market can be especially destabilising since forward sales require that currencies be delivered only upon expiry of the forward contracts. Speculators may thus continue to short a currency, subject to a typical margin requirement of approximately 10 per cent of the nominal value of the forward contract, for as long as such sales appear to be profitable, or for as long as forward buyers of the currency can be found to complete the forward contract. In the advanced stages of an exchange crisis, forward discounts tend to be pushed to the point where the cost of forward sales in relation to the likelihood of gains acts as a self-constraining mechanism. Continued support by the central bank in the forward exchange market, however, will tend to undermine this mechanism and may well contribute to a higher level of forward sales and more acute speculative pressures than would be the case in the absence of such intervention. These problems were particularly evident in the period immediately preceding the devaluation of sterling in November 1967, when heavy sales of forward sterling were absorbed by the Bank of England in an attempt to limit the widening forward discount to which sterling was increasingly being pushed. The rapid growth of the Bank's forward liabilities, however, convinced speculators that such large-scale intervention could not be sustained indefinitely and so reinforced expectations of an imminent sterling realignment. The inevitable devaluation enabled speculators to profit from the difference between the supported forward rate at which sterling had been sold and the new administered spot rate at which it could be repurchased. This latter rate was established at £1 = \$2.40, thus enabling profits of, for example, 30 cents to be gained for each pound which had been sold forward at a supported exchange rate of £1 = \$2.70 (Figure 2.1).

Weak currency speculation may also be conducted through the spot market by selling the weak currency outright and/or by creating weak currency liabilities (borrowings) which are then used to establish short positions in that currency. Speculators who expect sterling to be devalued will sell their sterling holdings and/or borrow sterling and sell it spot for whichever currency is expected to appreciate most against sterling. If the speculators' expectations prove correct and sterling is devalued from, for example, £1 = \$2.80 to £1 = \$2.40, speculative profits will amount to 40 cents for each pound sold plus any interest accumulated during the period that

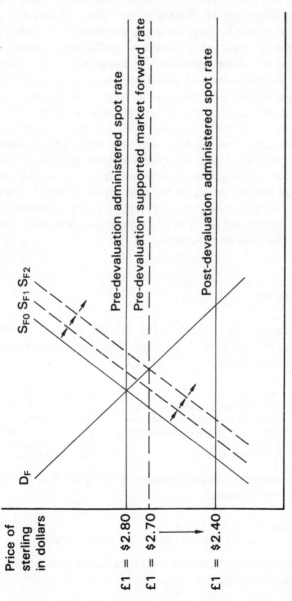

Figure 2.1: Demand for and supply of forward sterling. Successive forward sales of sterling push the forward rate further from the administered spot rate of £1 = $2.80 and enable speculators to profit from the difference between the supported forward rate of £1 = $2.70 and the new administered spot rate of £1 = $2.40.

dollars were held less the opportunity cost of holding or acquiring sterling. Profits will be substantial if a large devaluation is effected in a short period with relatively low opportunity costs.

Speculators who sell weak currencies in either the spot or forward markets are often referred to as **bears** and their pessimistic currency expectations as **bear sentiment**. Such sentiments frequently proved extremely profitable during the years of administered exchange rates (the so-called era of **fixed** or **pegged exchange rates** which ended in 1973), when central monetary authorities were committed to maintaining their currencies at predetermined levels known as **par values**, even though these values might no longer accurately reflect market demand and supply. The Bank of England's commitment to maintain sterling at a par value of £1 = $2.80 in the mid-1960s provided almost unparalleled speculative opportunities, since the exchange rate had become relatively overvalued and there was every prospect of a downward exchange realignment with little risk of any upward movement. Short sterling selling in both the spot and forward markets thus became an almost 'one-way bet' — a trial of strength between speculators and the Bank of England, the outcome of which was a decisive win for speculators.

EXAMPLE

Consider the dollar profits (π) which a successful bear speculator in sterling might potentially earn over three months, given:

Principal	(P)	= £1,000
Pre-devaluation sterling spot rate	($r_{£S0}$)	= £1 = $2.80
Post-devaluation sterling spot rate	($r_{£S1}$)	= £1 = $2.40
Three-month forward sterling rate	($r_{£F}$)	= £1 = $2.765
UK interest rate	(i_{UK})	= 10% p.a.
US interest rate	(i_{US})	= 5% p.a.

Forward speculation (forward sterling sales minus spot sterling repurchases):

$$\text{Net } \pi^* = P(r_{£F} - r_{£S1})$$
$$= £1,000 (\$2.765/£ - \$2.40/£) = \$365.$$

Spot speculation (spot sterling sales minus spot sterling repurchases):

36

Net π^* = $P(r_{£S0} - r_{£S1})$ = £1,000 ($2.80/£ - $2.40/£) = $400
plus accumulated dollar interest of:

P $\times r_{£S0}$ $\times i_{US}$ $\times$ 3/12 months
£1,000 $\times$ $2.80/£ $\times$ 5% $\times$ 3/12   = $35
less the opportunity cost of sterling of:

P $\times r_{£S0}$ $\times i_{UK}$ $\times$ 3/12 months
£1,000 $\times$ $2.80/£ $\times$ 10% $\times$ 3/12   = $70
                                          = $365

*Incidental expenses, such as forward margin requirements and trading costs, have been excluded from calculations.

Strong currency speculation

The basis of strong currency speculation is to 'buy cheap and sell dear'. It may be conducted in either the forward or spot exchange markets and involves the establishment of long positions in currencies which are expected to appreciate or be revalued.

Speculation in the forward market involves purchasing a currency forward in the expectation of selling it in the spot market after it has appreciated or has been revalued to a level above that of the original forward contract. The greater the difference between the forward rate and the new higher spot rate, the greater the speculative profits.

The defence of an undervalued currency in the forward exchange market is easier to sustain than that of an overvalued currency, since the onus of financing speculation shifts from the central bank to the individual speculator. Whereas the central bank of a weak currency is committed to the future delivery of scarce foreign exchange reserves, the central bank of a strong currency is merely committed to delivering domestic currency and hence responsibility for providing the foreign exchange necessary to meet maturing forward contracts is transferred to the individual speculator. Speculative attacks upon strong currencies are thus more easily contained than those directed towards weak currencies. This is shown in Figure 2.2, where the increased forward demand for Deutsche Marks is satisfied by the Bundesbank in exchange for a commensurate increase in the forward market supply of foreign exchange.

Strong currency speculation in the spot market involves the establishment of long positions in currencies which are expected to appreciate or be revalued. Speculators purchase currencies in the spot market in the hope of subsequently selling them at a new higher spot rate, thereby profiting from the difference between the two spot rates plus any interest accumulated during the holding period less the opportunity cost of acquiring the currency.

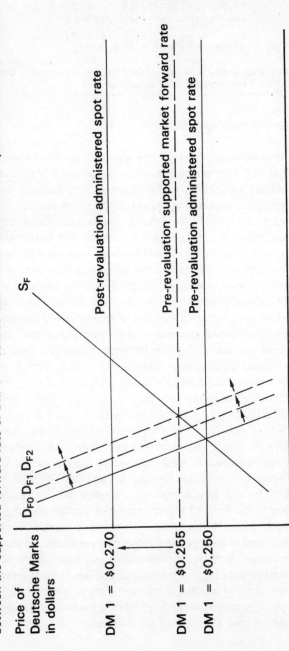

Figure 2.2: Demand for and supply of forward Deutsche Marks. Increasing forward demand for Deutsche Marks pulls the forward rate further from the administered spot rate of DM 1 = $0.25 and enables speculators to profit from the difference between the supported forward rate of DM 1 = $0.255 and the new administered spot rate of DM 1 = $0.27.

Price of Deutsche Marks in dollars

S_F

D_{F0} D_{F1} D_{F2}

DM 1 = $0.270

Post-revaluation administered spot rate

DM 1 = $0.255

Pre-revaluation supported market forward rate

DM 1 = $0.250

Pre-revaluation administered spot rate

Forward Deutsche Marks

Speculators who buy strong currencies in either spot or forward markets are often referred to as **bulls** and their optimistic currency expectations as **bull sentiment**.

EXAMPLE

Consider the dollar profits (π) which a successful bull speculator in Deutsche Marks might potentially earn over three months, given:

Principal	(P)	= \$1,000
Pre-revaluation DM spot rate	(r_{DMS0})	= DM 1 = \$0.250
Post-revaluation DM spot rate	(r_{DMS1})	= DM 1 = \$0.270
Three-month forward DM rate	(r_{DMF})	= DM 1 = \$0.254
German interest rate	(i_G)	= 3% p.a.
US interest rate	(i_{US})	= 10% p.a.

Forward speculation (forward Deutsche Mark purchases minus spot Deutsche Mark sales):

$$\text{Net } \pi^* = P\,\frac{r_{DMS1}}{r_{DMF}} - P$$

$$= P\left(\frac{r_{DMS1}}{r_{DMF}} - 1\right)$$

$$= \$1000\left(\frac{\$0.270/DM}{\$0.254/DM} - 1\right) \qquad = \$63.$$

Spot speculation (spot Deutsche Mark purchases minus spot Deutsche Mark resales):

$$\text{Net } \pi^* = P\,\frac{r_{DMS1}}{r_{DMS0}} - P$$

$$= P\left(\frac{r_{DMS1}}{r_{DMS0}} - 1\right)$$

$$= \$1000\left(\frac{\$0.27/DM}{\$0.25/DM} - 1\right) \qquad = \$80$$

plus accumulated DM interest of:

$$P\,\frac{r_{DMS1}}{r_{DMS0}} \times i_G \times 3/12 \text{ months}$$

39

$$\$1000 \; \frac{\$0.27/DM}{\$0.25/DM} \times 3\% \times 3/12 \qquad = \$8$$

less the opportunity cost of dollars of:

$$P \times i_{US} \times 3/12 \text{ months}$$
$$\$1000 \times 10\% \times 3/12 \qquad\qquad = \$25$$
$$\qquad\qquad\qquad\qquad\qquad\qquad = \$63.$$

*Incidental expenses, such as forward margin requirements and trading costs, have been excluded from calculations.

Adherence to a system of fixed exchange rates in the post-war period fostered a climate of international currency speculation in which both strong and weak currencies became subject to speculative attacks. These attacks were conducted through both spot and forward exchange markets where the vigorous defence of currencies, some of whose parities had become seriously misaligned, provided speculators with considerable opportunities to reap profits with minimal risks. The cumulative effect of these capital flows, whose impact varied in both magnitude and direction, was the progressive erosion and eventual disintegration of the post-war system of fixed exchange rates.

The post-1973 era of non-administered or **floating exchange rates** continued to generate speculative currency flows but these have tended to be less destabilising and more easily containable. This is because capital flows are now exposed to the greater likelihood of losses as well as attendant profits, since central monetary authorities are no longer committed to the defence of misaligned parities and currencies are now free to both appreciate and depreciate.

ARBITRAGE

The smooth and efficient flow of capital in foreign exchange markets is attributable partly to hedging and speculation and partly to **arbitrage**. In general terms, arbitrage is:

The simultaneous exploitation of opportunity cost differentials in one or more markets for profit.

Successful exploitation of these differentials by **arbitrageurs** generates profits but simultaneously destroys the very differentials from which these profits are derived, thereby eliminating temporary market discrepancies. This contributes to the smooth and efficient operation of international financial markets. There are several types of arbitrage, two of which have particular relevance to the foreign exchange market:

Foreign exchange arbitrage

Arbitrage in foreign exchange markets ensures that comparable foreign exchange rates vary minutely, if at all, amongst different markets.

The temporary emergence of exchange rate differentials in different markets for the same two currencies will generate **two-point arbitrage**. This will eliminate differentials as arbitrageurs purchase one currency at its lower rate in one market and simultaneously sell the same currency at the higher rate in the second market. Arbitrageurs thus profit from temporary differentials whose very existence is destroyed by their currency purchases and sales which respectively pull up and force down exchange rates to common levels.

EXAMPLE

Let the spot sterling exchange rate in London be
$$£1 = \$1.98 \ (\$1 = £0.505)$$
and the spot dollar exchange rate in New York be
$$\$1 = £0.50 \ (£1 = \$2.00)$$
These figures suggest that sterling is either undervalued in London or overvalued in New York and that the dollar is either overvalued in London or undervalued in New York. It is also possible that the true rate does, in fact, lie somewhere between the two. Since sterling is principally traded in London and the dollar in New York, it is probable that sterling is overvalued (relatively scarce) in New York ($£1 = \$2.00$) and that the dollar is overvalued (relatively scarce) in London ($\$1 = £0.505$). Provided that capital is free to flow between the two centres, arbitrageurs will attempt to exploit and hence profit from this differential by selling $1.98 in London

for £1.00, and reselling the £1.00 in New York for $2.00. This will generate profits of two cents per pound sterling transacted and will, *ceteris paribus*, force down dollar rates in London and sterling rates in New York to a possible common level of £1 = $1.99 or $1 = £0.5025.

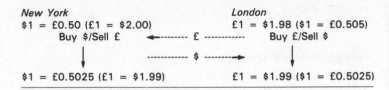

New York
$1 = £0.50 (£1 = $2.00)
    Buy $/Sell £

$1 = £0.5025 (£1 = $1.99)

London
£1 = $1.98 ($1 = £0.505)
    Buy £/Sell $

£1 = $1.99 ($1 = £0.5025)

Three-point (triangular) arbitrage arises when exchange rates are externally consistent (comparable rates in different centres) but internally inconsistent (exchange rates amongst different currencies are mutually inconsistent). Arbitrageurs will attempt to profit from these inconsistencies by buying and selling individual currencies and will, in the process, both eliminate these discrepancies and establish mutually consistent **cross-exchange rates** which are:

The price of a second currency expressed in terms of a third.

EXAMPLE

Let £1 = DM8
   £1 = $2
   $1 = DM4 (internally consistent)

If the dollar exchange rate were quoted at $1 = DM3.50, however, this would represent an internally inconsistent cross-exchange rate which would enable arbitrageurs to profit by selling, for example, DM7 for $2, reselling the $2 for £1 and finally reselling the £1 for DM8. This would generate profits of DM1 for every DM7 originally sold and would, in the process, contribute to the establishment of internally consistent cross-exchange rates as all three exchange rates adjust to mutually compatible levels:

	Sell	Buy
Position 1	DM7 ------------→ $2	
Position 2	$2 ----------------→ £1	
Position 3	£1 ----------------→ DM8	

Arbitrage profit is DM8 − DM7 = DM1.

Interest arbitrage

Arbitrage is also important to foreign exchange markets because it links them to domestic capital markets. Arbitrage ensures that, in the absence of capital controls and market imperfections, capital will flow to its most profitable market-determined use, thereby enabling international capital markets to be considered efficient to the extent that the price of capital reflects its international opportunity cost. The mechanism by which this is achieved is **interest arbitrage** which is:

The simultaneous exploitation of interest rate differentials in one or more markets for profit.

Arbitrageurs ensure that capital flows to its most profitable use by monitoring interest rates and exploiting any differentials which emerge between low and high cost financial centres. By simultaneously borrowing in, or by transferring arbitrage owned capital[4] from the former and lending in the latter, arbitrageurs are able to profit from these differentials which are systematically narrowed and eventually eliminated as interest rates are raised and lowered in the low and high cost centres respectively.

Uncovered interest arbitrage

This is:

The simultaneous, exchange rate uncovered exploitation of interest rate differentials in one or more markets for profit.

It arises when arbitrageurs are willing both to exploit interest rate differentials and to assume exchange rate risks (by not covering themselves against these risks).

The direction of uncovered arbitrage flows between any two centres (A and B) is determined by the **uncovered interest differential** (UD) which, for centre 'A', for example, can be expressed as:

43

$$UD_A = i_A - i_B.$$

Capital will be arbitraged uncovered from centre 'B' to centre 'A' whenever the uncovered differential is in favour of centre 'A' (UD_A is positive) and from centre 'A' to centre 'B' whenever the uncovered differential is unfavourable to centre 'A' (UD_A is negative).

The level of uncovered arbitrage profits generated will depend on both interest rate differentials and fluctuations in spot exchange rates:

$$\begin{matrix} \text{Arbitrage profits} \\ \text{in centre 'A'} \end{matrix} = \begin{matrix} \text{Anticipated revenue} \\ \text{in centre 'A'} \end{matrix} - \begin{matrix} \text{Opportunity costs} \\ \text{in centre 'B'} \end{matrix}$$

$$\pi_A = \frac{P}{r_{AS0}} (1 + i_A)r_{AS1} - P(1 + i_B) \qquad (2\text{-}1)$$

where:

π_A = Arbitrage profits in centre 'A'
P = Principal arbitraged
i_A = Interest rate in centre 'A'
i_B = Interest rate in centre 'B'
r_{AS0} = Initial spot exchange rate of centre 'A''s currency in terms of centre 'B''s
r_{AS1} = Final spot exchange rate of centre 'A''s currency in terms of centre 'B''s

Arbitrage profits will increase if the final spot exchange rate of centre 'A''s currency in terms of centre 'B''s appreciates ($\uparrow r_{AS1}$) and decrease if centre 'A''s currency in terms of centre 'B''s depreciates ($\downarrow r_{AS1}$). Profits will remain unchanged and equal to the pure interest rate differential ($i_A - i_B$) if spot exchange rates remain unchanged ($r_{AS0} = r_{AS1}$). Arbitrage profits in centre 'A' will thus be greater/less than the pure interest rate differential ($i_A - i_B$) as r_{AS1} is greater/less than r_{AS0}.

EXAMPLE

	Centre 'B' (US)	Centre 'A' (UK)
	i_B = 4% p.a.	i_A = 10% p.a.

Position 1 Borrow dollars — Sell dollars spot/ Buy sterling spot → Invest sterling

Position 2 Repay dollars ← Sell sterling spot/ Buy dollars spot — Disinvest sterling

Let

$$P = \$100$$
$$i_A = 10\% \text{ p.a.}$$
$$i_B = 4\% \text{ p.a.}$$
$$r_{AS0} = r_{AS1} = £1 = \$2.80$$

Substituting into equation 2-1 gives:

$$\pi_A^* = \frac{\$100}{\$2.80/£} (1+0.1) \, \$2.80/£ - \$100 \, (1+0.04)$$

$$= \$6.$$

* Incidental expenses, such as trading costs, have been excluded from calculations.

Arbitrage profits of six percentage points will be earned by borrowing dollars at 4% p.a. in the US and investing the converted sterling proceeds at 10% p.a. in the UK. Net profits of $6 p.a. will thus be earned for each $100 converted into sterling, invested in the UK and reconverted into dollars, *provided* that exchange rates remain unchanged.

Arbitrage flows conducted on an uncovered basis, however, expose arbitrageurs to exchange rate risks, since it cannot be assumed that exchange rates will remain unchanged. The establishment of either long or short positions in foreign currencies will expose arbitrageurs to the risk of losses if the currency in which long positions are established depreciates or if the currency in which short positions are established appreciates. (The 'risk' of profits again does not generally present problems.) Arbitrageurs who, for example, borrow dollars in the US (short positions) and invest the converted sterling proceeds in the UK (long positions) expose themselves to the risks of a sterling depreciation, which will reduce the dollar value of their sterling assets, or a dollar appreciation, which will increase the sterling value of their dollar liabilities. Thus if sterling depreciates to £1 = \$2.70 (r_{AS1} = \$2.70) in the example given, arbitrage profits would decrease from \$6 p.a. to \$2.07 p.a.

Arbitrageurs who accept these risks and trade them against the possibility of increased profits resulting from favourable exchange rate movements are speculating in the same way (although with potentially lesser intent) as operators who buy and sell currencies in the spot market for pure speculative profits.

Covered interest arbitrage

Arbitrageurs who are not willing to assume exchange rate risks but who still wish to exploit interest rate differentials resort to **covered interest arbitrage** which is:

The simultaneous, exchange rate covered exploitation of interest rate differentials in one or more markets for profit.

The risk of unfavourable exchange rate movements is eliminated in this case by closing open foreign exchange positions through recourse to forward exchange rates. Long positions are closed by selling forward the currency in which the asset is denominated while short positions are closed by buying forward the currency in which the liability is incurred. This introduces forward exchange rates as a second variable when determining the profitability and hence direction of arbitrage flows.

Forward exchange rates respond principally, although not exclusively, to arbitrage pressures and will tend to adjust until **forward interest parity** is attained, at which point there will no longer be any incentive to arbitrage capital between financial centres since the **covered interest differential** between these centres will have been reduced to zero. At this point, **covered interest parity** will have been established, which is:

The equalisation of covered interest rates.

The introduction of forward cover as a second arbitrage variable reduces the tendency for interest rate differentials between centres

46

to be completely eliminated, since capital flows will now respond to covered as opposed to uncovered differentials. Capital will thus flow towards centres with **positive covered differentials** and away from centres with **negative covered differentials**. This will tend to lower interest rates in high interest rate centres and raise them in low interest rate centres, whilst simultaneously strengthening the spot exchange rate and weakening the forward exchange rate of the currencies in the high interest rate centres. The effect of these flows on the US/UK example given above would be to raise interest rates in the US and lower them in the UK, whilst simultaneously strengthening the spot and weakening the forward sterling exchange rates. These exchange rate changes would reduce the arbitrage attractiveness of the UK relative to the US, since more dollars would be required to buy sterling spot and more sterling would be required to repurchase the dollars forward. These flows will tend to continue, *ceteris paribus*, until the covered interest rate differential in favour of the UK is reduced to zero and covered interest rate parity is established.[5]

Static arbitrage equilibrium in international capital markets is thus entirely consistent with the continuing existence of uncovered interest rate differentials. Indeed, equilibrium may even be consistent with capital flows from *high* to *low* interest rate centres if the forward discounts of high interest rate centres' currencies are large enough to absorb the centres' positive interest rate differentials or if the forward premiums of the low interest rate centres' currencies are large enough to compensate for the centres' negative interest rate differentials. Such flows may occur at times of exchange rate uncertainty when speculative and hedging considerations are large enough to outweigh those of a purely arbitrage nature.

The direction of covered arbitrage flows between any two centres (A and B) is thus determined by both interest rates and forward exchange rates. The covered differential in centre 'A' (CD_A), for example, may be expressed in the approximation:[6]

$$CD_A = (i_A - i_B) + F_A$$

where:

F_A represents the forward annual percentage premium or discount of centre 'A''s currency in terms of centre 'B''s.

The covered differential in centre 'A' is thus equal to the interest

47

rate in centre 'A' minus the interest rate in centre 'B' plus the forward percentage premium or discount of centre 'A''s currency in terms of centre 'B''s. Capital will be arbitraged from centre 'B' to centre 'A' whenever the covered differential is in favour of centre 'A' (CD_A is positive) and from centre 'A' to centre 'B' whenever the covered differential is unfavourable to centre 'A' (CD_A is negative).

EXAMPLE 1

Let

i_A = 10 % p.a.
i_B = 4 % p.a.
F_A = − 3 % p.a.

Since

$$CD_A = (i_A − i_B) + F_A$$

then

$$CD_A = (10\% − 4\%) + (−3\%) = 3\%.$$

Capital will flow to centre 'A' and will continue to flow (*ceteris paribus*) until the covered differential in favour of centre 'A' is reduced to zero through a combination of lower interest rates in 'A', higher interest rates in 'B' and a wider forward discount for centre 'A''s currency as spot demand strengthens the spot exchange rate and forward sales weaken the forward exchange rate. *

EXAMPLE 2

Let

i_A = 10 % p.a.
i_B = 4 % p.a.
F_A = −8% p.a.

Since

$$CD_A = (i_A - i_B) + F_A$$

then

$$CD_A = (10\% - 4\%) + (-8\%) = -2\%.$$

Capital will flow away from centre 'A' since the forward discount on centre 'A''s currency of 8% is large enough to absorb the positive differential of 6% in favour of centre 'A'. These flows will continue (*ceteris paribus*) until interest rates change or until the forward discount on centre 'A''s currency is narrowed.*

---

*Incidental expenses, such as trading costs, have been excluded.

The level of profits generated by covered interest arbitrage is determined simultaneously with the direction of covered arbitrage flows, since both profits and the direction of flows depend on interest rates and forward exchange rates:

$$\begin{array}{ccc}
\text{Covered arbitrage} \\
\text{profits in centre 'A'}
\end{array} = \begin{array}{c}
\text{Revenue from} \\
\text{centre 'A'}
\end{array} - \begin{array}{c}
\text{Opportunity costs} \\
\text{in centre 'B'}
\end{array}$$

$$\pi_A = \frac{P}{r_{AS}} (1+i_A) \, r_{AF} - P(1+i_B) \qquad (2\text{-}2)$$

where:

π_A = Covered arbitrage profits in centre 'A'
P = Principal arbitraged
i_A = Interest rate in centre 'A'
i_B = Interest rate in centre 'B'
r_{AS} = Spot exchange rate of centre 'A''s currency in terms of centre 'B''s
r_{AF} = Forward exchange rate of centre 'A''s currency in terms of centre 'B''s

EXAMPLE

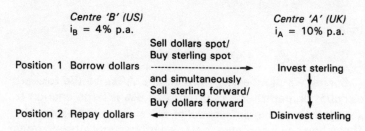

Centre 'B' (US)
i_B = 4% p.a.

Centre 'A' (UK)
i_A = 10% p.a.

Position 1 Borrow dollars

Sell dollars spot/
Buy sterling spot

Invest sterling

and simultaneously
Sell sterling forward/
Buy dollars forward

Position 2 Repay dollars

Disinvest sterling

Let

    P   = $100
    i_A = 10% p.a.
    i_B = 4% p.a.
    r_{AS} = £1 = $2.80
    r_{AF} = £1 = $2.73

Substituting into equation 2-2 gives:

$$\pi_A{}^* = \frac{\$100}{\$2.80/£}\ (1+0.1)\ \$2.73/£\ -\ \$100(1+0.04)$$

$$= \$3.25.$$

Gross arbitrage profits of six percentage points can still be earned by borrowing dollars at 4% p.a. in the US and investing the converted sterling proceeds, which are first sold forward for dollars to eliminate the exchange risk, at 10% p.a. in the UK. Net arbitrage profits on this occasion, however, will consist of the $6 earned for each $100 arbitraged minus the cost ($2.75) of the discount on forward sterling sales.*

*Incidental expenses, such as trading costs, have been excluded from calculations.

The way capital flows respond to changes in interest rates and foreign exchange rates clearly shows that international financial markets are closely integrated and do not function in isolation. Policies designed to achieve limited domestic objectives should thus always be considered within the wider international framework of monetary ramifications.

SUMMARY

Spot transactions are conducted in the spot exchange market and involve the purchase and sale of foreign exchange for delivery within two working days. The exchange rates applying to these transactions are spot exchange rates.

Forward transactions are conducted in the forward exchange market and involve purchases and sales of currencies which are contracted in the present for receipt and delivery in the future. The rate at which future transactions are contracted in the present is the forward exchange rate which is quoted at either a premium or discount to the spot rate.

Hedging is the elimination or avoidance of foreign exchange risk. It is achieved by avoiding 'open' foreign exchange positions which are imbalances in foreign currency assets and liabilities. Imbalances can take the form of 'long' positions, which arise when foreign currency assets exceed foreign currency liabilities, or 'short' positions, which arise when foreign currency liabilities exceed foreign currency assets.

Speculation is the acceptance of foreign exchange risk. It is directed at both weak and strong currencies. Speculators who sell weak currencies are referred to as bears and their pessimistic currency expectations as bear sentiment. Speculators who buy strong currencies are referred to as bulls and their optimistic currency expectations as bull sentiment.

Arbitrage is the simultaneous exploitation of opportunity cost differentials in one or more markets for profit. Arbitrage in the foreign exchange market eliminates exchange rate differentials between two or more currencies. Arbitrage in capital markets eliminates interest rate differentials and is conducted on either an uncovered (open exchange risk) or covered (closed exchange risk) basis.

CONCEPTS FOR REVIEW

Arbitrage   Hedging
Arbitrageurs   Interest arbitrage

Bears	'Long' positions
Bear sentiment	Negative covered differentials
Bulls	'Open' positions
Bull sentiment	Par values
Covered interest arbitrage	Positive covered differentials
Covered interest differential	'Short' positions
Covered interest parity	Speculation
Cross-exchange rates	Spot exchange market
Fixed or pegged exchange rates	Spot exchange rates
Floating exchange rates	Spot transactions
Forward discount	Three-point (triangular) arbitrage
Forward exchange market	Two-point arbitrage
Forward exchange rate	Uncovered interest arbitrage
Forward interest parity	Uncovered interest differential
Forward premium	

QUESTIONS FOR DISCUSSION

1. Distinguish between spot and forward exchange rates. Explain the form in which the latter are expressed and their foreign exchange significance.
2. What is hedging and how is it used to eliminate foreign exchange risk?
3. Explain two possible means by which a bear attack might be mounted against a currency. Is the containment of speculative attacks against weak and strong currencies symmetrical?
4. How does arbitrage ensure that exchange rates are internally and externally consistent?
5. Will arbitrage result in the elimination of interest rate differentials?

Notes

1. Many currencies are not freely quoted (convertible) in foreign exchange markets because the governments of these currencies wish to retain control of the administered exchange rates which frequently reflect factors of a non-economic nature such as social and political considerations. Examples of these currencies are to be found particularly in the developing world and in the Soviet bloc.

2. The concept of reciprocity also applies to forward exchange rates such that if currency X is trading at a forward premium to currency Y, then Y

is trading at a forward discount to X.

3. Forward exchange rates generally reflect anticipated spot exchange rates and so sterling might be expected to sell at a forward discount in this example. A forward sterling premium of $0.10/£, however, would have converted the forward cover cost into a gain of $200 (£2,000 × $0.10/£).

4. Opportunity cost differentials are affected only to the extent that the opportunity cost of borrowed capital may be greater than arbitrageur-owned capital.

5. Factors accounting for the persistence of covered interest rate differentials include transactions costs, taxes, speculation and political risks.

6. The equilibrium condition for covered interest rate parity can be expressed as

$$\frac{R_{AF} (1 + i_A)}{R_{AS}} = (1 + i_B). \tag{2A-1}$$

Expressing R_{AF}/R_{AS} as $(1 + F_A)$ which is the forward annual percentage premium or discount of centre 'A''s currency in terms of centre 'B''s, and substituting in 2A-1 gives:

$$(1 + F_A) (1 + i_A) = (1 + i_B)$$

or

$$1 + F_A + i_A + F_A i_A = 1 + i_B. \tag{2A-2}$$

Since the term $F_A i_A$ tends to zero, equation 2A-2 approximates to:

$$(i_A - i_B) + F_A = 0.$$

The covered differential in centre 'A' can therefore be expressed as the approximation:

$$CD_A = (i_A - i_B) + F_A.$$

3

The Balance of Payments

The international flow of goods, services and capital is recorded in the **balance of payments**, which is:

A systematic record of a country's international transactions over a specified period.

In other words, the balance of payments records the domestic currency *value* of goods and services and the net *volume* of capital which have *flowed* into and out of a country over a specified period, usually twelve months. Although balance of payments measures are compiled and published on a quarterly and even monthly basis, short-term fluctuations mean that these are only a general guide to overall trends. Even annual payments measures, because of data deficiencies and inaccuracies, have to be revised, sometimes over several years and sometimes significantly in both size and scope.

APPLICATION

At a microeconomic level, balance of payments measures are used to: analyse the economic role of individual goods and services accounts; quantify variations in the magnitude and direction of capital flows; identify the sources and uses of foreign exchange.

These microeconomic applications describe individual international activities whose economic impact might be counterbalanced by activities recorded elsewhere in the balance of payments.

At a macroeconomic level, balance of payments measures relate to aggregate international activities and indicate whether an economy is in external equilibrium or whether the foreign sector is subjecting the domestic economy to expansionary or contractionary pressures (external disequilibrium). This enables balance of payments measures to be used as a basis for either restoring external equilibrium or using external disequilibrium as a macroeconomic policy variable to achieve, for example, domestic economic expansion.

The application and interpretation of balance of payments measures is subject to two qualifications:

Firstly, balance of payments measures include both final and *intermediate* goods and services. They are not therefore a direct indicator of economic welfare.

Secondly, imbalances in balance of payments measures reflect surpluses and deficits and *not* profits and losses. This is because balance of payments measures record the *flow* of goods, services and capital into and out of a country and not the *terms* under which these flows are conducted.

CONSTRUCTION

Balance of payments measures record international flows denominated in the currency of the country compiling the accounts. Exports and imports of goods and services are flows and are consequently recorded directly in balance of payments accounts. Capital assets and liabilities, in contrast, are stocks regardless of whether they are domestic or foreign (non-resident) owned, so that only increases or decreases in outstanding totals are recorded in the accounts.

The flows are recorded using the **'double-entry' system of book-keeping** which ensures that for every entry there is a corresponding entry (or entries) with sign reversed. Consequently, the sum of credits must always equal the sum of debits so that, on an *accounting* basis, the balance of payments must always balance.

Whether an individual transaction carries a positive (credit) or negative (debit) sign is determined by accounting convention:

**Credits denote decreases in assets or increases in liabilities.
Debits denote decreases in liabilities or increases in assets.**

The appearance of **credits** (positive signs) in a country's balance of payments will thus be associated with one or more of the following transactions:

55

Exports of goods and services
Decreases in foreign claims and assets
Increases in liabilities to foreigners.

The appearance of **debits** (negative signs) on the other hand will be associated with one or more of the following:

Imports of goods and services
Increases in foreign claims and assets
Decreases in liabilities to foreigners.

Credits and debits can also be used to identify potential sources and uses of foreign exchange:

Credits represent potential sources of foreign exchange.
Debits represent potential uses of foreign exchange.

For example, exports are a potential source of foreign exchange and are recorded as a credit, while capital outflows are a potential use of foreign exchange and are recorded as a debit.

The assigning of positive and negative signs to individual trade flows also helps to identify the direction of resource transfers:

Credits denote outflows of resources from a country.
Debits denote inflows of resources into a country.

For example, exports are an outflow of resources and are recorded as a credit, while imports are an inflow of resources and are recorded as a debit.

Regardless of the sectoral distribution of individual credits and debits, however, a country's balance of payments must always be in **accounting equilibrium** since total credits and debits must always balance.[1]

EQUILIBRIUM AND DISEQUILIBRIUM

Although the balance of payments must always be in accounting equilibrium, it does not always have to be in **economic equilibrium**. This is because the sum of autonomous credit transactions need not always equal the sum of autonomous debit transactions.

Autonomous transactions are undertaken for their own sake in response to diverse economic, social and even political stimuli. They are undertaken to generate income and improve economic welfare. They include exports and imports of goods and services, overseas investment, government aid and military assistance and certain categories of capital flows, and are recorded in balance of payments accounts as credits or debits according to the flows they represent.

Accommodating transactions, in contrast, are undertaken to compensate for autonomous transactions and essentially represent the financial counterpart of these transactions. They basically comprise private and official short-term capital flows which are recorded as credits or debits according to the flows they represent.

Balance of payments (economic) equilibrium arises when autonomous credits equal autonomous debits. Correspondingly, balance of payments disequilibrium arises when the adjustment process is unable to restore equality between autonomous credits and debits. An excess of credits relative to debits generates a **balance of payments surplus**, whilst an excess of debits relative to credits generates a **balance of payments deficit**. Both types of disequilibrium are accommodated by corresponding accommodating transactions, but with sign reversed. A balance of payments deficit will thus be financed by net accommodating (credit) transactions, and a balance of payments surplus will be counterbalanced by net accommodating (debit) transactions.

EXAMPLE

Consider a situation in which US imports of goods and services exceed US exports of goods and services. The resultant deficit of, for example, $10 million (net debits) represents an inflow of resources which has to be financed by a corresponding surplus of accommodating transactions (net credits) representing payments by, or outflows of, resources from the US. These transactions, illustrated in the table, can take several forms:

(i) Foreign exporters might be willing to accept payment in dollars and maintain these dollars on deposit with US banks, in which case the deficit will have been financed by an increase in US liabilities to private foreigners (credit). Alternatively, US importers might acquire foreign currencies by selling dollars either to foreign commercial banks (in which case the dollar will, *ceteris paribus*, tend to depreciate) or to foreign central banks if support is undertaken to prevent a depreciation of the dollar. In this case, the deficit will have again been financed by an increase in US liabilities, but to either private foreigners or official foreigners respectively (credit).

	$ millions
AUTONOMOUS TRANSACTIONS	
US deficit of goods and services	− 10
ACCOMMODATING TRANSACTIONS	
Increase in US liabilities to foreigners	+ 10
or	
Decrease in US foreign assets	+ 10
or	
Decrease in US official reserves of gold and foreign exchange	+ 10

(ii) The US might draw upon foreign assets held either directly as foreign currency claims on foreign private banks or indirectly as assets which are sold to acquire foreign currencies. In either case the deficit will be financed by a decrease in US foreign assets (credit).

(iii) The US might pay for its net imports of goods and services by drawing on its reserves of gold and foreign exchange, in which case the deficit will have been financed by a decrease in US official reserve assets (credit).

Balance of payments equilibrium is determined, for any given level of credits and debits, by the classification of international transactions as autonomous or accommodating. Classification depends upon the economic significance of the particular balance of payments measure which is to be derived. There is therefore no single measure of balance of payments equilibrium, but rather a spectrum of measures, determined by the size and number of transactions which are to be considered autonomous. These transactions are recorded above an **imaginary financing line** which separates them from accommodating transactions recorded below the line. The initial inclusion of a few selected transactions above the line, such as exports and imports of goods, produces a narrow measure of equilibrium of specific economic application. The inclusion of further transactions above the line, however, which is tantamount to shifting the imaginary line downwards, progressively broadens the measure of equilibrium until, ultimately, both autonomous and accommodating transactions are included above the line and the concept of economic equilibrium reverts to that of accounting equilibrium.

The positioning of this imaginary line in relation to autonomous and accommodating transactions (illustrated in Figure 3.1) determines the particular measure of balance of payments equilibrium obtained and hence the economic application to which balance of payments data may be put.

Figure 3.1: The imaginary balance of payments financing line. Panel (a) shows that the imaginary financing line is initially drawn below accounts *a* and *b*, which are considered autonomous (for example exports and imports of goods and services) and determine one measure of balance of payments surplus/deficit. Accounts *c*, *d* and *e* are considered accommodating, such that $a + b = c + d + e$. Panel (b) shows that the imaginary financing line has been moved down and drawn below accounts *a*, *b*, *c* and *d* which are now all considered autonomous and determine a second measure of balance of payments surplus/deficit. Account *e* is now considered accommodating (for example, official reserves) such that $a + b + c + d = e$.

Accounts

Imaginary financing line

$\left.\begin{matrix} a \\ b \end{matrix}\right\}$ Autonomous transactions: $a + b = $ Surplus/deficit

$\left.\begin{matrix} c \\ d \\ e \end{matrix}\right\}$ Accommodating transactions: $c + d + e$

(a)

Accounts

Imaginary financing line

$\left.\begin{matrix} a \\ b \\ c \\ d \end{matrix}\right\}$ Autonomous transactions: $a + b + c + d = $ Surplus/deficit

$e \}$ Accommodating transactions: e

(b)

MEASURES

Several different balance of payments measures can be derived, ranging in scope and application from narrow and specific to broad and general. Their derivation is determined by the selection and ordering of balance of payments data which, in a pure accounting format, are of little economic significance since such data must, by definition, always balance. This is illustrated in Table 3.1 which tabulates, as an example, US payments data for 1980 to 1983. Table 3.1 shows that total credits equal total debits and that accounting equilibrium has been established.

More informative, in economic terms, is the identification and separation of autonomous and accommodating transactions which places the former above and the latter below an imaginary financing line.

This approach may be used to derive four separate measures of the balance of payments which are illustrated, using US payments data, in Table 3.2. (US payments data are used because of the important role played by the US in international trade and because of the willingness of the rest of the world to use and hold dollars for international payments purposes.)

Each measure is derived by cumulatively adding the autonomous transactions included under each balance of payments category and can be expressed notationally using the following symbols:

X_G = Exports of goods
M_G = Imports of goods
X = Exports of goods and services
M = Imports of goods and services
T = Unilateral transfers
LTC = Long-term capital
STC = Short-term capital
U = Statistical discrepancy
SDR = Special Drawing Right
R_F = Reserve assets (foreign-owned)
R_D = Reserve assets (domestically-owned)

Merchandise trade balance ($X_G - M_G$)

This balance is the narrowest and most specific payments measure and reflects the value of commercial goods exported from and

Table 3.1: US balance of payments data, 1980–3.

($ billions)

	1980 Credit	1980 Debit	1981 Credit	1981 Debit	1982 Credit	1982 Debit	1983 Credit	1983 Debit
Merchandise exports	224.3		237.1		211.2		200.3	
Merchandise imports		249.8		265.1		247.7		261.3
Service exports	118.2		138.6		138.3		131.9	
Service imports		83.7		97.5		102.9		103.8
Unilateral transfers, net		7.1		6.8	19.6	8.1		8.7
Direct investment, net		2.3	13.5		5.4		6.4	
Portfolio investment, net	4.5		4.4				9.7	
Bank and non-bank reported claims, net		50.0		85.4		104.4		30.7
Bank and non-bank reported liabilities, net	17.6		43.0		63.5		47.7	
Other capital, net		5.2		5.1		6.1		5.0
Allocation of SDRs	1.2		1.1		–		–	
Statistical discrepancy	25.0		22.3		32.9		9.3	
Foreign official assets in the US, net	15.5		5.0		3.3		5.3	
US official reserve assets, net		8.2		5.2		5.0		1.2
TOTAL	406.3	406.3	465.0	465.1	474.2	474.2	410.6	410.7

Source: *Survey of Current Business.* (Totals might not add due to rounding.)

Table 3.2: US balance of payments measures, 1980–3.

	($ billions)			
	1980	1981	1982	1983
Merchandise exports	224.3	237.1	211.2	200.3
Merchandise imports	− 249.8	− 265.1	− 247.7	− 261.3
= MERCHANDISE TRADE BALANCE $(X_G - M_G)$	− 25.5	− 28.0	− 36.5	− 61.1
+				
Service exports	118.2	138.6	138.3	131.9
Service imports	− 83.7	− 97.5	− 102.9	− 103.8
= BALANCE ON GOODS AND SERVICES $(X - M)$	9.0	13.1	− 1.1	− 32.9
+				
Unilateral transfers, net	− 7.1	− 6.8	− 8.1	− 8.7
= BALANCE ON CURRENT ACCOUNT $(X - M + T)$	1.9	6.3	− 9.2	− 41.6
+				
Direct investment, net	− 2.3	13.5	19.6	6.4
Portfolio investment, net	4.5	4.4	5.4	9.7
Bank and non-bank reported claims, net	− 50.0	− 85.4	− 104.4	− 30.7
Bank and non-bank reported liabilities, net	17.6	43.0	63.5	47.7
Other capital, net (n.i.e.)	− 5.2	− 5.1	− 6.1	− 5.0
Allocation of SDRs	1.2	1.1	—	—
Statistical discrepancy	25.0	22.3	32.9	9.3
Foreign official assets, net	15.5	5.0	3.3	5.3
= OVERALL BALANCE $(X - M + T + LTC + STC + SDR + U + R_F)$	8.2	5.2	5.0	1.2
Official reserve assets, net (increase-):				
Gold	—	—	—	—
SDRs	—	− 1.8	− 1.4	− 0.1
Reserve position in IMF	− 1.7	− 2.5	− 2.6	− 4.4
Foreign currencies	− 6.5	− 0.9	− 1.0	3.3
= OFFICIAL RESERVES (R_D)	− 8.2	− 5.2	− 5.0	− 1.2

Source: *Survey of Current Business.* (Totals might not add due to rounding.)

imported into a country. It is compiled from customs returns and specifically excludes service transactions. The deficit of $61.1 billion recorded for the US in 1983, for example, indicates that the US exported fewer goods than it imported $(X_G < M_G)$ and that the net flow of resources (debits) into the US had to be financed by equivalent but opposite net changes (credits) in other sectoral accounts.

Balance on goods and services $(X - M)$

This balance is more wide-ranging and includes the following accounts:

Investment income, net. This entry records investment income paid to, and received from, other countries. It includes portfolio (securities) income, such as interest and dividends, and direct investment income in the form of profits generated by physical assets such as plant and machinery.

Military transactions, net. This account records the net value of overseas military expenditure.

Travel, transportation and other services, net. Included in this account are international receipts and payments arising from foreign commercial transactions, such as overseas travel and transportation, and foreign financial transactions such as royalties and fees.

These items are the service equivalent of merchandise exports and imports. The balance on services for the US in 1983, for example, amounted to a surplus of $28.1 billion and reduced the deficit on goods and services to $32.9 billion.

Balance on current account (X − M + T)

The existence of 'gifts' or unrequited transfers to the rest of the world necessitates the creation of a unilateral transfers account which records items such as remittances, pensions and non-military government grants. These items are the accounting counterpart of goods and services which a country has transacted with the rest of the world and for which no corresponding payment or receipt is expected.

The combining of unilateral transfers and goods and services produces the important Balance on Current Account whose regular publication attracts the attention of even the popular news media. It is important for three reasons:

Firstly, it indicates the value of resources, in the form of goods and services, which have been transferred to or from a country. The US deficit for 1983, for example, represents a net resource transfer of $41.6 billion from the rest of the world to the US.

Secondly, it excludes capital movements which tend to be volatile and hence more responsive to short-term influences than current account transactions. The balance is consequently a more reliable indicator of the underlying strength or weakness of a country's international payments position than either narrower merchandise trade or wider capital inclusive balances.

Thirdly, the balance provides an indication of the extent to which external demand augments or diminishes domestic aggregate demand and hence influences other macroeconomic variables such as prices and employment. A current account surplus will tend to increase or maintain aggregate demand, which in turn will tend to increase or maintain at current levels domestic prices or employment or both.[2] A deficit will tend to decrease or accommodate excess aggregate demand with corresponding contractionary or stabilising effects on domestic prices or employment or both.

It could be concluded from this that the balance on current account represents total autonomous transactions with all remaining transactions considered accommodating and hence entered below the imaginary financing line. But this is not correct, for whilst current account transactions are autonomous, not all capital account transactions are accommodating. The basic balance $(X - M + T + LTC)$ represents an attempt to resolve this problem by combining current account transactions with long-term capital flows[3] which, in contrast to short-term capital flows, are essentially autonomous in nature. Even this is not entirely satisfactory, however, since some long-term capital flows are accommodating (flows within the same sectoral account, such as portfolio capital, may be either autonomous or accommodating, depending on the motives underlying the instigation of these flows) whilst some short-term flows, such as bank lending, may be autonomous.

Various attempts at resolving this capital identification problem which, for the US, has been compounded by the dollar's role as an international payments medium and reserve currency, have involved recourse to such alternative payments measures as gross and net liquidity balances which measure changes in a country's international liquidity position. These have also not proved entirely satisfactory, however, and suggest that an 'overall' measure of the balance of payments is desirable.

Overall balance $(X - M + T + LTC + STC + SDR + U + R_F)$

This measure combines current account transactions with the following major categories of international (predominantly capital) transactions:

> Direct investment, net. This represents domestic net changes in overseas investment and foreign net changes in domestic investment in enterprises in which investors have a significant

interest or play a significant managerial role. It includes the reinvested earnings of both domestic and overseas incorporated affiliates. The US, for example, has traditionally been an important source of international direct investment with substantial US gross capital outflows recorded in the 1970s. These flows decelerated rapidly in the early 1980s, however, and, together with an equally rapid acceleration of foreign direct investment in the US, succeeded in converting the US into a net recipient of international direct investment with net inflows amounting to $6.4 billion in 1983.

Portfolio investment, net. This represents domestic net purchases of foreign financial assets and foreign net purchases of domestic financial assets. These assets consist of ownership instruments, such as equities, and credit instruments with original maturities of more than twelve months, such as bonds. Net portfolio investment in the US amounted to $9.7 billion in 1983.

Bank and non-bank reported claims, net. These consist predominantly of domestic bank lending overseas and, to a lesser extent, non-bank domestic and foreign currency deposits overseas. The outflow on this account for the US amounted to a substantial $30.7 billion in 1983 and was the largest capital outflow recorded in that year.

SUPPLEMENTARY NOTE — OVERSEAS BANK LENDING

The impact of overseas bank lending exerts an indeterminate impact on a country's economy, balance of payments and exchange rate. Three possibilities, using US bank lending as an example, can be considered:

(i) US overseas lending may be used to finance the purchase of US goods and services. In this situation bank lending is used to finance a higher level of autonomous transactions (exports for example) than would have been possible, ceteris paribus, *in the absence of such lending, in which case the net impact of these outflows on the US economy will essentially be expansionary.[4] The impact on the US overall balance, on the other hand, will be neutral — since exports and increases in claims will be offsetting transactions — while the dollar exchange rate will be unaffected since dollar flows will not enter the foreign exchange market.*

(ii) US overseas lending may be used to finance and subsequently refinance foreign purchases of goods and services from third party countries. The maintenance of these financing facilities as dollar claims on the US would be recorded in US payments data as bank reported liabilities to private foreigners which would be the statistical counterpart (with sign reversed) of the original increase in bank reported claims (lending). The net direct impact of increased US bank lending in this situation would be zero for the US economy and the balance of payments, but expansionary for those economies whose international trade had been financed. The dollar exchange rate would again be unaffected if transactions were denominated in dollars which remained outside foreign exchange markets.

(iii) US overseas lending may be used to finance foreign purchases of goods and services from third party countries using foreign currencies acquired from the respective central banks in exchange for the previously borrowed dollars. The resulting accumulation of dollar reserves would be recorded in US payments data as increases in foreign official assets in the US such as bank reported liabilities to foreign official agencies. These liabilities would be the statistical counterpart (with sign reversed) of the original increase in bank reported claims. The net direct impact on the US economy and the overall balance would again be zero, but on this occasion net dollar sales to central banks might weaken the dollar in foreign exchange markets. If central banks were subsequently to sell their dollars for US gold, bank reported liabilities to foreign official agencies would decrease with a corresponding increase in the overall deficit.

Bank and non-bank reported liabilities, net. These essentially comprise foreign private claims on domestic banks and, to a lesser extent, non-bank overseas borrowing. Bank reported liabilities are almost exclusively a financing item and may be used to finance inflows of resources into a country, such as imports, by persuading foreigners to accept and hold domestic currency claims as payment. The substantial increases in bank and non-bank reported liabilities recorded in the US between 1981 and 1983, for example, indicate that bank reported liabilities played a major accommodating role in US balance of payments financing.

Other capital, net. This account includes capital flows not included elsewhere, such as changes in government assets other than official reserve assets which are treated as a separate financing item. In the US example, these outflows amounted to $5.0 billion in 1983.

Allocation of **Special Drawing Rights** (SDRs). This minor account represents capital inflows in the form of international assets created by the IMF and used in the discharge of debts amongst member countries. These assets are administrative in origin and, since they represent a net addition to international liquidity, are accorded a separate entry in balance of payments data. SDR allocations to the US amounted to $1.2 billion and $1.1 billion in 1980 and 1981 respectively, after which the international allocation of SDRs was suspended.

Statistical discrepancy. This is a residual balancing item in payments accounts and reflects errors and omissions which are largely accounted for by the statistical undervaluation of service exports, such as transportation services, and the under-recording of private short-term capital flows which exert a particularly destabilising impact on balance of payments accounts since they tend to be both substantial and highly volatile. An example of this volatility was apparent in the US balance of payments during the dollar crises of 1971 and 1973, when foreign official dollar inflows and attendant exchange rate pressures accorded closely with large negative statistical discrepancies. A large statistical discrepancy (inflow) was also recorded in 1982. This amounted to a substantial $32.9 billion which, if identifiable, would most likely have represented short-term capital inflows and would thus have been recorded as increases in bank reported liabilities to foreigners.

Foreign official assets, net. These are foreign-owned assets denominated in the currency of the reporting country and maintained by foreign official institutions (principally central banks) to finance international trade, discharge international debts and support official intervention in foreign exchange markets. They are the liabilities counterpart of international foreign exchange reserves which are principally denominated in dollars, Deutsche Marks and Yen, of which the dollar is the major reserve currency. From the point of view of the reporting country, foreign official assets represent the contribution which foreign official institutions make to the overall balance and to the accumulation/depletion of official reserve assets. In the case of the US in 1983, for example, this contribution amounted to an inflow of \$5.3 billion, predominantly in the form of increases in holdings of US Treasury securities and liabilities reported by US banks.

The overall balance is the ultimate balance of payments measure, since at this point, all other sources of adjustment have been exhausted. It represents outflows/inflows which can now only be financed/accommodated by changes in official reserve assets.

Official reserves (R_D)

The official reserves balance is the counterpart (with sign reversed to 'square off' the entire balance of payments)[5] of the overall balance and represents changes in **official reserve assets**. These consist of gold, SDRs, reserve positions in the IMF and holdings of foreign currencies, one or more of which will decrease (credit)/increase (debit) to finance/accommodate overall deficits/surpluses. In 1983, for example, the US recorded a \$1.2 billion overall surplus. It was able to accommodate this surplus by increasing its stock of reserve assets and recording this as a counterbalancing item under 'official reserves'.

Balance of payments measures used by various countries do not differ significantly.[6] The differences that do exist consist of minor variations in terminology and occasional differences in definition and statistical coverage. These mean, however, that care must be exercised when balance of payments are compared internationally.

The overall similarity of balance of payments measures can be seen in Tables 3.3 and 3.4.

Table 3.3 illustrates UK balance of payments data and shows that the visible (merchandise) trade balance, combined with services, interest, profits, dividends and transfers, results in the current account balance which, when combined with investment, other capital transactions and a balancing item (statistical discrepancy) results in the overall balance. In 1983, for example, this amounted to a deficit of £0.8 billion, which necessitated official financing.

Table 3.4 summarises the Singapore balance of payments. It shows that in 1983, for example, Singapore's overall balance recorded a surplus of S\$2.2 billion, which was accommodated by an increase in official reserves.

Table 3.3: UK balance of payments measures, 1980-3.

	(£ billions)			
	1980	1981	1982	1983
Merchandise exports	47.4	51.0	55.6	60.6
Merchandise imports	− 46.1	− 47.6	− 53.5	− 61.7
= VISIBLE TRADE BALANCE	1.4	3.4	2.1	− 1.1
+				
Services	4.4	4.5	3.7	3.9
Interest, profits and dividends	− 0.2	1.1	1.2	1.7
Transfers	− 2.1	− 1.9	− 2.0	− 2.2
= CURRENT ACCOUNT BALANCE	3.5	6.9	4.9	2.3
+				
Investment and other capital transactions	− 1.3	− 7.3	− 3.3	− 3.4
Balancing item	− 0.8	− 0.4	− 2.9	0.3
= OVERALL BALANCE	1.4	− 0.7	− 1.3	− 0.8
OFFICIAL FINANCING	− 1.4	0.7	1.3	0.8

Source: *Monthly Digest of Statistics*. (Totals may not add due to rounding.)

Table 3.4: Singapore balance of payments measures, 1980-3.

	(S$ billions)			
	1980	1981	1982	1983
Exports of goods	38.9	41.4	41.5	42.9
Imports of goods	− 48.0	− 54.5	− 56.1	− 55.5
= MERCHANDISE TRADE BALANCE	− 9.1	− 13.1	− 14.6	− 12.6
+				
Balance of services	5.8	10.3	12.1	10.9
+				
Transfer payments	− 0.1	− 0.1	− 0.2	− 0.4
= CURRENT ACCOUNT BALANCE	− 3.3	− 2.9	− 2.8	− 2.1
+				
Capital flows	3.6	4.8	4.7	5.7
+				
Balancing item	1.2	—	0.6	− 1.4
= OVERALL BALANCE	1.4	1.9	2.5	2.2
OFFICIAL RESERVES	− 1.4	− 1.9	− 2.5	− 2.2

Source: Singapore Department of Statistics. (Totals may not add due to rounding.)

SIGNIFICANCE

Balance of payments measures are important as a means of identifying and quantifying external disequilibria and the attendant expansionary and contractionary forces to which individual economies are subjected.

Global current account balances must sum to zero since, definitional and statistical discrepancies notwithstanding, global surpluses and deficits must balance. Consequently, individual surpluses or deficits will generate corresponding deficits or surpluses elsewhere.

Current account surpluses are expansionary, since they stimulate domestic demand through injections of net foreign demand. They might consequently be pursued as an engine of domestic economic expansion to achieve internal equilibrium, even at the expense of lower levels of income and employment elsewhere. For example, in the late 1980s, the counterpart of large Japanese current account surpluses and low levels of unemployment have been large US current account deficits and high levels of unemployment.

Current account deficits, in contrast, are contractionary since they syphon aggregate demand from domestic to foreign markets. They are generally not actively pursued as a vehicle for domestic deflation, however, because they deplete foreign exchange reserves. The pursuit of current account deficits and surpluses as an instrument of macroeconomic policy is consequently asymmetrical.

Once a current account deficit has appeared in the balance of payments, it may be tolerated and action may not immediately be taken to correct it. This is because the deficit represents an inflow of resources into the country. Moreover, if the contractionary impact of the deficit can be offset through increases in domestic demand — for example by increased government expenditure — it might be possible to sustain the higher level of resource absorption at the pre-deficit level of national income. This can only be accomplished for as long as the external deficit can be financed either out of reserves or through overseas borrowing and/or aid.

Generally, then, the absorption of real resources from overseas is subject to reserve, borrowing and aid constraints. An exception to this is the case of **reserve centre countries** (principally the US but also including Germany, Japan and, increasingly less significantly, the UK), whose currencies are regarded as **vehicle** or **key currencies**, fulfilling at an international level those functions traditionally assigned to domestic currencies operating within conventional domestic frameworks. (These functions relate to money's primary role as a **numeraire** [unit of account] and medium of exchange and its secondary role as a store of value and means of deferred payment.)

Since the US dollar, for example, is the principal means of denominating and financing international transactions involving trade, capital flows and foreign exchange reserves, the rest of the world has to pay for the 'privilege' of acquiring dollars for international payments purposes. The cost of acquiring these dollars, or any other vehicle currency, is known as **seigniorage**, which is:

The value of resources relinquished, or foreign claims on domestic assets incurred, in exchange for units of vehicle currency.

The seigniorage cost to the rest of the world of acquiring a vehicle currency is equivalent to the seigniorage gain accruing to that currency's country from the absorption of foreign real resources and the acquisition of external financial claims. The annual value of this gain is determined by the return generated by these resources and claims minus the net cost (essentially interest payments) of servicing the liabilities created. These gains normally accrue for as long as deficits are incurred and claims acquired and will be extinguished upon the establishment of surpluses and the liquidation of outstanding claims. In the case of the US dollar, which is required on a continuing and even, perhaps, ever-increasing basis, these liabilities are unlikely to be liquidated in the short term. US seigniorage gains, therefore, which are consistent with the transfer of wealth from the rest of the world — including less developed nations — to the US, may be expected to continue until the dollar ceases to be used as the principal source of international liquidity and is replaced by a supranational financial asset such as the SDR.

SUMMARY

The balance of payments is a systematic record of a country's international transactions with both microeconomic and macroeconomic applications. It is an accounting concept based on 'double-entry' book-keeping which ensures that credits and debits always balance.

Its economic significance is based on the concept of balance of payments equilibrium which may be measured in different ways and is obtained by recording autonomous transactions above and accommodating transactions below an imaginary financing line.

Variations in classifying and combining these transactions account for the different measures of balance of payments equilibria which may range in scope and application from narrow and specific to broad and general.

Balance of payments imbalances subject domestic economies to

71

powerful expansionary and contractionary forces, and may result in seigniorage gains accruing to reserve centre countries.

CONCEPTS FOR REVIEW

Accommodating transactions
Accounting equilibrium
Autonomous transactions
Balance of payments
Balance of payments deficit
Balance of payments surplus
Balance on current account
Balance on goods and services
Credits
Debits
Double-entry system of
  book-keeping

Economic equilibrium
Imaginary financing line
Merchandise trade balance
Numeraire
Official reserve assets
Overall balance
Reserve centre countries
Seigniorage
Special Drawing Rights
Vehicle/key currency

QUESTIONS FOR DISCUSSION

1. If the balance of payments must always balance, in what sense can balance of payments deficits and surpluses arise?
2. Imports of goods and services and increases in bank lending are both recorded as debits in the balance of payments and yet their economic impacts differ. Discuss.
3. The overall balance and official reserves balance are numerically identical. What is the significance of this relationship?
4. Should current account surpluses be actively pursued?
5. How can creating SDRs resolve the 'problem' of seigniorage?

Notes

1. Data deficiencies and inaccuracies are recorded in a 'Statistical Discrepancy' account which ensures accounting equilibrium.
2. One billion dollars of US exports, for example, is estimated to support, on average, 25,000 jobs in the US.
3. Long-term capital flows consist of flows with an original maturity of more than twelve months.
4. The opportunity cost of overseas lending might be close to zero if US banks have excess reserves and domestic loan demand is depressed.

5. Accounting equilibrium necessitates the reversal of the order in which debits and credits are assigned to reserve assets. Consequently, debits denote increases and credits decreases in reserve assets.

6. One important difference, however, which the US shares principally with the other reserve countries (Germany, Japan and to a lesser extent the UK) is that its balance of payments includes a foreign official assets account, which is the domestic liabilities counterpart of foreign exchange reserves denominated in the currency of the reporting country. This account can be shifted out of the overall balance, which then becomes the official settlements balance, into the official reserves balance, which then becomes the official financing balance. This shows explicitly the extent to which *private* deficits/surpluses are financed/accommodated through *official* transactions or, in other words, the dollar's role as an international reserve currency.

Part Two

Exchange Rate Systems

Exchange rate systems establish the structural framework within which foreign exchange transactions are conducted.

Systems are essentially either inflexible, in which case the exchange rate is stabilised within predetermined limits, or flexible, in which case the exchange rate is free to respond to changes in market forces.

Various exchange rate systems have been resorted to (at times through default) in different periods. Each has met with varying degrees of success, prompted in part by the advantages and disadvantages inherent in each system and in part by the prevailing economic climate. Chapters 4 to 7 examine these systems within a chronological framework which reflects the changing nature of these economic conditions.

4

The Gold Standard

The golden era of the gold standard was 1880–1914, when it was recognised and subscribed to by most of the industrialised world. The system was centred on the UK which was the dominant industrial and trading power of the time and which had operated a gold standard since the early nineteenth century. The outbreak of the First World War in 1914 brought the system to an end, but its perceived successes fostered attempts in the immediate post-war period to restore it to its former prominence. The subsequent return to the gold standard by the UK in 1925, and by most other countries by 1927, proved short-lived, however, not least because of the problems of misaligned exchange rates and the less than propitious international financial climate. This, together with a succession of financial crises, prompted the UK to abrogate the gold standard in 1931. The US followed in 1933 and France in 1936, so that by the end of the decade the gold standard had been abandoned and consigned to the annals of economic history.

CHARACTERISTICS

An efficiently operating gold standard is characterised by a stable exchange rate fluctuating within narrow, clearly defined limits, and an automatic balance of payments adjustment mechanism operating through price changes.

OPERATION AND ADJUSTMENT MECHANISM

The widespread acceptance of the gold standard and its appeal even amongst some economists today is attributable to the standard's *alleged* ease of operation and the automatic nature of its balance of payments adjustment mechanism. These attributes are claimed to result automatically from adherence to the following rules of the gold standard: each currency should have a specified gold content which determines its par value; currencies should be readily convertible into and out of gold at their par value; there should be no restrictions on the import or export of gold; there should be no government intervention to counteract increases or decreases in the domestic money supply resulting from imports or exports of gold.

The operational essence of the gold standard is contained in the **quantity theory of money** which can be expressed as:

$$M_S V = P Q \qquad\qquad (4\text{-}1)$$

where:

M_S represents the quantity of money (gold) in the economy

V represents the income velocity of circulation of money or the average number of times that each representative monetary unit circulates to finance the transacting of final goods and services produced per period

P represents the average price of final goods and services produced per period

Q represents the volume of final goods and services produced per period

($P Q$ expresses national income).

Equation 4-1 implies that, provided that V remains constant ($\overline{V}$), changes in the gold stock will lead to changes in P or Q or both. Notationally:

$$\Delta M_S \, \overline{V} \rightarrow \Delta (P Q).$$

Changes in P and Q and potentially in V consequently have important implications for the operation of the gold standard.

Firstly, if wages and prices are perfectly flexible both upwards and downwards and V is constant, and if this ensures full employment, then changes in the gold stock will lead to changes in prices with an unchanged volume of final goods and services. Under the gold standard, therefore, a balance of payments deficit, which reduces the stock of gold as a result of the need to finance net imports, will lower domestic prices, which in turn will discourage imports and encourage exports. This will eventually restore balance of payments equilibrium with unchanged real income (output) and employment levels. (Similar but opposite changes apply to balance of payments surpluses.) The widespread appeal of the gold standard was thus contained in the automatic nature of the adjustment mechanism which allegedly restored balance of payments equilibrium whilst maintaining full employment. Notationally:

$$\downarrow(X-M) \to \downarrow M_S \to \downarrow P \to \uparrow(X-M) \to \to (X-M=0) \text{ with } \bar{Q}.$$

Secondly, if wages and prices are imperfectly flexible downwards, the effect of changes in the gold stock will not be confined to changes in prices but will also extend to include changes in the volume of final goods and services. Since the effect of a reduction in the gold stock prompted by a balance of payments deficit will now be distributed between price and output changes, prices will be unable to accommodate the full impact of the gold outflow. Balance of payments equilibrium will consequently not be restored through price changes alone and the automatic nature of the adjustment mechanism will have been undermined. In this case, the gold standard has become consistent with persistent balance of payments deficits and sustained reductions in output and employment. Notationally:

$$\downarrow(X-M) \to \downarrow M_S \to \downarrow P \to (X-M<0) \text{ with unemployment.}$$
$$ \downarrow Q \longrightarrow$$

Thirdly, the income velocity of circulation of money might not remain constant. Decreases in the stock of money might encourage economising in the use of money, so that changes in the money stock might be counterbalanced by opposite changes in velocity. For example, the effect of a balance of payments deficit, which reduces the stock of gold, might not be confined to changes in prices and the volume of final goods and services, but might partly extend to include counterbalancing increases in the income velocity of circulation of gold. Since the effect of a reduction in the gold stock is now distributed among price, output and velocity changes, prices will again be unable to accommodate the full impact of the gold outflow. Balance of payments equilibrium will therefore not be restored through price changes alone and the automatic nature of the adjustment mechanism will again be undermined. Notationally:

$$\downarrow(X-M)\rightarrow\downarrow M_S\rightarrow\downarrow Q\rightarrow\rightarrow(X-M<0) \text{ with unemployment.}$$

with $\downarrow P$ and $\uparrow V$ forming feedback loops.

The alleged 'automatic' adjustment mechanism, therefore, does not function under certain conditions.

The adjustment mechanism and its potential shortcomings apply in the operation of both a simple gold-specie standard and a more sophisticated gold-bullion standard.

Gold-specie standard

The dominant characteristic of this standard, which might be expected to apply to underdeveloped economies such as existed in pre-industrial days, is that currency in circulation consists of gold coins whose intrinsic value (gold content) and nominal or face value are equal. Under this system, increases in net imports, for example, are financed directly with gold coins which are melted down and exported. This reduces the domestic money supply and initiates the standard's automatic adjustment mechanism.

Gold-bullion standard

More sophisticated economies are likely to adopt the **gold-bullion standard**, in which money is not confined to gold coins but includes notes and bank deposit liabilities, both of which are backed in varying degrees by gold.

In its simplest form, such a standard would operate with notes which were fully backed by gold and so would operate in a manner similar to that of a gold-specie standard, except that notes would first have to be converted into gold before they could be used to finance imports.

A second, more sophisticated version, however, uses gold only as a partial backing for both notes and commercial banks' deposit liabilities which also become the principal form of money. The extent of such partial backing constitutes the economy's **gold**

reserve ratio, which has two important implications for the operation of the gold standard:

(i) The link between gold, income and the balance of payments will be potentially further weakened since changes in the gold reserve ratio may be implemented to counteract the contractionary/expansionary effects of deficits/surpluses. For example, the contractionary impact of a net gold outflow prompted by a balance of payments deficit might be offset by lowering the gold reserve ratio, thereby enabling the existing money supply to be supported by a smaller stock of gold. The reduction in the ratio will further weaken the link between the balance of payments and national income and will further undermine the automatic operation of the balance of payments adjustment mechanism.

(ii) The development of money, in the form of bank deposit liabilities, introduces the possibility that payments deficits will be financed through transfers of deposits from residents to non-residents. If non-residents can be persuaded to hold domestic currency claims, for example through higher domestic interest rates, the transfer of gold from residents to non-residents (net outflows) will be reduced or possibly even circumvented entirely.

The inclusion of notes and deposit liabilities in the money supply implies that payments for imports will no longer be confined to the melting-down and shipping of gold coins but will now extend to a choice of financing consisting of gold, domestic and foreign currency. This choice results in the creation of **gold export and import points** and the maintenance of exchange rates within these narrowly defined limits.

The operation of these points is illustrated, using the dollar and sterling as an example, in Figure 4.1. Assume that the gold content (par value) of the dollar and sterling is one ounce and two ounces respectively. The exchange rate is thus \$1 = £0.50. Assume also that gold conversion and transatlantic shipping costs amount to £0.01 per ounce of gold. Since the rules of the gold standard oblige the central banks of both the US and the UK to buy and sell their respective currencies at par value without restriction, the exchange rate of the dollar cannot move beyond an upper limit of £0.50 plus £0.01 (\$1 = £0.51) or a lower limit of £0.50 minus £0.01 (\$1 = £0.49).

If a UK deficit were then to increase the demand for dollars (D_1), this would have to be satisfied from market sources and the sterling exchange rate would depreciate to \$1 = £0.51. Further increases in the deficit might further increase demand (D_2) and

81

prompt an attempted further depreciation of sterling beyond $1 = £0.51. At an exchange rate above this level, however, UK importers will no longer be prepared to buy dollars in the foreign exchange market since each dollar will cost more than £0.51 and it will be cheaper to acquire dollars in the US with gold. Importers will thus use sterling to purchase gold from the UK central bank and ship it to the US where, for a total cost of £0.51 — par value (£0.50) plus conversion and shipping costs (£0.01) — it will be sold for $1. There will be no incentive, therefore, for British importers to pay more than £0.51 for each dollar purchased. This exchange rate becomes the (UK) **gold export point** (point a) which is:

The lowest value of a currency's exchange rate, beyond which further supplies of foreign exchange are acquired through the export and sale of domestic gold.

Correspondingly, a decrease in the UK deficit reduces the demand for dollars (D_4) and prompts US importers to start shipping and selling US gold for sterling at an exchange rate of $1 = £0.49. This exchange rate becomes the (UK) **gold import point** (point b), which is:

The highest value of a currency's exchange rate, beyond which further supplies of the currency are provided through the import and purchase of foreign gold.

Changes in the supply of foreign exchange (dollars) similarly contribute to movements towards gold export and import points (Figure 4.1(b)).

Regardless of whether balance of payments fluctuations are caused by changes in deficits or surpluses, therefore, a currency's exchange rate will remain within its gold export and import points, which are determined by the currency's par value and the cost of converting and shipping gold.

Gold export/import points can now be used to compare the choice and impact of balance of payments adjustments using gold, domestic and foreign currency.

(i) Balance of payments disturbances which are small enough to be accommodated within gold export/import points will be financed through changes in the demand for and supply of foreign exchange.

(ii) Balance of payments disturbances which are too large to be accommodated within gold export/import points will be financed

Figure 4.1: Gold export/import points and demand- and supply-induced exchange rate fluctuations. An increase in the demand for dollars (D_1) in panel (a) up to point a is satisfied by a conventional market-induced extension in the supply of dollars. Further increases beyond this point (D_2) will prompt an *attempted* appreciation of the dollar above the exchange rate of $1 = £0.51. This does not occur, however, for it becomes cheaper for potential buyers to acquire dollars by selling sterling for gold in the UK and shipping the gold to the US where it is sold for dollars, since the total cost of the transaction (£0.51) will be limited to the par value of sterling plus conversion and shipping costs. Point a thus becomes the gold export point from the UK and, analogously, point b the gold import point from the US. Similar considerations apply to supply-induced exchange rate fluctuations (panel b).

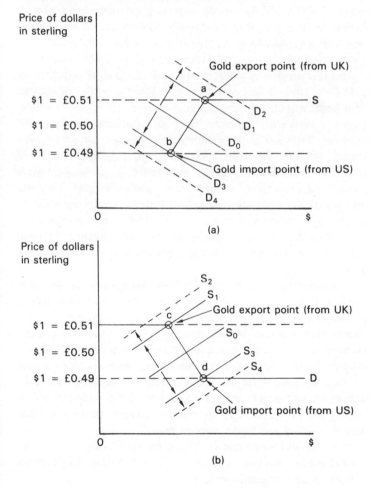

(a)

(b)

through net gold flows, such that net imports will generate gold outflows (depletion of gold reserves) and net exports gold inflows (accumulation of gold reserves). The magnitude of these flows and the macroeconomic impact of the corresponding payments imbalances will depend on the manner in which the economy responds to these flows: if there is perfect correspondence between net gold flows, changes in the money stock and changes in prices, net gold flows may be expected to restore external equilibrium automatically; if there is imperfect correspondence between net gold flows and changes in the money stock or if there is perfect correspondence between net gold flows and changes in the money stock but this does not extend to changes in prices, then changes in net gold flows will be unable to restore external equilibrium. A deficit, for example, might eventually have to be restored through devaluation (reduction in the gold content of the currency) or, even more drastically, through the abrogation of the gold standard.

(iii) If it is considered that capital flows are a close substitute for gold flows, then deficit countries, on whom the burden of external adjustment will tend to fall since gold reserves are relatively scarce, might raise domestic interest rates in an attempt to stem gold outflows. Increases in domestic interest rates will attract overseas capital, which increases the supply of foreign exchange, and this will tend to accommodate the net demand for foreign exchange, relieve pressure on exchange rates and stem the outflow of gold. They will also potentially persuade residents of surplus creditor countries to accept payments directly in the currency of the debtor country and to maintain these receipts as claims on the debtor country. This will again relieve pressure on exchange rates and stem the outflow of gold.

The increase in interest rates in both cases, however, will only serve to *finance* and not *correct* the balance of payments deficit. Consequently, financing policies which rely on raising domestic interest rates can only be sustained for as long as non-residents are prepared to hold claims denominated in the currency of the debtor country. Such policies are not without cost, moreover, for not only do they undermine the automatic nature of the gold standard's adjustment mechanism, they also shift part of the burden of adjustment from debtor country to creditor country through induced capital outflows and higher interest rates.

It was in this manner that the UK, as the gold standard's principal reserve centre, was able to finance part of its balance of payments deficits in the nineteenth century.

ADVANTAGES

Firstly, a gold standard provides stable exchange rates which are conducive to trade since they eliminate a further source of price instability and, in contrast to the economic chaos which prevailed during the 1930s, foster a measure of economic stability.

Secondly, provided that operational rules are followed, an efficiently operating gold standard allegedly ensures automatic balance of payments adjustment through price changes.

Thirdly, the standard imposes fiscal orthodoxy on governments which, in different circumstances, might resort to more expansionist measures to achieve desired policy objectives, even at the expense of external equilibrium.

DISADVANTAGES

Firstly, the burden of balance of payments adjustment is shifted from the exchange rate to domestic economic variables. This subordination of the domestic economy to external economic factors is one of the most serious criticisms of the gold standard, since it is consistent with severe deflation and, quite possibly, high unemployment in defence of overvalued exchange rates.

Secondly, the problem of selecting an appropriate par value is compounded by the complexity and volume of trade and capital flows and by the existence of both traded and non-traded goods. The adoption of an overvalued par value, for example, will tend to generate persistent balance of payments deficits and chronic unemployment.

Thirdly, the emergence of a misaligned par value (actual or perceived) may encourage speculation of sufficient magnitude to effect an exchange rate realignment. Such speculation tends to be asymmetrical, for whilst surplus countries are able, in the short run at least, to accumulate gold reserves, deficit countries are only able to support overvalued par values and gold outflows for as long as these flows may be financed out of existing or borrowed reserves. The undermining of market confidence by gold outflows which were initially containable might thus contribute to an acceleration of outflows which eventually culminate in a self-fulfilling exchange rate realignment. Such was the outcome of a succession of speculative attacks mounted on sterling in the early 1930s.

Fourthly, the gold standard is dependent on adequate but not excessive supplies of new gold. This is tantamount to tying the growth of the world economy to the continued supply of what is essentially just a popular metal.

Fifthly, the mining and processing of gold involves a real resource cost which may also be expected to increase as economic growth and accompanying increases in the demand for gold bring forth marginal mines with progressively higher operating costs.

Finally, the unequal geographical distribution of gold deposits generates substantial seigniorage gains for individual countries. These gains are neither competed away nor reversed since gold, once acquired with real goods and services, remains a permanent financing feature of the international monetary system.

DEMISE OF THE GOLD STANDARD

Despite the alleged advantages of the gold standard, the post-war return to it in the mid-1920s was relatively short-lived. There were several reasons for this:

The restoration of sterling's gold link in 1925 at its pre-war parity of £1 = \$4.86 most probably represented an overvaluation of sterling since, amongst other reasons, Britain was being confronted at the time with shrinking export markets and declining overseas investment revenues.

It was also true that London's previously unassailable position as the gold standard's reserve centre was being increasingly challenged by New York, whose development fostered increased capital mobility and exchange rate volatility.

These specific factors were compounded by the general uncertainty of the Great Depression which created an economic climate in which financial confidence was easily shaken. It was in these circumstances that a succession of financial crises, beginning with a banking crisis in Austria in May 1931, spread across Europe to the UK where sustained gold outflows culminated in the UK's abrogation of the gold standard in September 1931.

SUMMARY

The gold standard is an exchange rate system characterised by stable exchange rates, fluctuating within narrow, clearly defined limits and, if functioning efficiently, an automatic balance of payments adjustment mechanism operating through price changes. These attributes are alleged to result automatically if: currencies have a specified gold content; currencies are readily convertible into and out of gold; there are no restrictions on the import and export of gold and there is no government intervention to counteract changes in gold stocks.

The operation of the gold standard is explained by the quantity theory of money, such that balance of payments-induced changes in gold stocks (money) will change domestic prices which in turn will automatically correct the original external disturbance. The automatic nature of the adjustment process will be undermined, however, by an imperfect correspondence between changes in gold stocks and changes in prices, so that the gold standard becomes consistent with persistent external and internal disequilibria.

The adjustment mechanism applies to both a gold-specie standard, in which gold coins are melted down and shipped to pay for imports, and a gold-bullion standard, in which gold is used as partial backing for notes and commercial banks' deposit liabilities. In this latter case, exchange rates will fluctuate within gold export/import points which are determined by the currency's par value and the cost of converting and shipping gold.

External disturbances which are small enough to be accommodated within gold export/import points will be financed through changes in the demand for and supply of foreign exchange. Larger disturbances will be financed with net gold flows, for which partial substitution might be made with interest rate-induced capital flows. In this case, capital flows will have financed, but not corrected, the disturbances and the automatic nature of the gold standard's adjustment mechanism will have been further undermined.

The principal advantages of an efficient gold standard are that it provides stable exchange rates and automatic balance of payments adjustment through price changes. The principal disadvantage of the system is that the burden of adjustment is shifted from the exchange rate to domestic economic variables. This is potentially consistent with persistent balance of payments deficits and chronic unemployment.

The apogee of the gold standard was 1880–1914. Attempts to return to the standard after the First World War proved unsuccessful and the gold standard was eventually abandoned in the 1930s.

CONCEPTS FOR REVIEW

Gold-bullion standard	Gold reserve ratio
Gold export point	Gold-specie standard
Gold import point	Quantity theory of money

QUESTIONS FOR DISCUSSION

1. Use the quantity theory of money to explain the gold standard's alleged automatic balance of payments adjustment mechanism.
2. Under what circumstances might the automatic nature of this adjustment mechanism fail to operate?
3. Why are gold export/import points consistent with stable foreign exchange rates?
4. Explain the likely economic responses, under a gold standard, to a balance of payments deficit.
5. In what way do capital flows finance but not correct external disequilibria?

5

Fixed Exchange Rates

After the gold standard was abandoned in the 1930s, there was a period of exchange rate chaos. In response, a system of fixed exchange rates was introduced after the Second World War, following an international financial conference held at Bretton Woods, New Hampshire, USA in 1944. This so-called 'Bretton Woods' system, which survived for almost 30 years under the auspices of the IMF, may be used as a specific framework within which to examine the wider issues of fixed exchange rates in general.

Contrary to what its name suggests, a **fixed exchange rate** does not involve exchange rates which are permanently fixed or immutable. It represents, rather, a system in which:

Exchange rates are permitted to fluctuate within narrow bands centred around par values, both of which are fixed but not immutable.

Par values may be adjusted in response to structural changes which result in persistent balance of payments deficits or surpluses. Such imbalances represent **fundamental disequilibria** and may be defined as:

Balance of payments imbalances which cannot be corrected at the prevailing exchange rate without recourse to exchange controls or substantial income or price adjustments.

So while the Bretton Woods system precluded the use of exchange rate realignments as a means of correcting *temporary* balance of payments disequilibria, it did permit realignments as a means of correcting *fundamental* disequilibria. An example of this was the 14.3 per cent devaluation of sterling in 1967, undertaken to correct persistent balance of payments deficits.

Band spreads are changed much less frequently, since such changes are interpreted as symptomatic of deeper economic malaise and so are implemented only as a last resort. The eventual widening of the Bretton Woods band of maximum permitted exchange rate fluctuations from 2 per cent to 4.5 per cent in December 1971 preceded the collapse of the entire system of fixed exchange rates by just 15 months!

A fixed exchange rate system requires an international numeraire to provide a value framework within which the relative values of individual currencies may be determined. The Bretton Woods system was established as a **gold exchange standard** in which gold determined the value of the dollar whose conversion into gold at a rate of $35 per ounce was guaranteed by the US. The US thus became banker to the rest of the world, which used gold and dollars on an interchangeable basis. Other currencies were tied to gold either directly or indirectly via the dollar, and the dollar became the principal intervention currency in foreign exchange markets.

Despite the growth of US external liabilities and an attendant decline in the US gold reserve ratio, the gold exchange standard continued to operate until March 1968, when intensified speculative demand for gold and an accelerating decline in US gold reserves precipitated an international gold crisis. This was resolved through the establishment of a **two-tier gold market**, which separated official (central bank) and private gold transactions. The former continued to be transacted at the official price of $35 per ounce, but the latter were conducted in a free market with no attempt being made to stabilise the price at the official level through official purchases or, more likely, sales of gold. This effectively established a **de facto dollar exchange standard** in which the dollar maintained its role as an international numeraire, but in which privately held dollars could no longer be converted into gold, only other currencies. The rest of the world was thus faced with the simple choice of holding dollars or dollar-denominated assets — a state of affairs which was legitimised in August 1971 when President Nixon announced the 'suspension of official dollar convertibility' and effectively placed the world on an **official dollar exchange standard**.

CHARACTERISTICS

A well-managed fixed exchange system is characterised by: a stable exchange rate maintained, through official intervention, within narrow, clearly defined limits; long-term exchange rate stability with infrequent changes in par values, and adjustment to temporary balance of payments disequilibria through changes in official reserves, interest rates, incomes and prices and to fundamental disequilibria through changes in par values.

OPERATION

The operation of a fixed exchange rate system with or without dollar convertibility is illustrated, using sterling exchange rates as an example, in Figure 5.1. The par value for sterling (£1 = \$2.80) is the rate which prevailed between 1949 and 1967. The upper and lower limits, beyond which the spot exchange rate cannot move, were set at £1 = \$2.82 and £1 = \$2.78 respectively and thus became the **upper and lower intervention points** at which official intervention in the market was forthcoming to maintain exchange rate stability.

Panel (a) in Figure 5.1 shows that a continued increase ($D_1 \rightarrow D_2$) in the US demand for sterling, prompted by increases in either British exports to the US or capital inflows from the US, threatens to pull the exchange rate from point (b) to point (c), which lies beyond the upper intervention point of £1 = \$2.82. The authorities must intervene in the market to prevent movement beyond this point by providing official assistance in the form of increased supplies of sterling. This is shown as a shift to the right in the supply curve (S_1), which now becomes the market supply curve (S_0) plus official intervention (I) and which serves to contain the exchange rate at upper intervention point (d).

The impact of this increased supply of sterling, which can be provided by either the US or UK monetary authorities regardless of whether a gold exchange or dollar exchange standard prevails, will be felt at two levels. At a primary level, the impact is independent of the prevailing exchange rate standard. US sales of sterling will deplete US sterling reserves by $Q_2 - Q_1$, while UK sales of sterling will augment UK dollar reserves by the sterling equivalent of $Q_2 - Q_1$. At a secondary level, the impact of sterling sales will depend on the type of exchange rate standard operating. Under a

Figure 5.1: Upper intervention points under a system of fixed exchange rates. Increased demand for, or reduced supply of, sterling threatens to pull the exchange rate beyond the upper limit of £1 = \$2.82 (point b in panels (a) and (b)). This necessitates official market intervention in the form of increased supplies of sterling to maintain the rate at or below £1 = \$2.82 at points d in panel (a) and b in panel (b), which become the upper intervention points.

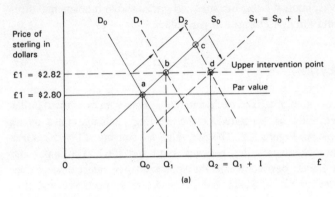

(a)

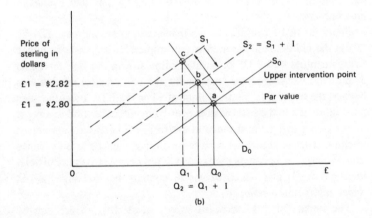

(b)

gold exchange standard the US can acquire further supplies of sterling by selling either gold or dollars to the UK monetary authorities, while under a dollar exchange standard, only the latter option is available. The choice confronting the UK under a gold exchange standard is between holding reserves in the form of dollar-denominated assets or converting these dollars into gold purchased from the US, while under a dollar exchange standard only the former option is available.

Decreases in the market supply of a currency produce similar results to increases in market demand. This is illustrated in panel (b), which shows that continuing decreases in the market supply of sterling ($S_0 \rightarrow S_1$), prompted by decreases in either UK imports from the US or UK capital outflows to the US, threaten to pull the exchange rate from point (a) to point (c) which lies beyond the upper intervention point of £1 = \$2.82. Official market intervention to prevent this is again necessary and takes the form of an increase in the supply of sterling. This is shown as a downward shift in the supply curve to S_2 which now becomes the market supply curve (S_1) plus official intervention (I). US sterling reserves will again decrease by $Q_2 - Q_1$, or UK dollar reserves will increase by the sterling equivalent of $Q_2 - Q_1$. The implications for reserve holdings/conversions will also be similar to those for increases in the market demand for sterling.

Under either a gold or dollar exchange standard, therefore, the efficient operation of a fixed exchange rate system and the maintenance of domestic currencies at or below their upper intervention points involves the sale of domestic currencies and the purchase of dollars. This requires confidence in the dollar and additionally, in the case of a dollar exchange standard, willingness on the part of the international community to continue accumulating dollar reserves. It was the loss of this confidence and the sheer magnitude of the dollar glut (the so-called dollar 'overhang') that eventually contributed to the collapse of the dollar exchange standard of fixed exchange rates.

The operation of lower intervention points, again using sterling exchange rates as an example, is illustrated in Figure 5.2.

A continuing increase in the UK supply of sterling ($S_1 \rightarrow S_2$ in panel (a)), prompted by increases in either British imports from the US or capital outflows to the US, threatens to push the exchange rate from point (b) to point (c) which lies below the lower intervention point of £1 = \$2.78. The authorities must prevent this by intervening in the market and providing official support in the form of

Figure 5.2: Lower intervention points under a system of fixed exchange rates. Increased supplies of, or reduced demand for, sterling threaten to push the exchange rate below the lower limit of £1 = $2.78 (point b in panels (a) and (b)). This necessitates official market intervention in the form of increased demand for sterling to maintain the rate at or above £1 = $2.78 at points d in panel (a) and b in panel (b), which become the lower intervention points.

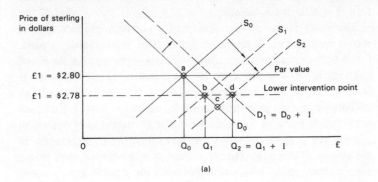

(a)

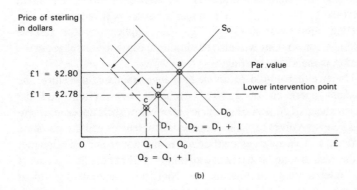

(b)

increased demand for sterling. This is shown by an upward shift in the demand curve to D_1, which now becomes the market demand curve (D_0) plus official intervention (I) and which serves to contain the exchange rate at lower intervention point (d). The impact of these support measures is to increase US reserves of sterling by $Q_2 - Q_1$ or decrease UK reserves of dollars by the sterling equivalent of $Q_2 - Q_1$.

Similarly, a continuing reduction in the demand for sterling

($D_0 \rightarrow D_1$ in panel (b)), prompted by decreases in either British exports to the US or capital inflows from the US, threatens to push the exchange rate from point (a) to point (c) which lies below the lower intervention point. Official intervention is again necessary and takes the form of an increase in the demand for sterling which is depicted as an upward shift in the demand curve to D_2 which now becomes the market demand curve (D_1) plus official intervention (I). US sterling reserves will again increase by $Q_2 - Q_1$ or UK dollar reserves decrease by the sterling equivalent of $Q_2 - Q_1$.

The impact of these intervention measures, for both increases in the market supply of, and decreases in the market demand for sterling, is the augmentation of US sterling reserves or the depletion of UK dollar reserves. Under a gold exchange standard, the US will either hold these reserves as sterling-denominated assets or use them to purchase gold from the UK. Under a dollar exchange standard, only the former option will be available. The UK, on the other hand, can acquire further dollar reserves with either gold or sterling under a gold exchange standard, but only with sterling under a dollar exchange standard.

Under either a gold or dollar exchange standard, therefore, the efficient operation of a fixed exchange rate system and the maintenance of domestic currencies at or above their lower intervention points involves the purchase of domestic currencies and the sale of dollars. This requires either an adequate international supply of dollar reserves or willingness on the part of the US to acquire additional foreign currency reserves in exchange for dollars. The problems which confronted the international monetary system in the immediate post-war period — in contrast to those of the late 1960s and early 1970s caused by a surplus of dollars — resulted from a shortage of dollars prompted by a trade imbalance heavily in favour of the US.

Regardless of the source or nature of foreign exchange disturbances, therefore, official intervention under a system of fixed exchange rates will ensure that exchange rates remain within predetermined parity bands and that the effects of such disturbances will be absorbed by changes in gold or foreign exchange reserves. Unlike gold export and import points, which are partly determined by 'natural' factors such as the cost of shipping gold, the intervention points or parity bands of fixed exchange rate systems are purely administrative and reflect both the degree of flexibility which is desired in the system and the opportunity cost of the official reserves (in terms, for example, of relinquished resources) necessary to finance official intervention.

ADJUSTMENT MECHANISM

The adjustment process under fixed exchange rates, as with the gold standard, works by either financing or correcting disequilibrium in the balance of payments. It operates in five ways:

In the initial stages of disequilibrium, a change in the level of official reserves will finance/accommodate the deficit/surplus and hence partially insulate the economy from the impact of the disturbance.

If the monetary authorities perceive the imbalance (for example, a balance of payments deficit) to be temporary and sterilise its contractionary effect, the economy will revert to external equilibrium with a net reserve loss if the deficit is subsequently corrected or a zero reserve loss if the deficit is over-corrected by an amount equal to the original deficit.

If, however, the imbalance is not corrected and the authorities continue to sterilise its contractionary effect, the deficit will continue to be financed out of official reserves for as long as the deficit persists.

The second element of the adjustment process operates through changes in domestic liquidity and interest rates. Official intervention to support a depreciating domestic currency (deficit) reduces both foreign exchange reserves and the market supply of domestic currency, since the former is used to purchase the latter in the foreign exchange market. This reduces domestic liquidity and raises domestic interest rates. (The opposite applies to an appreciating domestic currency.)

If the monetary authorities again perceive the imbalance (deficit) to be temporary, but do not sterilise its contractionary effect, the intervention-induced increase in domestic interest rates will stimulate capital inflows which will finance the payments imbalance. In this situation, increases in domestic interest rates will finance, but not correct, the payments imbalance.

Additionally, however, increases in domestic interest rates will tend to decrease national income which, through induced decreases in imports, will reduce the deficit and so contribute to the restoration of external equilibrium. In this situation, increases in domestic interest rates will also contribute to the correction of the payments imbalance.

A third element of the adjustment process operates through the direct impact of payments imbalances on national income, since current account deficits/surpluses decrease/increase national income.

(This may be contrasted with the indirect impact operating through changes in interest rates.) Income changes will induce changes in imports (exports may also be indirectly affected) which will tend to decline as income declines and increase as income increases, thereby contributing to the correction of the payments imbalance and the restoration of external equilibrium.

A fourth element of the adjustment process is changes in domestic prices. Balance of payments deficits/surpluses may be expected to decrease/increase domestic prices relative to those in the rest of the world, either through an absolute change or, more likely, through changes in differential inflation rates. Relative price decreases will tend to make imports more and exports less expensive, while relative price increases will have the opposite effect. These changes will, in turn, tend to reduce the size of the original deficit/surplus and thus contribute to the correction of the payments imbalance and the restoration of external equilibrium.

The final element of the adjustment mechanism involves changes in the par values of currencies which, under fixed exchange rates, are implemented only in response to persistent or fundamental balance of payments disequilibria. Devaluation lowers a currency's value relative to other currencies, thereby making imports more and exports less expensive, and revaluation exerts the opposite effect. Devaluation will thus tend to reduce balance of payments deficits and revaluation will tend to reduce balance of payments surpluses. Similar results might be expected from domestic price deflation/inflation, but whereas this involves price adjustments which are distributed throughout the economy and which might prove both inefficient and socially and politically inexpedient, exchange rate realignments initially confine price changes to the relative prices of traded goods and so may represent a more efficient and possibly less painful means of correcting external disequilibrium.

ADVANTAGES

The advantages of a system of fixed exchange rates are similar to those of a gold standard:

Firstly, the system provides a measure of exchange rate stability and so eliminates a further source of uncertainty and price instability.

Secondly, fixed exchange rates help insulate the economy against economic disturbances (monetary shocks) and thus contribute to economic stability.

97

Thirdly, the establishment of par values, to which the international financial community is committed, not only encourages international trade but also contributes to an economic climate which is conducive to long-term international investment.

Fourthly, finite official reserves and the prospect of devaluation impose fiscal orthodoxy upon governments which might otherwise be more willing to resort to budget deficits to achieve declared expenditure objectives.

Finally, fixed exchange rates provide a potentially more efficient economic framework within which objectives, such as the efficient allocation of capital resources, might more readily be achieved.

DISADVANTAGES

Fixed exchange rate systems suffer from a number of potentially serious disadvantages:

Firstly, exchange rate realignments tend to be resorted to only after all other corrective measures have failed. The subordination of internal to external economic objectives, which may precede currency realignments, might thus subject economies to adjustment burdens which may prove both economically and socially costly.

Secondly, a system of fixed exchange rates is not necessarily self-equilibrating. The coexistence, for example, of export bottlenecks and dependence on strategic imports such as energy may contribute to a situation in which the adjustment process is unable to eliminate persistent payments deficits at prevailing exchange rates.

Thirdly, the inherent inflexibility of fixed rate systems may prevent economies from responding sufficiently rapidly to changing economic conditions. If the 1974 oil crisis had occurred under a system of fixed exchange rates, for example, the system might have been exposed to insupportable financing burdens.

Fourthly, notwithstanding the problem of selecting an appropriate par value, the inflexibility of fixed exchange rates may exacerbate the distortions which result from structural changes in economic activity. Policies (such as increased taxation) designed to curb imports, relieve exchange rate pressures and conserve scarce foreign exchange reserves, which are implemented to correct what is erroneously perceived as a temporary balance of payments deficit, may thus merely exacerbate the contractionary impact of a decline in, for example, a staple export industry, if this decline is structural rather than cyclical in origin.

Fifthly, the emergence of a partially or temporarily misaligned exchange rate may precipitate destabilising capital flows of sufficient magnitude to convert a prospective into a realised currency realignment. Such destabilising flows became an increasingly common feature of the Bretton Woods system of fixed exchange rates and culminated in sustained capital flows out of dollars in the first quarter of 1973.

Sixthly, the efficient operation of a fixed exchange rate system requires individual countries to hold reserve assets to stabilise foreign exchange rates. Official holdings of reserve assets, which for the period 1980 to 1983 are illustrated in Figure 5.3, involve social benefits and costs.

The social benefit of reserve holdings in any given period reflects the social return (including explicit interest receipts) which may be expected to accrue from the efficient operation of the exchange rate system.

The social cost, on the other hand, depends on the form in which reserves are held. The social opportunity cost will be close to zero if the reserves are held in the form of administratively created supranational assets such as SDRs. The cost of holding reserves in the form of national currencies such as the dollar, however, will amount to the return foregone on the goods and services relinquished in order to obtain these reserves. This cost is equivalent to the gross seigniorage gain accruing to the country issuing the reserve currency.

Optimal individual reserve holdings will thus be determined by the volume of reserves which equates marginal social return with marginal social cost. Departures from this equality, such as might arise from excess dollar reserve holdings prompted by persistent US balance of payments deficits, will be suboptimal and will result in the misallocation of resources.

Finally, the pursuit of economically prudent policies by selective countries might not even be sufficient to ensure economic and exchange rate stability within these countries, since fixed exchange rates will rapidly transmit to these countries the destabilising repercussions of less prudent economic policies pursued by other countries operating within the system. This problem is particularly acute in the case of differential inflation rates and is amply demonstrated by the difficulties Germany experienced in attempting to accord high priority to the maintenance of low inflation rates in the 1960s and 1970s. These attempts subjected the Deutsche Mark to considerable revaluationary pressures which were initially resisted but which,

Figure 5.3: Official holdings of reserve assets, 1980–3. Gold is valued at its free market price, fluctuations in which account for fluctuations in official holdings which remained virtually unchanged in physical terms.

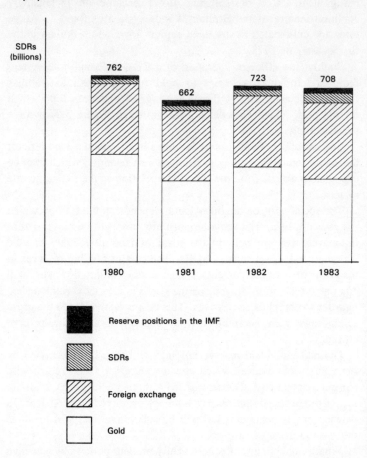

Source: *IMF Annual Report 1984.*

through intervention-induced increases in domestic liquidity, eventually threatened to undermine Germany's low inflation rate objective. The conflict between inflation and revaluation was reconciled partly by a combination of reserve augmentation and liquidity sterilisation measures and partly by the periodic revaluation of the Deutsche Mark.

100

THE DEMISE OF FIXED EXCHANGE RATES (BRETTON WOODS)

The collapse of the Bretton Woods system of fixed exchange rates in March 1973 was prompted by a number of diverse, yet inter-related factors:

Firstly, the increased incidence of US balance of payments deficits undermined the stability of the system through substantial increases in international dollar liquidity (US liabilities to foreign official institutions increased by $27 billion in 1971 alone).

Secondly, the US exhibited little resolve to introduce measures to contain these burgeoning deficits. Neither domestic deflation nor dollar devaluation was considered an economically (politically) viable solution, and the 'adopted' policy of 'benign neglect' merely served to perpetuate international economic instability.

Thirdly, a succession of exchange rate crises, commencing with the devaluation of sterling in 1967 and extending to other currencies, undermined confidence in the political and economic survival of Bretton Woods.

Finally, and in conjunction with the first three factors, the excessive growth of international dollar liquidity increased the unwillingness of international asset holders to continue accumulating dollars. This prompted a sustained movement out of dollars into other convertible currencies. Central banks were neither able nor willing to accommodate this movement at prevailing exchange rates and eventually closed the foreign exchange markets.

When the foreign exchange markets reopened on March 19th, 1973, the international monetary system had embarked upon a course of floating exchange rates.

SUMMARY

A fixed exchange rate system is characterised by stable exchange rates which are permitted to fluctuate within narrow bands centred around par values, both of which are fixed but not immutable.

Exchange rates are maintained within their upper and lower intervention points through official intervention in the foreign exchange market. This involves central bank sales of an appreciating currency and purchases of a depreciating currency.

The adjustment process consists of both financing and corrective components. Temporary payments imbalances can be financed either with reserves or through interest rate changes, while corrective measures can be effected through interest rate, income and price changes. Persistent or fundamental disequilibria can be corrected through exchange rate realignments.

The principal advantage of a fixed exchange rate system is that it provides a measure of exchange rate stability and hence eliminates a further source of uncertainty and price instability. The principal disadvantage of the system is that it subordinates internal economic objectives to external ones. This can result in adjustment burdens which are economically and socially costly.

The Bretton Woods system of fixed exchange rates collapsed in 1973 because of excessive international dollar liquidity and substantial and sustained conversions of dollars into other currencies. It was replaced by a system of floating exchange rates.

APPENDIX: PURCHASING POWER PARITY (PPP) DOCTRINE

The PPP doctrine sets out to explain the determination of equilibrium foreign exchange rates on the basis of domestic and foreign prices. It states that since the price of a currency reflects its general purchasing power, the rate of exchange between currencies must reflect their relative internal purchasing powers measured in terms of their relative general price levels.

There are two versions of the doctrine:

Absolute version

This postulates that a country's equilibrium exchange rate reflects the ratio of general domestic to general foreign price levels. This can be expressed as:

$$r = \frac{P_D}{P_F} \qquad (5A\text{-}1)$$

where:

   r is the exchange rate expressed as the domestic currency price of a unit of foreign currency

   P_D is a measure of domestic prices

   P_F is a measure of foreign prices.

EXAMPLE

If the general level of dollar (domestic) prices in the US is 250 and that of sterling (foreign) prices in the UK is 100, the PPP predicted equilibrium exchange rate will be:

$$r = \frac{P_D}{P_F} = \frac{250}{100} = \$2.50/£.$$

Qualifications

In practice, the actual exchange rate may deviate from the predicted equilibrium exchange rate because of factors such as the existence of non-traded goods. Consequently, the absolute version of the PPP doctrine is generally considered invalid as an accurate predictor of equilibrium exchange rates and associated par values.

Relative version

This postulates that *changes* in a country's equilibrium exchange rate reflect *changes* in the ratio of general domestic to general foreign price levels. This can be expressed as:

$$r_1 = \frac{\left[\frac{P_D}{P_F}\right]_1}{\left[\frac{P_D}{P_F}\right]_0} \times r_0 \qquad (5A\text{-}2)$$

where subscripts 1 and 0 refer to current and base periods respectively.

EXAMPLE

If the general level of dollar (domestic) prices in the US increases from 250 to 500 and that of sterling (foreign) prices in the UK from 100 to 125, the PPP predicted equilibrium exchange rate will be:

$$r_1 = \frac{\left[\dfrac{P_D}{P_F}\right]_1}{\left[\dfrac{P_D}{P_F}\right]_0} \times r_0 = \frac{\dfrac{500}{125}}{\dfrac{250}{100}} \times \$2.50/\pounds = \$4.00/\pounds.$$

This indicates that more units of domestic currency will be required to purchase one unit of foreign currency since domestic prices have increased relative to foreign prices and the international purchasing power of the domestic currency has decreased (exchange rate depreciation).

Qualifications

Whether the relative version of the doctrine is an efficient predictor of equilibrium exchange rates and associated par values depends on whether disturbances originate in the real or monetary sectors of the economy.

Changes in real factors, such as trade barriers and relative internal price structures, will cause deviations between actual and predicted rates, so that the doctrine will be an inefficient predictor.

Changes in monetary factors, such as increases in the money supply, will not cause deviations between actual and predicted rates, so that the doctrine becomes an efficient predictor. Consequently, countries which, for example, pursue long-run expansionary monetary policies, can expect to experience long-run depreciations in the exchange rates of their currencies.

In both cases, however, the actual exchange rate may deviate from the predicted rate if the latter is based on a disequilibrium rate in the base period.

The qualifications attached to the PPP doctrine suggest that it can only be used, if at all, as a general guide to the determination of long-run foreign exchange rates and par values.

CONCEPTS FOR REVIEW

De facto dollar exchange standard

Fixed exchange rate system

Fundamental disequilibria

Official dollar exchange standard

Purchasing power parity doctrine

Gold exchange standard   Two-tier gold market
Lower intervention point   Upper intervention point

QUESTIONS FOR DISCUSSION

1. In what sense are par values and intervention points fixed but not immutable under a system of fixed exchange rates?
2. Explain the operation of and potential problems associated with intervention to stabilise an appreciating currency.
3. How might changes in interest rates simultaneously finance and contribute to the correction of balance of payments deficits?
4. Assess the economic implications of a par value which has become structurally overvalued.
5. How might fixed exchange rates transmit economic instability?

6

Floating Exchange Rates

The system of floating exchange rates which emerged in 1973 was initially widely regarded as temporary. More than a decade later, despite frequent and persistent calls from economists and politicians alike for a return to fixed exchange rates, the system is still operating internationally and has achieved both theoretical and practical legitimacy.

The system's survival is partly explained by the lack of potentially viable alternatives but, more significantly perhaps, by the inherent advantages of a system able to absorb and diffuse the economic vicissitudes which have characterised the international monetary system since the early 1970s.

CHARACTERISTICS

A system of freely floating exchange rates is characterised by: an exchange rate which fluctuates freely in response to changes in the demand for and supply of foreign exchange; balance of payments adjustment principally through exchange rate and interest rate changes, and the absence of international reserves of gold and foreign exchange.

OPERATION

Freely floating exchange rates are the least complex of exchange rate systems and accord most closely with a competitive market model in which official intervention to support exchange rates is absent and exchange rates are free to respond to changes in market conditions and hence to changes in the factors underlying the demand for and supply of foreign exchange. These factors may originate in either the product market, such as crop failures, or the money market, such as interest rate changes, but in either case they will be rapidly, if not instantaneously, incorporated into the prevailing structure of exchange rates. At any given moment, therefore, floating exchange rates may be expected to incorporate and reflect all publicly disseminated information relevant to the determination of exchange rates and, to this extent, they may be considered allocatively efficient.

The implication of this is that floating exchange rates will be more volatile than fixed exchange rates since official intervention will not dampen the effects of exchange rate oscillations. Exchange rate volatility is thus not in itself inherent in a system of floating exchange rates but is a result of ever-present economic uncertainty and the absence of official stabilising measures.

Figure 6.1, for example, shows the potential impact on the sterling exchange rate of a hypothetical failure in the UK wheat crop. The failure leads to an increase in UK wheat imports from the US, the effect of which is to increase the demand for dollars and, correspondingly, increase the market supply of sterling from S_0 to S_1. This effect is common to both fixed and floating exchange rate systems, but whereas under fixed exchange rates official attempts to stabilise the exchange rate would shift the demand curve to D_1 (D_0 plus official intervention [I]) and stabilise the exchange rate at the prevailing rate of £1 = \$2.00, under floating exchange rates there is no attempt to stabilise the exchange rate and sterling depreciates to a market determined level of, for example, £1 = \$1.90. With fixed exchange rates, therefore, the increased UK demand for US wheat is financed out of UK dollar reserves amounting to the dollar equivalent of ($Q_2 - Q_0$), while in the case of floating exchange rates the increased demand for US wheat is accommodated through a combination of higher sterling prices for US wheat (since sterling has depreciated) and a contraction in the demand for wheat in response to these higher market prices.

Floating exchange rates thus permit the impact of changes in the underlying demand for and supply of foreign exchange to be fully manifested in the foreign exchange market. For any given change in economic variables, therefore, greater exchange rate volatility may be expected under a system of floating exchange rates.

Figure 6.1: Foreign exchange rates under a system of floating and fixed exchange rates. Under a system of floating exchange rates, an increase in the supply of sterling (S_1) causes the exchange rate to depreciate to £1 = \$1.90. Under a system of fixed exchange rates, official intervention stabilises the exchange rate at £1 = \$2.00.

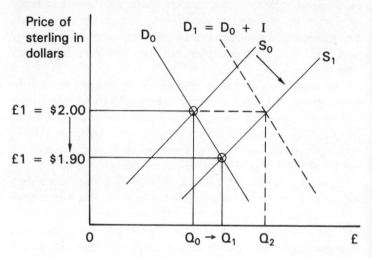

ADJUSTMENT MECHANISM

Balance of payments adjustments under floating exchange rates can occur on current account, capital account, or both. Regardless of the adjustment mix, however, equilibrium must always be restored within the overall balance, since the absence of official intervention and hence the absence of accruals or depletions of official reserves precludes the official reserve financing/accommodating of deficits/surpluses.

The principal means of securing external equilibrium under a system of floating exchange rates is through exchange rate changes, since the exchange rate is an economic variable, subordinated to domestic economic variables, whose function is to accommodate changes in the demand for and supply of foreign exchange.

Floating exchange rates secure external equilibrium through changes in the prices of exports and imports relative to foreign and domestic prices respectively. An autonomous decrease in exports, for example, will precipitate an exchange rate depreciation which will decrease relative export prices/increase relative import prices. If changes in these relative prices do not change the general level of prices (P_G), the depreciation will correct the incipient deficit and restore external equilibrium at the original level of national income. In notational form:

$$\downarrow X \rightarrow \downarrow r \rightarrow \downarrow P_X \uparrow P_M \rightarrow \uparrow X \downarrow M \rightarrow \rightarrow (X - M = 0) \text{ with } \overline{P}_G.$$

It is possible, however, that the depreciation-induced increase in import prices might, through institutional channels such as organised labour, initiate a cost-push increase in general prices. This will reduce the stock of real money balances and increase domestic interest rates. The increase in domestic interest rates will reduce capital outflows ($\downarrow K$), which will partly finance the incipient deficit, but which will also cause the exchange rate to appreciate. This will partly offset the current account improvement to the balance of payments, as a result of which external equilibrium will be secured through a combination of current account correction and capital account financing but at a reduced level of national income. Notationally:

$$\downarrow X \rightarrow \downarrow r \rightarrow \downarrow P_X \uparrow P_M \rightarrow \uparrow X \downarrow M \rightarrow\rightarrow\rightarrow\rightarrow\rightarrow\rightarrow\rightarrow\rightarrow\}$$
$$\rightarrow \uparrow P_G \rightarrow \downarrow M_S \rightarrow \uparrow i \rightarrow \downarrow K \rightarrow\rightarrow\} \text{ External Equilibrium}$$
$$\rightarrow \downarrow X \uparrow M \rightarrow\rightarrow\rightarrow\rightarrow\}$$

The second means of securing external equilibrium under a system of floating exchange rates is through interest rate changes. These will finance/accommodate incipient deficits/surpluses. An autonomous increase in capital outflows, for example, will generate an exchange rate depreciation. If the economy is already at full employment, the resulting increase in exports/decrease in imports will take the economy to over-full employment with inflationary consequences. The monetary authorities might attempt to avoid this situation by raising interest rates just enough to offset part of the original capital outflow through induced capital inflows. At the same time, the remaining capital outflow-induced depreciation of the exchange rate will encourage exports/discourage imports and offset the contractionary impact on national income of the policy-induced increase in interest rates. In this situation, balance of payments equilibrium will be secured partly through capital account financing and partly through current account correction.

The third and final means of securing external equilibrium is through income changes. This contribution is not precise, however, since there is no determinate relationship between changes in income and changes in imports under floating exchange rates, because of the effect of exchange rate changes on the relative prices of imports. To the extent, however, that imports decrease as income decreases and increase as income increases, income changes will contribute to the securing of external equilibrium.

ADVANTAGES

Firstly, provided that the system is allowed to work efficiently, floating exchange rates may be expected to adjust automatically to ensure balance of payments equilibrium.

Secondly, since floating exchange rates reflect the market-determined prices of currencies and since theory predicts that market-determined prices will contribute to the efficient allocation of resources, floating exchange rates might be expected to increase the allocative efficiency of international resource utilisation.

Thirdly, floating exchange rates may encourage stabilising speculation which limits the size of exchange rate fluctuations. This is illustrated in Figure 6.2, which shows that speculative purchases of sterling, for example, may limit (stabilise) the currency's potential depreciation. A temporary increase in the supply of sterling from S_0 to S_1 might prompt speculative currency purchases ($D_0 \rightarrow D_1$) in the belief that the exchange rate will revert to its anticipated equilibrium level of £1 = $1.50 and hence enable speculators to profit from the difference between this rate and the prevailing rate at which sterling was purchased. These purchases might confine the depreciation of sterling to £1 = $1.48, which is eight cents higher than the rate of £1 = $1.40 which might have prevailed in the absence of stabilising speculation. (Analogous reasoning would apply to speculation which stabilises potential currency appreciations.)

Fourthly, floating exchange rates facilitate domestic economic autonomy by removing the external constraint of balance of payments equilibrium. Domestic policies of full employment, for example, might thus be pursued whilst the exchange rate is permitted to fluctuate to maintain external equilibrium.

Fifthly, the absence of the need to maintain official reserves eliminates the opportunity cost of reserve holdings and official intervention in foreign exchange markets.

Sixthly, continual exchange rate adjustments eliminate the

Figure 6.2: Stabilising speculation under a system of floating exchange rates. Any tendency for the supply curve for sterling to shift, for example to the right from S_0 to S_1, might induce speculators, who consider the shift to be only temporary, to buy sterling in the hope of reselling it when the exchange rate reverts to the anticipated equilibrium of £1 = \$1.50. Speculative sterling purchases will shift the demand curve from D_0 to D_1 and hence support sterling at £1 = \$1.48 compared to the £1 = \$1.40 which might have prevailed in the absence of stabilising speculation.

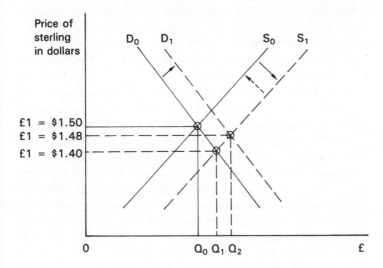

discrete parity adjustments and hence instability which are potentially associated with fixed exchange rate systems and which may reflect the failure of monetary authorities to predict exchange rates more accurately than market operators.

Seventhly, the symmetry of floating exchange rates, which provides scope for both the appreciation and depreciation of individual currencies, is less conducive to the large-scale capital flows and speculative profits associated with the asymmetrical adjustment of fixed exchange rates.

Finally, the absence of official intervention and foreign exchange controls may enhance social, political and economic welfare.

DISADVANTAGES

Firstly, temporary or cyclical exchange rate instability will transmit price instability which may discourage trade and hence reduce economic welfare. The more inelastic the demand for and supply of foreign exchange, the greater the exchange rate volatility for any given change in demand or supply and hence the greater the potential price instability associated with this volatility.

Secondly, destabilising speculation might exacerbate exchange rate volatility by pushing the exchange rate progressively further from equilibrium. Such speculation is essentially short-run, however, and can only be sustained for as long as speculators are prepared to incur the increasing losses resulting from market forces pushing the exchange rate towards its true market-determined equilibrium level and away from the 'equilibrium' level incorrectly perceived by speculators.

Thirdly, the absence of balance of payments constraints might foster the pursuit of domestic economic policies inimical to the long-run maximisation of economic welfare. This might arise, for example, if expansionary economic policies are pursued for short-run social or political gains at the expense of long-run price stability and external constraints, such as depletion of foreign exchange reserves, are removed by allowing the exchange rate to fluctuate to maintain external equilibrium.

Finally, floating exchange rates might represent a second-best option in relation to the social benefits arising from fixed exchange rates and the establishment of an optimal currency area. These benefits might be expected to result from the production economies of unified product markets, the more efficient allocation of capital resources and economies in the use of financial (monetary) and real (administrative) resources.

PROSPECTS

The present system of floating exchange rates has been in existence since 1973 and is likely to remain, despite frequent calls to the contrary, in the foreseeable future. This is because of its inherent flexibility and ability to operate within a framework of billion-dollar international currency markets which can mobilise large-scale destabilising capital flows at relatively short notice.

There is presently no viable alternative which is sufficiently

resilient to withstand these large-scale capital flows and yet sufficiently flexible to provide the liquidity and efficient resource allocation necessary to finance international commerce and minister to the
needs of an increasingly integrated and complex international
monetary system.

SUMMARY

A system of freely floating exchange rates is characterised by
exchange rates which are free to respond to changes in the demand
for and supply of foreign exchange. This implies greater exchange
rate volatility than under a fixed exchange rate system in which
official intervention dampens the magnitude of exchange rate fluctuations.

Balance of payments adjustments must always occur within the
overall balance because of the absence of official reserve intervention to finance/accommodate deficits/surpluses.

The adjustment process consists of corrective and financing
elements. Incipient disequilibrium is corrected through exchange
rate changes, which change the relative prices of exports and
imports, and is financed through interest rate changes, which induce
capital flows. Income changes will also contribute to the adjustment
process.

The principal advantage of floating exchange rates is that they
adjust automatically to secure balance of payments equilibrium.
Their principal disadvantage is that they transmit price instability
which may discourage trade and reduce economic welfare.

Floating exchange rates were implemented in 1973. Their present
existence is attributable to their basic flexibility and ability to
operate within a framework of potentially destabilising capital
flows. Their likely future existence is attributable to the lack of a
viable alternative.

APPENDIX: FLOATING EXCHANGE RATE VARIATIONS

One important variation of floating exchange rates is **managed
floating** in which the exchange rate is not permitted to float freely
but is subject to discretionary intervention to avoid excessive
exchange rate fluctuations which are presumed to be temporary or
cyclical. These fluctuations are expressed in terms of either a major

trading currency, such as the dollar, or a basket of currencies weighted to reflect the trading importance of each constituent currency.

Intervention might be undertaken to avoid either excessive exchange rate appreciations, which might undermine international trading competitiveness, or excessive exchange rate depreciations, which might increase the risk of inflation. In both situations, intervention requires the maintenance of official reserves.

Notwithstanding the inefficiencies of an incorrectly perceived target exchange rate, the abuse of managed floating may contribute to the serious misallocation of economic resources. A managed downward float, for example, implemented to achieve full employment through current account surpluses, will export unemployment to other countries. Such **'competitive devaluations'** or **dirty floating** contributed to the high unemployment and exchange rate instability which characterised the international monetary system in the inter-war years.

CONCEPTS FOR REVIEW

Competitive devaluation   Floating exchange rates
Dirty floating   Managed floating

QUESTIONS FOR DISCUSSION

1. Are floating exchange rates inherently volatile?
2. In what way are floating exchange rates consistent with both stabilising and destabilising speculation?
3. How is the adjustment process under floating exchange rates undermined by general price increases?
4. Is the removal of the external constraint of balance of payments equilibrium an advantage or disadvantage of floating exchange rates?
5. Why might 'dirty floating' result in resource misallocation?

7

Alternative Exchange Rate Systems

In an attempt to improve upon the economic efficiency of conventional exchange rate systems, various alternative systems have been adopted at different times. They are usually either combinations of the features of conventional systems or modifications of them.

CRAWLING PEG

The crawling peg or gliding parity is an attempt to combine the advantages of fixed exchange rates with the flexibility of floating exchange rates.

The essence of the system is an exchange rate which is pegged at a given value but which is allowed to crawl (glide) in response to changing market conditions. The crawl may be triggered by persistent revaluation or devaluation exchange rate pressures — prompted, for example, by differential inflation rates — or by predetermined changes in foreign exchange reserves. Because of this ability to adapt to market pressures, the system affords relatively frequent but modest exchange rate adjustments, with potentially minimal economic dislocation.

An example of how a crawling peg operates is given, using hypothetical sterling exchange rates and increasing market sales of sterling, in Figure 7.1. Initial demand (D_0) and supply (S_0) establish a sterling exchange rate of £1 = $1.50. Increased sterling sales, shown as S_1 in panel (a), subject sterling to devaluationary pressures which are absorbed through official support measures in the form of official sterling purchases. These shift the sterling demand curve to D_1, which represents market demand D_0 plus official support. Further increases in sterling sales and support operations might eventually shift the supply and demand curves to S_4 and D_4 respectively, at which point official support is withdrawn and sterling is devalued to £1 = \$1.48 to establish a new market equilibrium at Q^*. The decision to withdraw support and devalue sterling at Q_4 might be triggered by the size of the loss of exchange reserves which amounts to the sterling equivalent of $Q_4 - Q_0$.

The possible re-emergence of increased sterling sales in the next period (t_2) might precipitate a second sterling devaluation to £1 = \$1.45. Recurrent increases in sterling sales in successive periods ($t_1 \rightarrow t_5$), for example, might prompt a succession of frequent, modest devaluations which constitute a **downward crawling peg**. This is shown as devaluation path A in panel (b).

Currencies experiencing revaluationary pressures may similarly be subject to periodic revaluations, although the absence of reserve loss constraints might reduce the frequency of these adjustments. An **upward crawling peg** is shown as revaluation path B in panel (b).

Crawling pegs offer two comparative advantages over conventional exchange rate systems:

Firstly, they potentially avoid the economic instability associated with the infrequent and discrete adjustments which characterise fixed exchange rates;

Secondly, they reduce the uncertainty and volatility which characterise floating exchange rates.

The net effects of crawling peg adjustments might be expected to be similar to those of fixed and floating exchange rates, but without the former's economic dislocation and the latter's exchange rate volatility. The orderly adjustment paths depicted in panel (b), however, might not be achieved if crawling pegs generate substantial currency flows in anticipation of exchange rate realignments. These flows might prompt monetary authorities to accelerate their currency realignments, thereby creating an erratic adjustment process and exposing market operators to unsystematic economic costs.

The purported benefits of fixed rate stability and floating rate flexibility might thus prove difficult to realise in practice under a system of crawling pegs. Indeed, the system might merely succeed in combining the disadvantages of fixed and floating exchange rates with few, if any, of the advantages. This is perhaps why few countries have actually adopted the crawling peg system of exchange rates.

Figure 7.1: Exchange rate determination with crawling pegs. The withdrawal of official support ($D_4 \rightarrow D_0$) following successive increases in sterling sales ($S_0 \rightarrow S_4$), results in the devaluation of sterling to £1 = $1.48 at equilibrium quantity Q*. Repeated modest devaluations will result in a downward crawling peg which is shown as devaluation path A. Similarly, repeated modest revaluations will result in an upward crawling peg shown as revaluation path B.

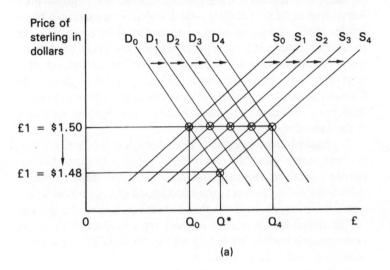

(a)

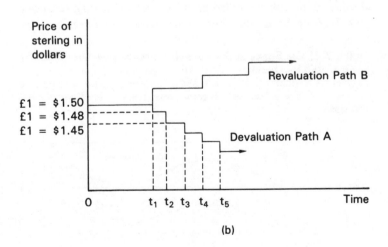

(b)

SNAKE IN THE TUNNEL

The exchange rate system referred to as the **Snake in the Tunnel** is essentially of historical interest, having been introduced in April 1972 and abandoned in March 1973.

The system represented an attempt to exploit the advantages of fixed exchange rate stability within a wider framework of floating exchange rate flexibility. It emerged in response to the **Smithsonian Agreement** of December 1971, which widened the maximum range within which currencies were permitted to fluctuate against the dollar from 1 per cent to 2.25 per cent above and below the dollar's newly established central value and so created an excessively wide band of 4.5 per cent within which the currencies of the EEC could fluctuate in relation to each other. It was in an attempt to narrow this band, whilst maintaining flexibility against the dollar, that the Snake in the Tunnel was created.

The Snake limited to 2.25 per cent, through official intervention, the band within which the currencies of initially Belgium, France, Germany, Holland, Italy and Luxembourg could fluctuate in relation to each other. The Tunnel represented a band of 4.5 per cent within which these currencies could float collectively against the dollar.

The system thus succeeded in providing a measure of European exchange rate stability while maintaining the flexibility of a European joint float against the dollar.

In March 1973, however, the collapse of Bretton Woods and the floating of the dollar resulted in the Tunnel's becoming redundant and therefore being abandoned. The Snake was retained as the

Figure 7.2: The Snake in the Tunnel. Currencies within the Snake were limited to a band of 2.25% within which they could fluctuate in relation to each other. These same currencies were limited to a Tunnel of 4.5% within which they could collectively float against the dollar.

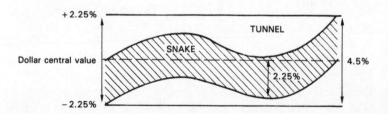

European Joint Float, which eventually became the precursor of the more sophisticated European Monetary System.

EUROPEAN MONETARY SYSTEM

The **European Monetary System** (EMS) became operational in March 1979. Although it may be considered a logical successor to the European Joint Float, it is economically more complex and represents a stronger political commitment than its 'simple' exchange rate predecessor. It is essentially an attempt to achieve greater European monetary stability and hence take a further step towards European Monetary Union which would involve the co-ordination of monetary and fiscal policies and the adoption of a common European currency unit.

The essence of the EMS is a system of fixed but adjustable exchange rates. Its operation is technically complex and consists of two elements: a grid system and a currency basket.

Under the grid system, the participating countries of Belgium, Luxembourg, Denmark, France, Holland, Ireland, Italy and West Germany, each declare a central rate for their currency against every other currency. This establishes a grid of bilateral central rates, within which the margin of fluctuation on either side of bilateral central rates is limited to 2.25 per cent. (Italy adopted a wider, more flexible margin of 6 per cent.) In other words, the exchange rate of the strongest currency can appreciate by no more than 2.25 per cent above that of the weakest currency, while that of the weakest currency can depreciate by no more than 2.25 per cent below that of the strongest currency. (At these margins, intervention by the participating central banks is obligatory and unlimited.) The declared central rate remains unchanged throughout these fluctuations. The grid consequently ensures that the bilateral exchange rates of any pair of currencies are maintained within a maximum band of 4.5 per cent (12 per cent for the lira), while the entire system is permitted to fluctuate against external currencies such as the dollar in response to changing market conditions.

The currency basket forms the basis of the **European Currency Unit** (ECU), which is an average of all participating currencies (including, additionally, sterling) weighted on the basis of trade, GNP and selected financial quotas. The ECU plays a key role in the EMS. In particular, it acts as a numeraire in which central rates are denominated and as a reference point for the 'divergence indicator'.

119

This acts as a supplement to the grid of bilateral central rates and intervention limits and indicates the extent to which an individual currency's exchange rate diverges from the weighted average of *all* other currencies. This is measured as the divergence of the currency's exchange rate, expressed in ECUs, from its declared ECU central rate. A currency reaches this narrower 'divergence threshold', which potentially reduces the permissible band of fluctuation, when it deviates by 75 per cent of its maximum theoretical divergence against all other currencies. At this point, the monetary authorities of the relevant currency are required to implement corrective measures — these include diversified intervention, changes in monetary policy or, ultimately, parity realignment — or (politically more significant) explain the absence of such measures.

Initial fears that the EMS would subject inflation-prone economies to excessive deflationary pressures or that it would intensify inflationary pressures through intervention-induced liquidity creation appear to have been unfounded. Moreover, despite several realignments, the system has survived and contributed to a reduction in the exchange rate variability of member currencies and to the prevention of greater economic divergence in the monetary policies of member countries.

The system has thus apparently succeeded in achieving an initial degree of exchange rate stability and it remains to be seen whether this success can be translated into more effective European economic integration and, ultimately perhaps, the realisation of European Monetary Union.

SUMMARY

Alternative exchange rate systems represent attempts to improve upon the economic efficiency of conventional exchange rate systems by combining or modifying their operating characteristics.

The crawling peg is an exchange rate system which attempts to combine the advantages of fixed exchange rates with the flexibility of floating exchange rates. It consists of an exchange rate pegged at a given value but which is allowed to crawl in response to changing market conditions. The system potentially avoids the economic instability associated with the infrequent and discrete adjustments which characterise fixed exchange rates, while reducing the uncertainty and volatility which characterise floating exchange rates. Few countries, however, have adopted the system.

The Snake in the Tunnel represented an attempt to exploit the advantages of fixed exchange rate stability within a wider framework of floating exchange rate flexibility. The Snake limited to 2.25 per cent the band within which participating European currencies could fluctuate in relation to each other, while the Tunnel represented a band of 4.5 per cent within which these currencies could collectively float against the dollar. The system was introduced in April 1972 but abandoned in March 1973 following the floating of the dollar.

The European Monetary System became operational in March 1979 and is an attempt to achieve greater European monetary stability and to move closer to European Monetary Union. The system consists of a grid of bilateral central rates, around which fluctuation margins of ±2.25 per cent have been established, and a European Currency Unit, which serves as the system's numeraire and which, through a 'divergence threshold', potentially reduces the permissible band of exchange rate fluctuations. Despite several exchange rate realignments, the system appears to have succeeded in achieving an initial degree of exchange rate stability.

CONCEPTS FOR REVIEW

Downward crawling peg
European Currency Unit
European Joint Float
European Monetary System

Smithsonian Agreement
Snake in the Tunnel
Upward crawling peg

QUESTIONS FOR DISCUSSION

1. Why might the paths of upward and downward crawling pegs prove asymmetrical for a common level of exchange rate instability?
2. Why did the floating of the dollar in March 1973 result in the abandoning of the Snake in the Tunnel?
3. How does the grid of bilateral central rates limit exchange rate fluctuations in the European Monetary System?

121

Part Three

Equilibrium and the Adjustment Process

Internal equilibrium is essentially a state of full employment with price stability, while external equilibrium is equality between external autonomous debit and credit transactions. Internal and external equilibrium do not necessarily occur together but they are interdependent, so that the correction of external disequilibrium will affect internal equilibrium.

External disequilibrium is an imbalance of resources flowing into or out of a country in any given period. Its correction depends on the exchange rate system in operation and the adjustment process adopted:

Under fixed exchange rates, the elasticities approach to external equilibrium focuses on the price elasticities of traded goods and services. It concentrates on exchange rate changes as a means of achieving the directional and value changes necessary to restore external equilibrium. The income approach incorporates the effects of income changes into the adjustment process, while the absorption approach introduces to the analysis the relationship between external disequilibrium and discrepancies between national income and expenditure (the domestic absorption of goods and services). These three current account approaches to the adjustment of external disequilibrium are examined in Chapter 8.

The adjustment process becomes more complex when capital flows are introduced, since internal and external equilibrium will then be influenced by both current and capital account balances. Chapter 9 reviews the macroeconomic theory necessary to undertake this more complex analysis.

This theory is then applied in Chapters 10 and 11, which examine the mechanics of the capital mobility approach to internal and external equilibrium, under both fixed and floating exchange rates. To reflect the post-war interest in the macroeconomic role of money, the monetary approach is illustrated in Chapter 12. This approach perceives external disequilibrium as a monetary phenomenon prompted by money stock imbalances.

8

External Disequilibrium and Current Account Adjustment

The elasticities, income and absorption approaches to external disequilibrium apply to current account adjustments under fixed exchange rates. Particular emphasis is placed on balance of payments *deficits*, since the adjustment process, through reserve depletion rather than reserve augmentation, subjects deficit countries to greater corrective pressures than surplus countries.

THE ELASTICITIES APPROACH

Characteristics

This is the use of exchange rate realignments to achieve the directional and value changes necessary to restore external equilibrium which, on current account, is equality between import expenditures and export receipts.

Devaluation lowers and revaluation raises the value (purchasing power) of domestic currency relative to foreign currencies. This compensates for relatively inflated or deflated domestic prices and can generally be expected to contribute to the restoration of external equilibrium.

Operation

Overvalued exchange rates, by lowering the domestic price of imports relative to import substitutes and raising the price of exports relative to export substitutes, encourage imports/discourage exports and create balance of payments deficits. Undervalued exchange rates have the opposite effect.

The object of exchange rate changes is to correct these misalignments and restore equality between import expenditures and export receipts expressed in either domestic or foreign currency. Devaluation, for example, raises the domestic price of imports and lowers the foreign price of exports. This reduces imports and increases exports and, depending on the price elasticities of demand for imports and exports, improves the balance of payments. Devaluation is thus intended to reduce an excess of import expenditures relative to export receipts and revaluation to reduce an excess of export receipts relative to import expenditures.

Expenditures on both domestic imports and foreign imports (domestic exports) are determined by the volume and the prices of the goods and services transacted. Expenditures thus depend on the price elasticity of demand for imports (domestic and foreign), which is a measure of the responsiveness of changes in the quantity of imports demanded to changes in price. This can be expressed as:

$$Em = \frac{\text{Percentage change in quantity of imports demanded}}{\text{Percentage change in the price of imports}}$$

Figure 8.1 uses the UK and US as examples to express the value of UK (domestic) imports and US (foreign) imports (UK exports) in both sterling and dollars and show the stylised impact of a sterling devaluation. (Revaluation would have the opposite effect.)

Devaluation raises the sterling price of domestic (UK) imports from P_0 to P_1 and reduces the quantity demanded from Q_0 to Q_1 (panel a). Sterling expenditure on imports will decrease if $Em_D > 1$ and increase if $Em_D < 1$. Dollar expenditure on domestic imports will necessarily decrease, however, since the dollar price of domestic imports remains unchanged (P_0) but the quantity demanded decreases from Q_0 to Q_1 (panel c).

Correspondingly, devaluation lowers the dollar price of foreign (US) imports from P_0 to P_1 and increases the quantity demanded from Q_0 to Q_1 (panel d). Dollar expenditure on imports will increase if $Em_F > 1$ and decrease if $Em_F < 1$. Sterling expenditure on foreign imports will necessarily increase, however, since the sterling price of foreign imports remains unchanged (P_0) but the quantity demanded increases from Q_0 to Q_1 (panel b).

Figure 8.1: Devaluation and its effects on the balance of payments.
The net effect of a sterling devaluation is to decrease sterling
expenditure on domestic imports if $Em_D > 1$ and to increase it if
$Em_D < 1$ (panel a). Sterling expenditure on foreign imports
increases (panel b). Dollar expenditure on domestic imports
decreases (panel c), while dollar expenditure on foreign imports
increases if $Em_F > 1$ and decreases if $Em_F < 1$ (panel d).

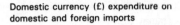

Domestic currency (£) expenditure on
domestic and foreign imports

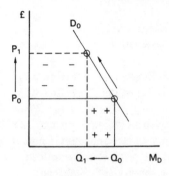

UK domestic imports
(UK demand for US exports)
(a)

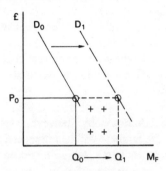

US foreign imports
(US demand for UK exports)
(b)

Foreign currency ($) expenditure on
domestic and foreign imports

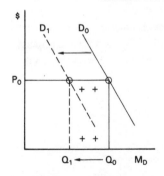

UK domestic imports
(UK demand for US exports)
(c)

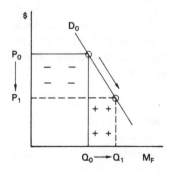

US foreign imports
(US demand for UK exports)
(d)

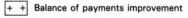

Balance of payments improvement

Balance of payments deterioration

The net effect for an individual country of an exchange rate realignment, therefore, depends on the price elasticities of demand for domestic and foreign imports and can be summarised as:

Domestic Currency Expenditure

	Devaluation	Revaluation
Domestic imports (panel a)	$\downarrow (Em_D > 1)$	$\uparrow (Em_D > 1)$
	$\uparrow (Em_D < 1)$	$\downarrow (Em_D < 1)$
Foreign imports (panel b)	$\uparrow$	$\downarrow$

Foreign Currency Expenditure

	Devaluation	Revaluation
Domestic imports (panel c)	$\downarrow$	$\uparrow$
Foreign imports (panel d)	$\uparrow (Em_F > 1)$	$\downarrow (Em_F > 1)$
	$\downarrow (Em_F < 1)$	$\uparrow (Em_F < 1)$

Additionally, however, the effectiveness of an exchange rate realignment will be influenced by income-induced changes in import expenditures, which might counteract the price elasticity effects.

More specifically, therefore, the ability of exchange rate realignments to improve the balance of payments depends on:

(i) the price elasticity of demand for domestic and foreign imports;

(ii) income-induced changes in domestic and foreign imports.

The operation of exchange rate realignments can be analysed using a simplified two-country model (the UK and US) and a specific (sterling) devaluation intended to correct a (UK) balance of payments deficit.

Case 1

Assumptions

Sterling is devalued from £1 = $3 to £1 = $2
The price of UK fish exports to the US is £10/kilo
The price of US computer exports to the UK is $600/unit
The UK price elasticity of demand for imports from the US exceeds unity ($Em_{UK} > 1$)
The US price elasticity of demand for imports from the UK

exceeds unity ($Em_{US} > 1$)

Income-induced changes in domestic and foreign imports are absent

Export supply constraints are absent (export supply elasticities are infinite).

The devaluation of sterling leaves the sterling price of UK exports (£10/kilo) and the dollar price of US exports ($600/unit) initially unchanged. It raises, however, the sterling price of UK imports (computers) from £200 ($600/$3/£) to £300 ($600/$2/£) and lowers the dollar price of US imports (fish) from $30 (£10 × $3/£) to $20 (£10 × $2/£). Consequently, UK purchases of computers will decrease and US purchases of fish will increase.

These changes are illustrated in Figure 8.2. The UK demand for imports contracts from 5 units to 3 units when devaluation raises the sterling price of imports from £200 to £300 (the dollar price of $600 remains unchanged), while the US demand for imports extends from 20 kilos to 100 kilos when devaluation lowers the dollar price of imports from $30 to $20 (the sterling price of £10 remains unchanged).

The impact of these changes on the UK and US balance of payments is also illustrated in Figure 8.2. UK import expenditures — equivalent to US export receipts — decrease from £1,000 (5 × £200) to £900 (3 × £300), while UK export receipts — equivalent to US import expenditures — increase from £200 (20 × £10) to £1,000 (100 × £10). The UK balance of payments thus moves from a deficit of £800 to a surplus of £100. Correspondingly, US import expenditures — equivalent to UK export receipts — increase from $600 (20 × $30) to $2,000 (100 × $20), while US export receipts — equivalent to UK import expenditures — decrease from $3,000 (5 × $600) to $1,800 (3 × $600). The US balance of payments thus moves from a surplus of $2,400 to a deficit of $200.

Changes in the balance of payments may also be analysed in terms of the demand for and supply of foreign exchange, thus relating the impact of exchange rate realignments directly to the foreign exchange market. This is illustrated in Figure 8.3, which transforms UK and US import expenditures into the demand for and supply of dollars respectively, and UK and US export receipts into the demand for and supply of sterling respectively. The devaluation of sterling causes the UK demand for dollars to contract from $3,000 (5 units of imports at $600 each) to $1,800 (3 units at $600) and the US supply of dollars to extend from $600 (20 kilos of imports at $30

129

Figure 8.2: Devaluation and changes in import demand (elastic). The devaluation of sterling from £1 = $3 to £1 = $2 causes UK import (computer) demand to contract from 5 units to 3 units and UK import expenditure to decrease from £1,000 (5 × £200) to £900 (3 × £300). Correspondingly, US import (fish) demand extends from 20 kilos to 100 kilos and US import expenditure increases from $600 (20 × $30) to $2,000 (100 × $20). The impact on the UK and US balance of payments is:

UK

	£1 = $3	£1 = $2
UK import expenditure (−)	5 × £200 = £−1,000	3 × £300 = £− 900
UK export receipts (+)	20 × £ 10 = £+ 200	100 × £ 10 = £+1,000
Deficit (−)/Surplus (+)	£− 800	£+ 100

US

	£1 = $3	£1 = $2
US import expenditure (−)	20 × $ 30 = $− 600	100 × $ 20 = $−2,000
US export receipts (+)	5 × $600 = $+3,000	3 × $600 = $+1,800
Deficit (−)/Surplus (+)	$+2,400	$− 200

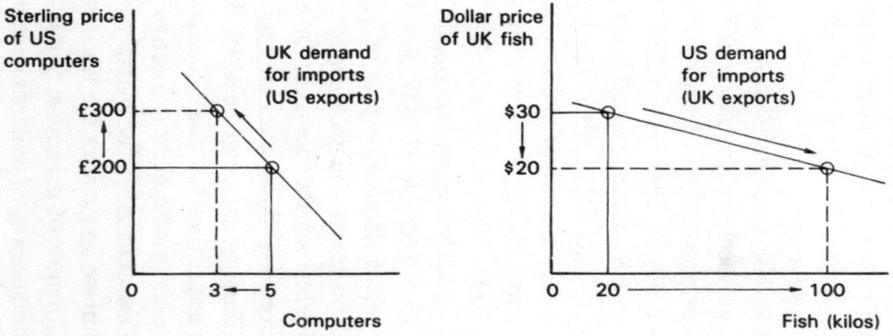

per kilo) to $2,000 (100 kilos at $20 per kilo). Correspondingly, the UK supply of sterling contracts from £1,000 (5 units of imports at £200 each) to £900 (3 units at £300 each) and the US demand for sterling extends from £200 (20 kilos of imports at £10 per kilo) to £1,000 (100 kilos at £10 per kilo).

The impact of these changes on the UK and US balance of payments is also illustrated in Figure 8.3. The net supply of sterling (£800) is transformed into net demand (£100) and the UK balance of payments correspondingly moves from deficit to surplus, while the net demand for dollars ($2,400) is transformed into net supply ($200) and the US balance of payments correspondingly moves from surplus to deficit.

The devaluation of sterling has thus succeeded in reducing (over-correcting) the excess of UK import expenditures relative to export receipts. This success, however, was based on the assumption that the price elasticity of demand for imports exceeded unity for both the UK and the US. The implications of relaxing this assumption are considered in Case 2.

Case 2

Assumptions:

As in Case 1, except that:

The UK price elasticity of demand for imports from the US is less than unity ($Em_{UK} < 1$)
The US price elasticity of demand for imports from the UK is also less than unity ($Em_{US} < 1$).

The implications of relaxing the assumption of elastic import demand may be highlighted — and also expositionally simplified — by reducing still further the UK price elasticity of demand for imports from the US from 'less than unity' ($Em_{UK} < 1$) to zero ($Em_{UK} = 0$). This indicates that the UK demand for imports is now perfectly inelastic and that the UK will continue to import the same volume of imports regardless of the sterling price of these imports. Consequently, devaluation will *increase* rather than decrease UK import expenditures as the sterling price of imports rises. Correspondingly, US demand for imports will still increase but, because $Em_{US} < 1$, this increase will be insufficient to compensate

131

Figure 8.3: Devaluation and the demand for and supply of foreign exchange. The devaluation of sterling from £1 = $3 to £1 = $2 causes the UK demand for dollars to contract from $3,000 to $1,800 and the US supply of dollars to extend from $600 to $2,000. The excess demand for dollars of $2,400 in the foreign exchange market is thus transformed into excess supply amounting to $200. Correspondingly, the UK supply of sterling contracts from £1,000 to £900 and the US demand for sterling extends from £200 to £1,000. This transforms the £800 excess supply of sterling into excess demand of £100. The impact on the UK and US balance of payments is:

UK	£1 = $3	£1 = $2
Demand for sterling (+)	£+ 200	£+ 1,000
Supply of sterling (−)	£− 1,000	£− 900
Net demand (+)/supply (−)	£− 800	£+ 100

US	£1 = $3	£1 = $2
Demand for dollars (+)	$+ 3,000	$+ 1,800
Supply of dollars (−)	$− 600	$− 2,000
Net demand (+)/supply (−)	$+ 2,400	$− 200

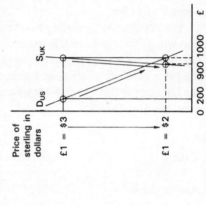

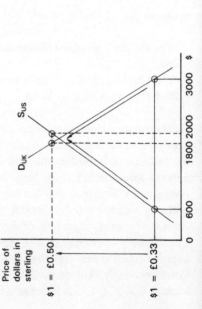

for the decrease in the dollar price of these imports. Consequently, devaluation will *decrease* rather than increase US import expenditures as the dollar price of imports falls.

These changes are illustrated in Figure 8.4. The UK demand for imports (computers) remains at 5 units when devaluation raises the sterling price of imports from £200 to £300, while the US demand for imports (fish) extends modestly from 20 kilos to 25 kilos when devaluation lowers the dollar price of imports from $30 to $20.

The impact of these changes on the UK and US balance of payments is also illustrated in Figure 8.4. UK import expenditures *increase* from £1,000 (5 × £200) to £1,500 (5 × £300), while UK export receipts barely increase from £200 (20 × £10) to £250 (25 × £10). The UK balance of payments thus *deteriorates* from a deficit of £800 to a deficit of £1,250. Correspondingly, US import expenditures *decrease* from $600 (20 × $30) to $500 (25 × $20), while US export receipts remain *constant* at $3,000 (5 × $600). The US balance of payments surplus thus increases from $2,400 to $2,500.

The impact of devaluation on the foreign exchange market is illustrated in Figure 8.5, which shows that UK demand for dollars remains at $3,000 (5 × $600), while the US supply of dollars *contracts* from $600 (20 × $30) to $500 (25 × $20). Correspondingly, the UK supply of sterling *extends* from £1,000 (5 × £200) to £1,500 (5 × £300), while the US demand for sterling extends only modestly from £200 (20 × £10) to £250 (25 × £10).

The impact of these changes on the UK and US balance of payments is also illustrated in Figure 8.5. The net supply of sterling *increases* from £800 to £1,250 and the UK balance of payments *deteriorates*, while the net demand for dollars *increases* from $2,400 to $2,500 and the US balance of payments surplus *strengthens* further. The devaluation of sterling has thus produced a perverse effect which increases both the UK deficit and the US surplus.

The normal devaluation response (Case 1) and the perverse devaluation response (Case 2), which are reconciled in terms of the underlying UK and US price elasticities of demand for imports, may be generalised into the **Marshall-Lerner condition**:

Devaluation will improve a country's balance of payments if the sum of the domestic (Em_D) and foreign (Em_F) elasticities of demand for imports exceeds unity ($Em_D + Em_F > 1$).[1]

133

Figure 8.4: Devaluation and changes in import demand (inelastic). The devaluation of sterling from £1 = $3 to £1 = $2 leaves UK import (computer) demand unchanged at 5 units ($Em_{UK} = 0$) but causes UK import expenditure to *increase* from £1,000 (5 × £200) to £1,500 (5 × £300). Correspondingly, US import (fish) demand extends from 20 kilos to 25 kilos but, because $Em_{US} < 1$, US import expenditure *decreases* from $600 (20 × $30) to $500 (25 × $20). The impact on the UK and US balance of payments is:

UK

	$£1 = \$3$		$£1 = \$2$	
UK import expenditure (−)	5 × £200 =	£ −1,000	5 × £300 =	£ −1,500
UK export receipts (+)	20 × £ 10 =	£ + 200	25 × £ 10 =	£ + 250
Deficit (−)/Surplus (+)		£ − 800		£ −1,250

US

US import expenditure (−)	20 × $ 30 =	$ − 600	25 × $ 20 =	$ − 500
US export receipts (+)	5 × $600 =	$ +3,000	5 × $600 =	$ +3,000
Deficit (−)/Surplus (+)		$ +2,400		$ +2,500

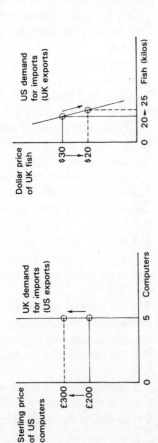

Figure 8.5: Devaluation and the demand for and supply of foreign exchange. The devaluation of sterling from £1 = $3 to £1 = $2 leaves the UK demand for dollars unchanged at $3,000 but causes the US supply of dollars to contract from $600 to $500. This *increases* the excess demand for dollars in the foreign exchange market from $2,400 to $2,500. Correspondingly, the UK supply of sterling *extends* from £1,000 to £1,500 whilst the US demand for sterling extends only modestly from £200 to £250. This *increases* the excess supply of sterling from £800 to £1,250. The impact on the UK and US balance of payments is:

UK	£1 = $3	£1 = $2
Demand for sterling (+)	£+ 200	£+ 250
Supply of sterling (−)	£− 1,000	£− 1,500
Net demand (+)/supply (−)	£− 800	£− 1,250

US	£1 = $3	£1 = $2
Demand for dollars (+)	$+3,000	$+3,000
Supply of dollars (−)	$− 600	$− 500
Net demand (+)/supply (−)	$+2,400	$+2,500

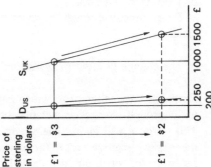

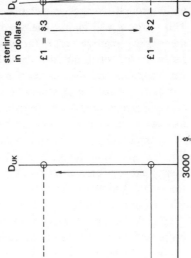

This condition (notwithstanding the initial imbalance) was satisfied in Case 1 (Em_{UK} + Em_{US} > 1) and so the devaluation of sterling reduced the UK balance of payments deficit. The condition (notwithstanding the initial imbalance) was not satisfied in Case 2, however, (Em_{UK} + Em_{US} < 1), so that devaluation exacerbated the UK deficit.

The second factor which influences the ability of exchange rate realignments to improve the balance of payments and which, by extension, influences the adequacy of the Marshall-Lerner condition, is income-induced changes in imports which are likely to counteract the impact of exchange rate realignments. These changes may occur in three ways:

First, directly through the **marginal propensity to import** (m) which is:

The change in import expenditure per unit change of income.

Exchange rate realignments which improve the balance of payments will, through changes in net injections, change national income. This, in turn, will induce changes in imports which will counteract the original improvement in the balance of payments. Devaluations, for example, which improve the balance of payments, will increase net injections and the resulting increases in national income will induce counteracting increases in imports.[2] For example, if 25 per cent of changes in income are spent on imports (m = 0.25), a $100 increase in income will increase imports by $25.

Secondly, through *changes* in the marginal propensity to import. For example, if exchange rate-induced inflation causes the proportion of extra income spent on imports to increase from 25 per cent (m = 0.25) to 40 per cent (m = 0.4), a $100 increase in income will increase imports by a further $15 from $25 to $40.

Finally, through changes in the *weighted average* marginal propensity to import, resulting from exchange rate-induced changes in the distribution of national income. This might arise, for example, if devaluation were to redistribute income to economic sectors with relatively high marginal propensities to import. In this case, the redistribution of $100 of income from low (0.25) to high (0.75) propensity to import sectors would increase net imports by $50 (−$100 × 0.25 + $100 × 0.75).

These changes may be analysed in terms of a third generalised case:

Case 3

Assumptions:

As in Case 1, except that:

Devaluation-induced income changes restore UK import demand to its original level.

The effect of income-induced import changes is illustrated in Figure 8.6. The devaluation of sterling from £1 = $3 to £1 = $2 results in an increase in UK income which shifts the UK demand curve for imports from D_{UK0} to D_{UK1} (panel a). This represents a counteracting increase in imports which are assumed restored to their original level of 5 units, even though their sterling price has increased from £200 to £300. The increased demand for imports causes the UK demand curve for dollars to shift to the right (from D_{UK0} to D_{UK1} in panel b), which restores the UK demand for dollars to its original level of $3,000 (5 × $600) at the new exchange rate of $1 = £0.50. If the US supply of dollars remains unchanged at the post-devaluation level of $2,000 (100 × $20) — assuming the absence of income feedbacks — the excess demand for dollars amounts to $1,000. Correspondingly, the UK supply curve for sterling shifts to the right (from S_{UK0} to S_{UK1} in panel c) and the supply of sterling increases to £1,500 (5 × £300) at the new exchange rate of £1 = $2. If the US demand for sterling remains unchanged at the post-devaluation level of £1,000 (100 × £10), the excess supply of sterling amounts to £500.

The impact of these changes on the UK and US balance of payments is also illustrated in Figure 8.6, which shows that the net supply of sterling and the net demand for dollars are only reduced to £500 and $1,000 respectively. This may be contrasted with the balance of payments position in Case 1 above, in which devaluation transformed an £800 UK deficit into a £100 UK surplus and a $2,400 US surplus into a $200 US deficit. The income-induced increase in UK imports resulting from the sterling devaluation has thus counteracted the improvement in the UK balance of payments and prevented the restoration of external equilibrium.[3]

137

Figure 8.6: Devaluation and income-induced changes in the demand for and supply of foreign exchange. The devaluation of sterling from £1 = $3 to £1 = $2 results in an increase in income which shifts the UK demand curve for imports (computers) from D_{UK0} to D_{UK1} (panel a). This restores import demand to 5 units and shifts the UK demand curve for dollars from D_{UK0} to D_{UK1} (panel b). At the new exchange rate, the UK demand for dollars reverts to $3,000 (5 × $600) which, with an unchanged US supply of dollars of $2,000, creates excess dollar demand of $1,000. Correspondingly, the UK supply of sterling increases to £1,500 (5 × £300) at the new exchange rate which, with unchanged US demand of £1,000, creates an excess supply of sterling of £500 (panel c). The impact on the UK and US balance of payments is:

UK	£1 = $3	£1 = $2
Demand for sterling (+)	£+ 200	£+ 1,000
Supply of sterling (−)	£− 1,000	£− 1,500
Net demand (+)/supply (−)	£− 800	£− 500

US		
Demand for dollars (+)	$+ 3,000	$+ 3,000
Supply of dollars (−)	$− 600	$− 2,000
Net demand (+)/supply (−)	$+ 2,400	$+ 1,000

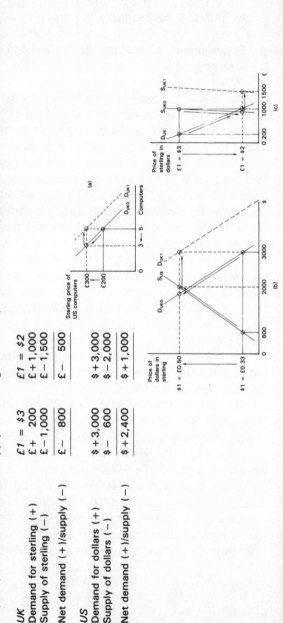

Summary

Exchange rate realignments change the value of domestic currencies relative to foreign currencies and restore external equilibrium by restoring equality between import expenditures and export receipts. Their ability to achieve this depends on the price elasticity of demand for domestic and foreign imports and income-induced changes in domestic and foreign imports.

THE INCOME APPROACH

Characteristics

The income approach incorporates the effects of income changes into the adjustment process and can be used as a second means of restoring external equilibrium. Income changes can contribute either positively (improvement) or negatively (deterioration) to the correction of external disequilibrium, but in both cases their effects are likely to be incomplete, so that they will have to be supplemented with, or act as a supplement to, alternative corrective measures such as exchange rate realignments.

Operation

National income is determined by the sum of consumption, investment, government and net foreign expenditure on goods and services. These components can be expressed as:

$$C = C^* + cY \qquad (8\text{-}1)$$

where

    C is aggregate consumption
    C^* is autonomous consumption
    c is the marginal propensity to consume
    Y is national income.

$$I = I^* \qquad (8\text{-}2)$$

where I is autonomous investment.

139

$$G = G^*$$ (8-3)

where G is autonomous government expenditure.

$$X = X^*$$ (8-4)

where X is exogenous exports determined by external factors such as foreign incomes.

$$M = M^* + mY$$ (8-5)

where:

M is aggregate imports
M* is autonomous imports
m is the marginal propensity to import which links changes in imports (induced) to changes in income. It is assumed to be positive and less than unity, so that imports are an increasing function of income.

Since national income is expressed as:

$$Y = C + I + G + (X - M),$$ (8-6)

substituting equations (8-1) to (8-5) into equation (8-6) gives:

$$Y = C^* + cY + I^* + G^* + X^* - (M^* + mY)$$

$$= \frac{C^* + I^* + G^* + X^* - M^*}{1 - c + m}$$

and

$$\Delta Y = \frac{\Delta C^* + \Delta I^* + \Delta G^* + \Delta X^* - \Delta M^*}{1 - c + m}.$$ (8-7)

The **open economy multiplier** appears in equation 8-7 as:

$$\frac{1}{1 - c + m}.$$

It is smaller than its closed economy counterpart $\left(\dfrac{1}{1-c}\right)$ because of the inclusion of the marginal propensity to import (m) which is an additional leakage of demand (overseas) from the circular flow of income. More specifically:

$$\frac{1}{1 - c + m} < \frac{1}{1 - c}$$

or

$$\frac{1}{s + m} < \frac{1}{s}$$

where s is the marginal propensity to save $(1 - c)$.

Equation 8-7 may now be expressed as:

$$\Delta Y = \frac{\Delta C^* + \Delta I^* + \Delta G^* + \Delta X^* - \Delta M^*}{s + m}. \tag{8-8}$$

Equation 8-8 determines the impact on national income of changes in any of the components of national income. For example, increases in exogenous exports (ΔX^*) increase national income, while increases in autonomous imports (ΔM^*) decrease national income. Notationally:

$$\Delta C^*, \ \Delta I^*, \ \Delta G^*, \ \Delta X^*, \ \Delta M^* \ \rightarrow\rightarrow \ \Delta Y.$$

Equation 8-8 can also be used to determine the impact of changes in the components of national income on external equilibrium. The current account balance (B) can be expressed as:

$$B = X - M \tag{8-9}$$

and

$$\Delta B = \Delta X - \Delta M. \tag{8-10}$$

Substituting equations 8-4 and 8-5 into 8-10 gives:

$$\Delta B = \Delta X^* - (\Delta M^* + m\Delta Y)$$

or

$$\Delta B = \Delta X^* - \Delta M^* - m\Delta Y. \tag{8-11}$$

Equation 8-11 determines the direct impact of changes in exogenous exports and autonomous imports as well as the indirect impact, through changes in induced imports, of changes in all the components of national income, on external equilibrium. Notationally:

$$\Delta X^*, \Delta M^* \rightarrow\rightarrow\rightarrow\rightarrow\rightarrow\rightarrow\rightarrow\rightarrow\rightarrow\rightarrow\rightarrow\rightarrow\rightarrow\rightarrow\rightarrow\rightarrow\rightarrow\rightarrow\rightarrow \left.\right\}$$
$$\Delta X^*, \Delta M^*, \Delta C^*, \Delta I^*, \Delta G^* \rightarrow \Delta Y \rightarrow \Delta M \rightarrow\rightarrow \left.\right\} \quad \Delta B.$$

Equation 8-11 can be consolidated by substituting into it equation 8-8 and rearranging the terms to get:

$$\Delta B = \frac{s}{s+m}(\Delta X^* - \Delta M^*) - \frac{m}{s+m}(\Delta C^* + \Delta I^* + \Delta G^*). \quad (8\text{-}12)$$

Equation 8-12 clearly shows that changes in both the direction and magnitude of national income will affect external equilibrium.

Directional changes involving increases in exogenous exports and decreases in autonomous imports, consumption, investment and government expenditure will improve the current account. Opposite changes will have the opposite effect. Notationally:

$$\uparrow X^*, \downarrow M^*, \downarrow C^*, \downarrow I^*, \downarrow G^* \rightarrow\rightarrow \uparrow B.$$

The magnitude of changes depends on the marginal propensities to save and import. Since these are both likely to be positive and less than unity, changes in income (components) will be unable to effect complete changes in the external balance, so that the income adjustment process will be incomplete. For example, unless $m = 0$, there will be imperfect correspondence between external disturbances and changes in external equilibrium, and unless $s = 0$, there will be imperfect correspondence between internal disturbances and changes in external equilibrium.

The implications of these changes for external equilibrium are:

Firstly, income changes contributing positively to the restoration of external equilibrium will have to be supplemented with additional corrective measures such as exchange rate realignments. For example, balance of payments improvements occasioned by decreases in autonomous consumption might have to be supplemented with devaluation.

EXAMPLE

Consider the effect on a 35 unit balance of payments deficit of a 50 unit decrease in autonomous consumption intended to correct the deficit. Assume s = 0.3 and m = 0.2.

$$\Delta B = \frac{s}{s+m}(\Delta X^* - \Delta M^*) - \frac{m}{s+m}(\Delta C^* + \Delta I^* + \Delta G^*) \qquad (8\text{-}12)$$

$$= 0 - \frac{0.2}{0.3+0.2}(-50)$$

$$= 20.$$

Adjustment is incomplete since the 50 unit decrease in autonomous consumption induces only a 20 unit improvement in the balance of payments (decrease in induced imports). A deficit of 15 units ($-35 + 20$) remains, which could be completely eliminated either by further contractionary measures (decreases in consumption) or by a devaluation-induced increase in exports/decrease in imports.

Secondly, income changes contributing negatively to the restoration of external equilibrium will necessitate counteracting income changes to act as a supplement to the measures prompting the original change in the balance of payments. For example, a devaluation-induced improvement in the balance of payments will be partially offset by income-induced increases in imports. Additional income changes in the form of contractionary measures will therefore be required to reinforce the devaluation improvement and counteract the income-induced increase in imports.

EXAMPLE

Consider the effect on a 35 unit balance of payments deficit of a devaluation-induced 30 unit increase in exports and 10 unit decrease in imports. Assume s = 0.3 and m = 0.2.

$$\Delta B = \frac{s}{s+m} (\Delta X^* - \Delta M^*) - \frac{m}{s+m} (\Delta C^* + \Delta I^* + \Delta G^*) \quad (8\text{-}12)$$

$$= \frac{0.3}{0.3 + 0.2} (30 - [-10]) - 0$$

$$= 24.$$

Adjustment is incomplete since the 30 unit increase in exports and 10 unit decrease in imports induce only a 24 unit improvement in the balance of payments because of induced income increases and corresponding increases in induced imports. A deficit of 11 units ($-35 + 24$) remains, which could be completely eliminated either by contractionary measures, such as decreases in consumption, or by a further devaluation.

The net contribution (positive or negative) of income changes to the adjustment process and the restoration of external equilibrium will also be reinforced by domestic price changes (absolute or rate of change). Since these will tend to reflect domestic supply elasticities, income changes will be positively related to price changes which, through changes in exports and imports, will result in corresponding changes in the external account. Notationally:

$$\left.\begin{array}{l} \Delta X^*, \ \Delta M^* \ \rightarrow\} \\ \Delta X^*, \ \Delta M^*, \ \Delta C^*, \ \Delta I^*, \ \Delta G^* \ \rightarrow\rightarrow\rightarrow \ \Delta Y \ \rightarrow\rightarrow\rightarrow \ \Delta M \ \rightarrow\rightarrow\} \\ \qquad\qquad\qquad\qquad\qquad\quad \downarrow \qquad\qquad\qquad\qquad\quad\} \\ \qquad\qquad\qquad\qquad\qquad\quad \Delta P \rightarrow \Delta X, \ \Delta M \ \rightarrow\rightarrow\} \end{array}\right\} \Delta B.$$

For example, decreases in autonomous consumption, undertaken to correct an external deficit, will reduce income and, through a reduction in induced imports, improve the external balance. Income decreases will also subject prices to downward pressure which, in turn, will encourage exports/discourage imports and contribute to a further improvement in the external balance. In this case, price changes have reinforced a positive income effect. Notationally:

$$\left.\begin{array}{l} \downarrow C^* \rightarrow\rightarrow \ \downarrow Y \ \rightarrow\rightarrow\rightarrow\rightarrow\rightarrow\rightarrow\rightarrow\rightarrow \ \downarrow M \ \rightarrow\rightarrow\rightarrow\rightarrow \} \\ \qquad\qquad\qquad \searrow \qquad\qquad\qquad\qquad\qquad\qquad \} \\ \qquad\qquad\qquad\quad \downarrow P \rightarrow \ \uparrow X, \downarrow M \ \rightarrow\rightarrow\rightarrow\rightarrow\rightarrow\rightarrow\rightarrow \} \end{array}\right\} \uparrow (X - M)$$

Alternatively, a devaluation-induced improvement in the balance of payments will increase income which, in turn, will result in partially offsetting increases in induced imports and also in price increases, which will discourage exports/encourage imports and contribute to a further deterioration in the external balance. In this case price changes have reinforced a negative income effect. Notationally:

$$\downarrow r \rightarrow \uparrow X, \ \downarrow M \rightarrow \uparrow (X-M) \rightarrow \ \uparrow Y \rightarrow \uparrow M \rightarrow \rightarrow \rightarrow \ \}$$
$$\downarrow \qquad\qquad\qquad\qquad\qquad\qquad \} \downarrow (X-M)$$
$$\uparrow P \rightarrow \downarrow X, \ \uparrow M \rightarrow \ \}$$

Summary

Income changes contribute either positively or negatively to the correction of external disequilibrium. Positive changes are used directly to restore external equilibrium, while negative changes must be offset by counteracting positive changes. In both cases, income-induced price changes will reinforce the effects of income changes.

THE ABSORPTION APPROACH

Characteristics

The **absorption approach** relates external disequilibrium to discrepancies between national income and expenditure. Changes in domestic absorption are not necessarily in themselves a means of correcting external disequilibrium. They are, rather, a composite of exchange rate, income and expenditure changes and represent the combined application of these changes to the adjustment process and the restoration of external equilibrium.

Domestic absorption (A) is:

Aggregate domestic expenditure on goods and services.

Domestic absorption may be greater or less than national income. When absorption is greater than income, a country consumes more than it produces and this difference must be satisfied from overseas by an inflow of goods and services (deficit). Similarly, if absorption

145

is less than income, a country consumes less than it produces and this difference must be accommodated by an outflow of goods and services (surplus). Notationally:

$$Y = C + I + G + (X - M)$$
$$\text{(Income)} = \text{(Expenditure)}$$
$$A = C + I + G$$
(Domestic Absorption) = (Total domestic expenditure on goods and services)
$$B = X - M$$
(Current account balance) = (Exports minus imports)

$$Y = A + B \qquad (8\text{-}13)$$
(Income) = (Domestic Absorption plus Current Account Balance)

EXAMPLE

Assume:

$$C = 10$$
$$I = 5$$
$$G = 1$$
$$X = 4$$
$$M = 8$$

$$Y = C + I + G + (X - M)$$
$$= 10 + 5 + 1 + (4 - 8)$$
$$= 12.$$
$$A = C + I + G$$
$$= 10 + 5 + 1$$
$$= 16.$$
$$B = X - M$$
$$= 4 - 8$$
$$= -4.$$
$$Y = A + B$$
$$12 = 16 + (-4).$$

Application

A country which absorbs (consumes) less than it produces will experience external disequilibrium in the form of a balance of payments surplus. Notationally:

$$Y > A \twoheadrightarrow (+) B.$$

The surplus can be corrected either by reducing income through **expenditure-switching policies** such as revaluation, which reduces the transfer of resources overseas, or, less painfully, by increasing domestic absorption through **expenditure-augmenting policies** such as expansionary monetary or fiscal policy.

A country which 'lives beyond its means' absorbs more than it produces and so experiences external disequilibrium in the form of a balance of payments deficit. Notationally:

$$Y < A \twoheadrightarrow (- B).$$

The deficit can be corrected either by increasing income or, more painfully, by reducing absorption. The former increases the economy's supply of resources which, through expenditure-switching policies such as devaluation, can then be transferred overseas to correct the deficit. Increasing income in the short run, however, is not always possible because of domestic supply constraints. Alternatively, therefore, domestic absorption must be reduced through **expenditure-reducing policies**, such as contractionary monetary or fiscal policy, to release the resources necessary to improve the balance of payments. The application of absorption changes to the correction of external disequilibrium (deficits) consequently involves various combinations of exchange rate, income and expenditure changes which may be considered in terms of three possibilities:

(i) Positive income and absorption changes

$$\uparrow Y = \uparrow A + \uparrow B \qquad (\uparrow Y > \uparrow A).$$

This adjustment process involves income increases which exceed absorption increases, thereby enabling the increases in income which are not absorbed domestically to be channelled overseas to correct the balance of payments deficit. The process is effected by an expenditure-switching policy such as devaluation which, if successful, will increase exports by more than the induced decrease/increase in imports, so that income will increase by more than absorption and external disequilibrium will consequently be reduced. Notationally:

$$\downarrow r \rightarrow \uparrow(X - M) \rightarrow \uparrow Y > \uparrow A \rightarrow \uparrow B.$$

The process depends critically on the existence of unemployed resources, excess capacity or increases in productivity to provide the resources necessary to accommodate the increase in national income. In the absence of these resources and alternative macroeconomic policies, adjustment through devaluation alone will not be successful, since devaluation will stimulate aggregate demand which will, with fixed aggregate output, contribute to inflation and undermine the improvement in the balance of payments as attempts are made to satisfy excess demand through the overseas sector with increased imports. Alternative absorption approaches to the restoration of external equililbrium are consequently required.

EXAMPLE

Consider the impact on income, absorption and the balance of payments of a 30 unit devaluation-induced increase in exports. Assume $s = 0.3$, $m = 0.2$ and that autonomous imports remain unchanged.

From equation 8-8:

$$\Delta Y = \frac{\Delta X^*}{s + m}$$

$$= \frac{30}{0.3 + 0.2}$$

$$= 60.$$

From equation 8-11:

$$\Delta B = \Delta X^* - \Delta M^* - m\Delta Y$$
$$= 30 - 0.2 \,(60)$$
$$= 18.$$

From equation 8-13:

$$\Delta A = \Delta Y - \Delta B$$
$$= 60 - 18$$
$$= 42.$$

The increase in income (60 units) is greater than the increase in absorption (42 units), thereby allowing resources to be channelled overseas and providing a corresponding improvement (18 units) in the balance of payments.

(ii) Constant income and negative absorption changes

$$\overline{Y} = \ \downarrow A + \ \uparrow B.$$

This adjustment process involves reducing domestic absorption to release the resources necessary to correct external disequilibrium. (Net increases in income are precluded by domestic supply constraints.) Resources are transferred from the domestic sector to the foreign sector by combining expenditure-switching and expenditure-reducing policies. The former, if successful, will increase exports by more than the induced decrease/increase in imports, while the latter will release from domestic absorption the resources required to accommodate the increase in net exports.

The consequences of domestic supply constraints are that devaluation must be accompanied by domestic deflation if external disequilibrium is to be successfully corrected. Since domestic deflation involves the reduced domestic absorption of real goods and services, however, the correction of external disequilibrium will necessarily involve reductions in economic welfare until the adjustment process is complete.

EXAMPLE

Consider the impact on income, absorption and the balance of payments of a 30 unit devaluation-induced increase in exports. Assume: s = 0.3, m = 0.2, full employment, unchanged autonomous imports and a balance of payments deficit of 30 units.

The existence of full employment implies the necessity to neutralise the expansionary impact of the 30 unit increase in exports by domestic deflation in the form of, for example, a corresponding decrease in autonomous consumption.

From equation 8-12:

$$\Delta B = \frac{s}{s+m} (\Delta X^* - \Delta M^*) - \frac{m}{s+m} (\Delta C^* + \Delta I^* + \Delta G^*)$$

$$= \frac{0.3}{0.3+0.2} (30) - \frac{0.2}{0.3+0.2} (-30)$$

$$= 18 + 12$$
$$= 30.$$

From equation 8-13:

$$\Delta A = \Delta Y - \Delta B$$
$$= 0 - (+30)$$
$$= -30.$$

The reduction in absorption (-30) has been just sufficient to release the resources necessary to accommodate the increase in exports (30) without creating excess demand ($\bar{Y}$). The balance of payments deficit has thus been corrected, leaving the level of income unchanged.

(iii) Negative income and absorption changes

$$\downarrow Y = \downarrow A + \uparrow B \qquad (\downarrow Y < \downarrow A).$$

The burden of external adjustment is increasingly shifted to reductions in both income and domestic absorption as exchange rate devaluations become increasingly ineffective (for example, because of low import demand elasticities). The smaller the increase in devaluation-induced exports and the smaller the decrease in devaluation-induced imports, the larger must be income-induced decreases in imports for adjustment to be effective. The adjustment process consequently becomes increasingly expenditure-reducing, involving negative changes in both absorption and income, with larger decreases in absorption than income since absorption must decrease by at least as much as income and, additionally, by the reduction in imports. Ultimately, in the absence of increases in exports and decreases in autonomous imports, the entire burden of adjustment is transferred to decreases in income, absorption and induced imports.

Consider the impact on income, absorption and a 25 unit balance of payments deficit, of income and absorption changes designed to correct this deficit. Assume s = 0.3, m = 0.2 and that combined exports and autonomous imports remain unchanged.

Since combined exports and autonomous imports remain unchanged, the entire burden of adjustment is shifted to decreases in income and domestic absorption effected through, for example, reductions in autonomous consumption which reduce induced imports.

From equation 8-11:

$$\Delta B = \Delta X^* - \Delta M^* - m\Delta Y$$
$$25 = -0.2\Delta Y$$
$$\Delta Y = -125.$$

From equation 8-13:

$$\Delta A = \Delta Y - \Delta B$$
$$= -125 - (+25)$$
$$= -150.$$

Domestic absorption has thus decreased by 150 units to accommodate the 125 unit decrease in income and the 25 unit improvement in the balance of payments (reduced imports).

Absorption changes and import controls

The failure of market-oriented corrective measures such as devaluation to correct external disequilibrium (deficits) without excessive deflation may prompt recourse to alternative administrative corrective measures such as import controls. These constitute another form of expenditure switching and, by curbing imports directly, are intended to restore external equilibrium without recourse to excessive deflation. Three possibilities may be considered:

(i) Positive income and absorption changes

$$\uparrow Y = \uparrow A + \uparrow B \qquad (\uparrow Y > \uparrow A).$$

This is the most desirable possibility, since it involves increases in both income and domestic absorption. The unsatisfied import demand created by import controls is channelled to domestically produced import substitutes which, through the action of the multiplier, increase income and domestic absorption.

The successful application of import controls and income and absorption increases to the external adjustment process depends critically on the existence of unemployed resources or excess capacity to provide the resources necessary to accommodate the increase in income. The absence of such resources will shift the burden of adjustment to decreases in domestic absorption.

EXAMPLE

Consider the impact on income, absorption and the balance of payments of import controls which decrease autonomous imports by 10 units. Assume s = 0.3, m = 0.2 and unchanged exports.

From equation 8-8:

$$\Delta Y = \frac{-\Delta M^*}{s+m}$$

$$= \frac{-(-10)}{0.3+0.2}$$

$$= 20.$$

From equation 8-11:

$$\Delta B = \Delta X^* - \Delta M^* - m\Delta Y$$
$$= -(-10) - 0.2\,(20)$$
$$= 6.$$

From equation 8-13:

$$\Delta A = \Delta Y - \Delta B$$
$$= 20 - 6$$
$$= 14.$$

The autonomous decrease in imports (-10) — partly offset by an increase in induced imports (4) — has improved the balance of payments (6 units) and increased both income (20 units) and domestic absorption (14 units).

(ii) Constant income and negative absorption changes

$$\overline{Y} = {\downarrow}A + {\uparrow}B.$$

Import controls create excess demand when unemployed resources or excess capacity are absent. The restoration of external equilibrium consequently necessitates decreases in domestic absorption which can be achieved either through a contractionary monetary or fiscal policy or (improbably) through a corresponding increase in domestic saving. In both situations, external equilibrium will be restored with decreases in domestic absorption and unchanged income. (Since import controls may be expected to reduce autonomous imports directly, income-induced decreases in imports will not be required, so that decreases in both absorption and income (case (ii) above) will not apply.)

(iii) Income, absorption and the balance of payments unchanged

$$\overline{Y} = \overline{A} + \overline{B}.$$

This possibility arises if the unsatisfied import demand created by import controls is not sterilised but is channelled to domestically produced import substitutes whose supply cannot initially increase because of domestic supply (full employment) constraints. This results in excess demand which will both attract resources to these substitutes from the export sector thus reducing exports, and increase domestic prices, thereby contributing to further decreases in exports. Corresponding decreases in exports and imports will leave income, absorption and the balance of payments unchanged. Import controls will thus have failed to improve the balance of payments and restore external equilibrium.

Summary

Absorption changes illustrate the combined effect of exchange rate, income and expenditure changes on the external adjustment process.

External equilibrium can be restored through devaluation with increases in income and domestic absorption if domestic supply constraints are absent. External equilibrium will be restored through devaluation with constant income and decreases in domestic absorption if domestic supply constraints exist. External equilibrium will be restored with decreases in both income and domestic absorption as devaluation becomes increasingly ineffective (for example, because of low import demand elasticities). Ultimately, in the absence of devaluation-induced increases in exports and decreases in imports, the entire burden of external adjustment is transferred to decreases in income and absorption.

Absorption changes also illustrate the potential inability of import controls to restore external equilibrium if domestic supply constraints exist and import controls are not supplemented with domestic deflation.

These adjustment problems do not directly apply to external disequilibrium resulting from balance of payments surpluses, however, since decreases in net export receipts, unlike increases, are not subject to domestic supply constraints. Exchange rate revaluations, therefore, which satisfy the Marshall-Lerner condition, may be expected to reduce balance of payments surpluses, subject only to counteracting income changes which reduce imports. The smaller the marginal propensity to import, the smaller will be the income-induced decrease in imports and thus the more effective will be the revaluation-induced correction of external equilibrium.

These adjustment problems do not arise with floating exchange rates either, since adjustment is market-determined and automatic. The exchange rate responds to changes in the demand for and supply of imports and exports and so ensures that external equilibrium is automatically maintained.

SUMMARY

Under fixed exchange rates, the process of correcting external disequilibrium (deficits) involves transferring domestic resources overseas. These transfers can be analysed in several ways:

The elasticities approach focuses on exchange rate changes to achieve the directional and value changes necessary to restore external equilibrium. Its success depends on the absence of low import demand elasticities and counteracting income changes.

The income approach incorporates income changes into the adjustment process. These changes may either contribute to or detract from the adjustment process, but in either case their impact is likely to be incomplete, so that they will have to be supplemented with, or act as a supplement to, alternative measures of correcting external disequilibrium. Their net contribution (positive or negative) to the adjustment process depends on the direction of income changes, which is determined by the expansionary or contractionary profile of the economic variables causing income to change, and the magnitude of these income changes, which is determined by the size of the marginal propensities to save and import. Positive income changes, which improve the balance of payments, may be supplemented with additional corrective measures such as exchange rate realignments. Negative income changes, which counteract improvements in the balance of payments, may necessitate alternative income changes to supplement the measures prompting the original improvements in the balance of payments. In both cases, income-induced price changes will reinforce the effects of income changes.

The absorption approach relates external disequilibrium to discrepancies between income and expenditure. It is a composite of exchange rate, income and expenditure changes which are used in combination to restore external equilibrium. Domestic absorption is aggregate domestic expenditure on goods and services, so that a country which absorbs (consumes) less than it produces generates a balance of payments surplus. This can be corrected by either reducing income or increasing absorption. A country which absorbs more than it produces incurs a balance of payments deficit which can be corrected by either increasing income or reducing absorption. Increases in income generate increases in resources which, through expenditure-switching policies such as devaluation, are then transferred overseas to correct the deficit. The existence of domestic supply constraints, however, necessitates reductions in absorption, which, through expenditure-reducing policies such as contractionary monetary or fiscal policy, release the resources necessary to correct the external deficit. The burden of external adjustment is increasingly shifted to reductions in both income and absorption as expenditure-switching policies become increasingly ineffective.

Adjustment problems do not arise with floating exchange rates, since the exchange rate responds to changes in the demand for and supply of imports and exports and ensures that external equilibrium is automatically maintained.

CONCEPTS FOR REVIEW

Absorption approach

Domestic absorption

Elasticities approach

Expenditure-augmenting policies

Expenditure-reducing policies

Expenditure-switching policies

Income approach

Marginal propensity to import

Marshall-Lerner condition

Open economy multiplier

QUESTIONS FOR DISCUSSION

1. Explain why devaluation increases export receipts denominated in domestic currency. Under what circumstances might receipts not increase?
2. Will devaluation necessarily restore external equilibrium if the Marshall-Lerner condition is satisfied?
3. Why do income changes contribute both positively and negatively to the restoration of external equilibrium?
4. Distinguish between expenditure-switching and expenditure-adjusting policies.
5. Will import controls correct external disequilibrium?

Notes

1. The Marshall-Lerner condition applies when:

(i) Export supply elasticities are infinite. If these are not infinite, devaluation might improve the balance of payments even though the Marshall-Lerner condition is not satisfied.

(ii) The initial imbalance is not large. If this is not the case, and import values are large relative to export values, devaluation might still improve the balance of payments in foreign currency even though the Marshall-Lerner condition is not satisfied.

(iii) Income remains unchanged. If this is not the case, exchange rate-induced changes in income will induce changes in imports which will counteract the impact of the original exchange rate realignment.

2. The contractionary impact of induced increases in imports is mitigated by the 'foreign repercussions effect'. This results from increases in the devaluing country's exports induced by increases in foreign incomes prompted by the increase in the induced imports of the devaluing country.

3. The effect of income changes on the balance of payments can be expressed in the form of a more stringent Marshall-Lerner condition, such that:

$$Em_D + Em_F > 1 + m.$$

This indicates that devaluation will, *ceteris paribus*, improve the balance of payments if the sum of domestic and foreign elasticities of demand for imports exceeds unity plus the marginal propensity to import in the devaluing country.

9

Internal and External Equilibrium

Analysis of external disequilibrium and the adjustment process in Chapter 8 was confined to the current account. A more comprehensive treatment incorporates capital flows, but before this can be undertaken, it is necessary to review how equilibrium is established in closed and open economies within a framework of IS-LM curve analysis.

INTERNAL EQUILIBRIUM IN A CLOSED ECONOMY

Internal equilibrium is essentially:

Full employment national income with price stability.

National income in a closed economy is determined by the sum of consumption, investment and government expenditures on domestic goods and services. It can be expressed as:

$$Y = C + I + G. \tag{9-1}$$

Income received after taxation is either consumed or saved, so that

$$Y = C + S + T \tag{9-2}$$

and

$$C + S + T = Y = C + I + G$$

from which

$$S + T = I + G. \tag{9-3}$$

Equation 9-3 indicates that, in equilibrium, total leakages and injections must be equal. Changes in either leakages or injections will change equilibrium income. Increases in leakages/decreases in injections will decrease income, while decreases in leakages/increases in injections will have the opposite effect.

These changes, which apply to the goods market, can be combined with money market changes to provide an IS-LM curve framework within which fiscal and monetary policies can be individually applied to analysis of the adjustment process and the establishment of internal equilibrium.

IS curves reviewed

IS curves represent:

The different combinations of interest rates and income levels for which the goods market is in equilibrium.

The derivation of IS curves is illustrated in Figure 9.1, which shows that, when applied to a closed economy, IS curves represent equality between total leakages $(S + T)$ and total injections $(I + G)$ for different combinations of interest rates and income levels.

The inverse relationship between investment and the rate of interest is illustrated in quadrant (a) as the Marginal Efficiency of Investment (MEI) schedule to which government expenditure is added to provide total injections $(I + G)_0$ for any given rate of interest (i_0).

Total injections must equal total leakages in equilibrium and the 45° line in quadrant (b) relates total injections to total leakages which are illustrated in quadrant (c). The positive relationship between saving and income is depicted by a positively sloped savings function to which taxes are added to provide total leakages for that particular level of income (Y_0) which is consistent with the rate of interest (i_0) given in quadrant (a). The coincidence of this income level (Y_0) and interest rate (i_0) provides one point (A) on the IS curve in quadrant (d). Similarly, a higher rate of interest (i_1) in quadrant (a) will induce a lower level of investment (injections)

159

which will equate with a lower level of saving (leakages) which in turn will correspond to a lower level of income (Y_1). The coincidence of this higher interest rate and lower income level generates a second point (B) on the IS curve which may be derived by repeating the procedure for different combinations of interest rates and income levels. The resultant negatively sloped IS curve indicates that higher interest rates will, through reduced net investment, generate lower levels of income and vice versa. Points lying off the IS curve represent disequilibrium in the product market, such that points to the right of the curve (C) represent excess leakages ($S + T > I + G$) while points to the left of the curve (D) represent excess injections ($I + G > S + T$).

Figure 9.1: IS curve derivation in a closed economy. The IS curve depicts the different combinations of interest rates and income levels which represent equality between total leakages and total injections.

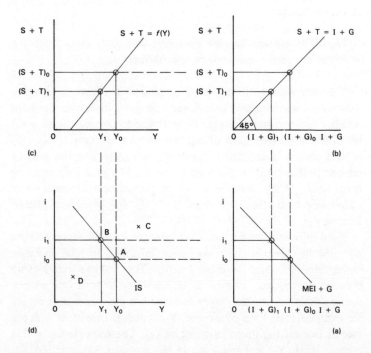

Movements along the IS curve

Changes in the rate of interest, operating through changes in investment, will induce movements along the IS curve and corresponding but opposite changes in income whose new values will depend on the size of the income multiplier. Notationally:

$$\uparrow i \to\to\to\to \downarrow I \to\to\to\to \downarrow Y$$
$$\downarrow i \to\to\to\to \uparrow I \to\to\to\to \uparrow Y.$$

Shifts of the IS curve

Changes in either leakages or injections will cause changes in interest rates or income levels or both and corresponding shifts in the IS curve. Increases in leakages and decreases in injections shift the IS curve to the left, while decreases in leakages or increases in injections shift the IS curve to the right. Notationally:

$$\uparrow S, \ \uparrow T, \ \downarrow I, \ \downarrow G \to\to\to\to \text{(Leftward shift in IS)}$$
$$\downarrow S, \ \downarrow T, \ \uparrow I, \ \uparrow G \to\to\to\to \text{(Rightward shift in IS).}$$

IS curves thus permit the expansionary and contractionary effects of changes in leakages and injections in general and fiscal policy in particular to be applied to analysis of the adjustment process and the establishment of internal equilibrium through changes in interest rates and income levels.

LM curves reviewed

LM curves represent:

> *The different combinations of interest rates and income levels for which the money market is in equilibrium.*

Money market equilibrium expresses equality between the supply of and demand for money for different combinations of interest rates and income levels.

The nominal supply of money (M_S) is assumed to be exogenously determined by the monetary authorities, so that:

$$M_S = M_S^*. \tag{9-4}$$

The Keynesian demand for money consists of three components:

161

The Transactions Demand for Money (m_t), which represents money demanded as a medium of exchange to finance commercial transactions. It is a direct function of national income.

The Precautionary Demand for Money, which represents money demanded to finance contingencies and is also a direct function of national income. It may be included in the transactions demand, both of which may be expressed as:

$$m_t = k(Y). \tag{9-5}$$

The Speculative or Asset Demand for Money (m_{sp}), which represents money demanded as an asset to act as a store of value. It is an inverse function of the rate of interest, since higher interest rates increase the opportunity cost of holding money and is expressed as:

$$m_{sp} = h(i). \tag{9-6}$$

The total demand for money (M_D) is expressed as:

$$M_D = m_t + m_{sp} \tag{9-7}$$

or (by substituting from equations 9-5 and 9-6):

$$M_D = k(Y) + h(i). \tag{9-8}$$

Equilibrium in the money market is established when the supply of, and demand for, money are equal, and is expressed as:

$$M_S = M_D. \tag{9-9}$$

Substituting for M_D from equation 9-8 gives:

$$M_S = k(Y) + h(i). \tag{9-10}$$

This equation is used to derive the LM curve for different combinations of interest rates and income levels. In Figure 9.2, quadrant (a) shows the inverse relationship between the rate of interest (i_0) and the speculative demand for money (m_{sp0}) which absorbs that level of the money supply (M_{S0}) not absorbed by the transactions demand for money (m_{t0}). This allocation of the money

Figure 9.2: LM curve derivation. The LM curve depicts the different combinations of interest rates and income levels which represent equality between the demand for, and supply of, money.

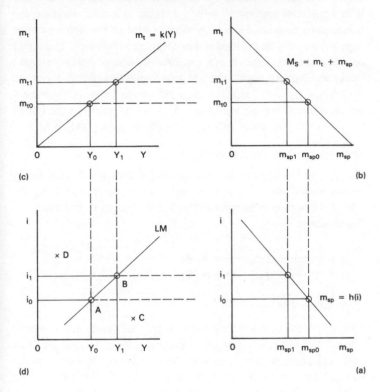

supply between the speculative and transactions demand for money is illustrated in quadrant (b). Quadrant (c) shows the positive relationship between the transactions demand for money and that level of income (Y_0) which is consistent with the rate of interest (i_0) given in quadrant (a). The coincidence of this income level and interest rate provides one point (A) on the LM curve in quadrant (d). Similarly, a higher initial rate of interest (i_1) in quadrant (a) will increase the opportunity cost of holding money and reduce the speculative demand for money (m_{sp1}). This reduced demand will correspond to an increased transactions demand for money (m_{t1}) — M_S unchanged — which in turn will correspond to a higher level of income (Y_1). The coincidence of this higher interest rate and higher income level generates a second point (B) on the LM curve which

163

may be derived by repeating the procedure for different combinations of interest rates and income levels. The resultant positively sloped LM curve indicates that higher income levels are associated with higher interest rates, since increases in income increase the transactions demand for money which, with an unchanged money supply, can only be satisfied out of speculative balances. These will be released as the interest rate (opportunity cost of holding money) increases. Points lying off the LM curve represent disequilibrium in the money market. Points to the right of the curve (C) represent excess demand for money ($M_D > M_S$), while points to the left of the curve (D) represent an excess supply of money ($M_S > M_D$).

Movements along the LM curve

Changes in the level of income, operating through changes in the transactions demand for money, will induce movements along the LM curve with corresponding directional changes in interest rates. Notationally:

$$\uparrow Y \rightarrow\rightarrow\rightarrow\rightarrow \uparrow m_t \rightarrow\rightarrow\rightarrow\rightarrow \uparrow i$$
$$\downarrow Y \rightarrow\rightarrow\rightarrow\rightarrow \downarrow m_t \rightarrow\rightarrow\rightarrow\rightarrow \downarrow i.$$

Shifts of the LM curve

Changes in the demand for money, supply of money and domestic prices (P_D) will cause changes in interest rates or income levels or both and corresponding shifts in the LM curve. Increases in the demand for money (transactions or speculative), decreases in the supply of money and increases in domestic prices (these reduce the real money supply) will shift the LM curve to the left, while decreases in the demand for money, increases in the supply of money and decreases in domestic prices will shift the LM curve to the right. Notationally:

$$\uparrow M_D, \quad \downarrow M_S, \quad \uparrow P_D \rightarrow\rightarrow\rightarrow\rightarrow \text{(Leftward shift in LM)}$$
$$\downarrow M_D, \quad \uparrow M_S, \quad \downarrow P_D \rightarrow\rightarrow\rightarrow\rightarrow \text{(Rightward shift in LM)}.$$

LM curves thus permit the expansionary and contractionary effects of changes in the demand for money, supply of money and domestic prices in general and monetary policy in particular to be applied to analysis of the adjustment process and the establishment of internal equilibrium through changes in interest rates and income levels.

Figure 9.3: IS-LM curves and internal equilibrium. Monetary and fiscal policy may be applied in different combinations to establish internal equilibrium.

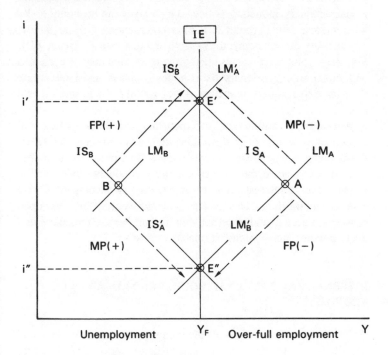

IS-LM curves combined

IS-LM curves may now be combined and applied to the analysis of internal equilibrium and the assignment (application) of stabilising monetary and fiscal policies. Internal equilibrium (IE) is illustrated in Figure 9.3 as a vertical schedule which combines different interest rates with the full employment level of national income (Y_F). Each point on the schedule (IS-LM curve intersection) represents a different combination of IS-LM curves. Points to the left of the schedule represent unemployment, while points to the right represent over-full employment, which is potentially inflationary. By changing the combination of IS-LM curves through the assignment of monetary and/or fiscal policy, the economy can be moved towards internal equilibrium on the IE schedule. Each policy

165

assignment consists of either an expansionary (+) or contractionary (−) monetary (MP) or fiscal (FP) policy. For example, point A represents over-full employment which may be corrected with either a contractionary monetary policy, which takes the economy to Y_F with interest rate i' (point E'), or a contractionary fiscal policy, which takes the economy to Y_F with interest rate i'' (point E''). Similarly, point B represents unemployment which may be corrected with either an expansionary fiscal policy (point E' and interest rate i') or an expansionary monetary policy (point E'' and interest rate i'').

Appropriate combinations of monetary and fiscal policy will consequently secure internal equilibrium in a closed economy. Other things being equal, lower interest rates will be preferred to higher interest rates, since the former are more conducive to economic growth. Lower interest rates, however, may be incompatible with external equilibrium. This creates potential conflict between open economy internal and external equilibrium which monetary and fiscal policies alone might be unable to resolve.

INTERNAL AND EXTERNAL EQUILIBRIUM IN AN OPEN ECONOMY

An open economy contains all the components of a closed one and in addition a foreign sector, comprising exports and imports. National income is determined by the sum of consumption, investment, government and foreign expenditures on domestic goods and services. It can be expressed as:

$$Y = C + I + G + X. \tag{9-11}$$

Income received after taxation is either consumed domestically, saved or expended overseas, so that

$$Y = C + S + T + M \tag{9-12}$$

and

$$C + S + T + M = Y = C + I + G + X$$

from which

$$S + T + M = I + G + X. \qquad (9\text{-}13)$$

SUPPLEMENTARY NOTE — IMPORT EXPENDITURES AND DOUBLE COUNTING

Each expenditure component of national income contains some element of import expenditure which is individually difficult to identify and eliminate. For example, aggregate consumption will include expenditure on consumer durables which contain both domestic and foreign manufactured components. To avoid 'double counting' and to ensure that aggregate demand accurately reflects expenditure on domestically *produced goods and services, component imports are removed in aggregate form. National income in equation 9-11 may thus be alternatively expressed as:*

$$Y = C + I + G + (X - M).$$

Equation 9-13 indicates that total leakages and injections must again be equal in equilibrium. It also illustrates two important financing possibilities created by the establishment of a foreign sector whose potential imbalances are accommodated with official reserves. These possibilities are best expressed by rearranging equation 9-13 so that:

$$(M - X) = (I - S) + (G - T). \qquad (9\text{-}14)$$

The first possibility is that domestic investment, which cannot be financed domestically because of insufficient saving $(I > S)$, may be financed through the overseas sector in the form of a balance of payments deficit $(M > X)$. Consequently, in the absence of a government sector or with a balanced budget, equation 9-14 may be expressed as:

$$M > X = I > S.$$

This financing possibility might apply, for example, to developing countries whose substantial investment needs can only be satisfied through imports and accompanying balance of payments deficits.

167

(The opposite might apply to developed countries, such as Japan, whose balance of payments surpluses are financed with excess saving.)

The second possibility arises when budget deficits $(G > T)$ become so large that they can no longer be financed out of domestic saving and have to be financed, instead, through the foreign sector in the form of a balance of payments deficit $(M > X)$. In the assumed absence of an excess of domestic saving $(I = S)$, equation 9-14 may be expressed as:

$$M > X = G > T.$$

This establishes a direct link between budget deficits and balance of payments deficits and illustrates, for example, how in the 1980s the US has been able to incur and sustain substantial budget deficits through balance of payments deficits.

Changes in leakages and injections can again be combined with money market changes to provide an IS-LM curve framework within which monetary and fiscal policies can be individually applied to the adjustment process and the establishment of internal and external equilibrium.

IS-LM curve analysis

The composition of the LM curve is essentially the same in closed and open economies.

The IS curve, however, differs in the open economy since it must incorporate the additional leakages and injections resulting from imports and exports respectively. The derivation of the IS curve in an open economy is illustrated in Figure 9.4. Quadrant (a) shows that the MEI + G curve shifts horizontally to the right (MEI + G + X) by the full amount of exports which are assumed exogenous and thus independent of domestic interest rates. The 45° line in quadrant (b) relates total injections to total leakages, which are shown in quadrant (c). The total leakages function $(S + T + M)$ shifts up to the left by an amount equal to the level of total imports. (The pivotal shift is also obtained by adding the marginal propensity to import to the marginal propensity to save, both of which determine the slope of the $S + T + M$ function.) The total level of leakages thus derived will correspond to that level of open economy income (Y_0°) which is consistent with the interest rate (i_0) given in

Figure 9.4: IS curve derivation in an open economy. The IS curve in an open economy is more steeply inclined because the marginal propensity to import, operating through induced imports (leakages), reduces the responsiveness of changes in income to changes in interest rates. Changes in income in an open economy will be correspondingly smaller than changes in a closed economy for any given change in interest rates.

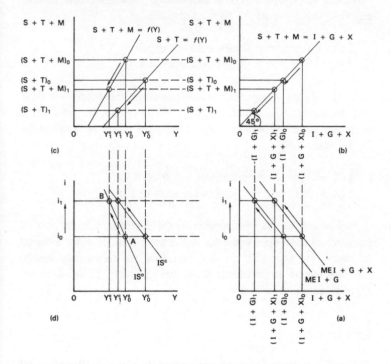

quadrant (a). The coincidence of this income level and interest rate provides one point (A) on the open economy IS curve (IS^o) in quadrant (d). The repetition of this process with higher interest rates generates a series of points, such as point (B), which when connected will determine the location of the IS curve. A comparison of the open economy (IS^o) and closed economy (IS^c) curves in quadrant (d) illustrates the former's comparative inelasticity which is caused by the dampening effect of the marginal propensity to import on the income multiplier process.

Shifts of the IS curve

The open economy IS curve will shift in response to closed economy changes in leakages and injections and, additionally, to changes in imports and exports. Increases in imports and decreases in exports will cause income to fall and shift the curve to the left, while decreases in imports and increases in exports will increase income and shift the curve to the right. Notationally:

$\uparrow$M, $\downarrow$X →→→→ (Leftward shift of IS)
$\downarrow$M, $\uparrow$X →→→→ (Rightward shift of IS).

On a balance of payments basis, therefore, increases in deficits and decreases in surpluses shift the IS curve to the left, while decreases in deficits and increases in surpluses shift the curve to the right. Notationally:

$\downarrow$(X − M) →→→→ (Leftward shift of IS)
$\uparrow$(X − M) →→→→ (Rightward shift of IS).

IS-LM curves may be applied to the determination of internal equilibrium in an open economy in the same manner as for a closed economy, but only after an additional tool has been established to take into account the existence of the foreign sector and an additional external equilibrium target.

EE curve

External equilibrium can be considered in terms of the **external equilibrium** (EE) curve, defined as:

The different combinations of interest rates and income levels for which the foreign sector is in equilibrium.

The concept of external equilibrium depends on the distinction between autonomous and accommodating transactions and the positioning of the imaginary financing line which separates the two. If current account flows are considered the only autonomous transactions, external equilibrium will be established when (abstracting from unilateral transfers) exports and imports are equal (X − M = 0). Alternatively, some capital account flows might be considered autonomous, in which case they should be included with current account transactions in the determination of external equilibrium. A third possibility considers all capital transactions autonomous. This dispenses with the need to distinguish between autonomous and accommodating capital flows and explicitly shifts the concept of external equilibrium to the overall balance where deficits/surpluses are financed/accommodated through decreases/increases in official reserves. The concept of **external equilibrium** may therefore be expressed as:

Equality between external autonomous debit and credit transactions on both current and capital account,

so that the external equilibrium curve now reflects combined current and capital account balances for which the combined demand for, and supply of foreign exchange are equal.

The current account balance, in the absence of unilateral transfers, is expressed as:

$$X - M = 0. \tag{9-15}$$

The capital account balance may be expressed as:

$$K = 0 \tag{9-16}$$

where K represents net capital *outflows*.

External equilibrium may thus be expressed as:

$$(X - M) - K = 0. \tag{9-17}$$

Equation 9-17 indicates that current account surplus/deficit/equilibrium must correspond to capital account deficit/surplus/equilibrium for external equilibrium to prevail (equality between the demand for and supply of foreign exchange).

The current account balance is inversely related to national income, since increases in income, operating through the marginal propensity to import, increase imports and hence cause the balance on current account to deteriorate.

Net capital outflows are inversely related and net capital inflows directly related to positive domestic interest rate differentials, so that increases in domestic interest rates (relative to international rates) will tend to decrease capital outflows and/or increase capital inflows, since the domestic capital market will, *ceteris paribus*, now

171

offer more attractive investment opportunities to capital which is internationally mobile. Decreases in domestic interest rates will have the opposite effect. The responsiveness of capital flows to changes in interest rate differentials reflects the interest rate elasticity of capital flows, which is influenced by factors such as risk, transaction costs and exchange controls. The diminished influence of these factors increases elasticity and hence capital mobility until, eventually, capital may become perfectly mobile. The increasing influence of these factors, on the other hand, reduces elasticity and capital mobility until, eventually, capital may become perfectly immobile, or remain mobile but become perfectly interest inelastic. Imperfect capital mobility, responding in varying degrees to interest rate changes, lies between these two extremes and represents the general case.

The EE curve, derived from equation 9-17, shows that, since the current account balance is inversely related to national income, and net capital outflows are inversely related to domestic interest rates, and since external equilibrium requires that current account and capital account balances change in the same direction, changes in income levels and interest rates will be positively related, so that the EE curve will be positively sloped. This is illustrated in Figure 9.5.

Quadrant (a) shows the inverse relationship between domestic interest rates (i_0) and capital outflows (K_0). In external equilibrium, capital outflows must correspond to a current account surplus and the 45° line in quadrant (b) relates these outflows to the current account surplus $(X - M)_0$ which is illustrated in quadrant (c). The inverse relationship between the current account balance and national income is indicated by a negatively sloped $(X - M)$ schedule, which depicts the payments surplus for that particular income level (Y_0) which is consistent with the rate of interest (i_0) given in quadrant (a). The coincidence of this income level and interest rate provides one point (A) on the EE curve in quadrant (d). Similarly, a higher rate of interest (i_1) in quadrant (a) will induce a lower level of capital outflow (K_1) which will equate with a smaller current account surplus $(X - M)_1$ which in turn will correspond to a higher level of income (Y_1). The coincidence of this higher interest rate and higher income level generates a second point (B) on the EE curve which may be derived by repeating the procedure for different combinations of interest rates and income levels. The resultant positively sloped EE curve indicates that higher income levels will, through induced imports, reduce the current account surplus and that higher interest rates will be required to reduce capital outflows to offset the current account deterioration and hence maintain external equilibrium. (Current account deficits will be offset by capital inflows [negative capital outflows $(-K)$].) Points lying off the EE curve represent external disequilibria: points to the right of the curve (C) represent external deficit $[(X - M) - K < 0]$, while points to the left of the curve (D) represent external surplus $[(X - M) - K > 0]$.

Figure 9.5: EE curve derivation. The EE curve represents the different combinations of interest rates and income levels for which the foreign sector is in equilibrium. The curve has a positive slope because external equilibrium at low interest rates and high levels of capital outflow can only be sustained with low income levels and relatively large current account surpluses.

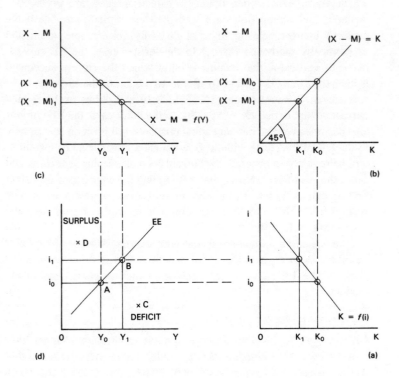

EE curves may be extended to include perfect capital mobility and immobility. These curves are illustrated in Figure 9.6, which shows three EE curves:

Curve EE_0 (panel [a]) corresponds to the curve derived in Figure 9.5 and represents imperfect capital mobility.

Curve EE_1 (panel [b]) represents perfect capital mobility (capital is perfectly interest rate elastic). The EE curve becomes horizontal at that interest rate (i_0) which equates domestic and international interest rates. Points lying above the curve represent external surplus $[(X - M) - K > 0]$ (excess capital inflows), while points lying below the curve represent external deficit $[(X - M) - K < 0]$ (excess capital outflows).

Curve EE_2 (panel [c]) represents perfect capital immobility which arises either when domestic capital markets are perfectly insulated and capital flows are zero or when capital is mobile but perfectly interest inelastic. (This might apply, for example, to illicit or politically motivated flows.) In the former case, the EE curve becomes vertical at that income level at which the current account is in equilibrium $(X - M = 0)$. Points to the left of the curve represent current account surplus $(X - M > 0)$ and points to the right current acount deficit $(X - M < 0)$. In the latter case, the EE curve also becomes vertical but net capital outflows will position the curve to the left of the curve without flows since a lower level of income will be required to generate the current account surplus necessary to offset these outflows. Net capital inflows will have the opposite positioning effect. Points to the left of the curve represent external surplus $[(X - M) - K > 0]$ and points to the right external deficit $[(X - M) - K < 0]$.

The EE curve is thus consistent with varying degrees of capital mobility. With a given $(X - M)$ function, this is reflected in the slope of the EE curve which becomes flatter as capital mobility increases.

Movements along the EE curve

Changes in the level of income, operating through changes in induced imports, will induce changes in the current account balance. These changes will have to be offset by interest rate-induced changes in capital flows to maintain external equilibrium. Since the current account balance is inversely related to income changes and capital outflows are inversely related to positive interest rate differentials, increases in income will precipitate movements along the EE curve with corresponding directional changes in interest rates. For

Figure 9.6: EE curves with varying degrees of capital mobility. Imperfect capital mobility is illustrated in panel (a) which shows that the EE curve is positively sloped. Perfect capital mobility is shown in panel (b) which shows that the EE curve is horizontal at that interest rate (i_0) which equates domestic and international interest rates. Perfect capital immobility is depicted in panel (c) which shows that the EE curve is vertical at that income level for which the foreign sector is in external equilibrium.

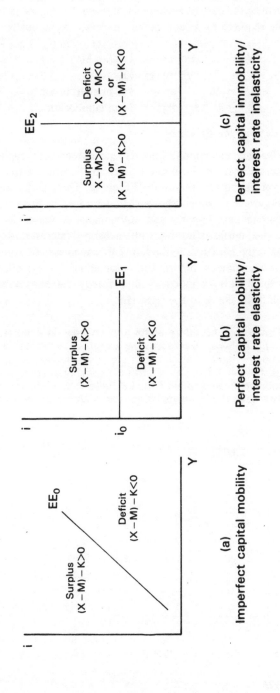

example, higher income levels will, through induced imports, reduce the current account surplus, so that higher interest rates will be required to reduce capital outflows. Notationally:

$\uparrow$Y $\rightarrow\rightarrow\rightarrow\rightarrow$ $\downarrow$(X − M)
$\uparrow$i $\rightarrow\rightarrow\rightarrow\rightarrow$ $\downarrow$K
$\downarrow$(X − M)   = $\downarrow$K in equilibrium
$\uparrow$Y $\leftarrow\leftarrow\leftrightarrow\rightarrow\rightarrow$ $\uparrow$i in equilibrium

Shifts of the EE curve

Changes in exports, imports and autonomous capital flows will cause changes in interest rates or income levels or both and corresponding shifts in the EE curve. These shifts are illustrated in Figure 9.7, which shows that decreases in exports, increases in autonomous imports and autonomous increases/decreases in net capital outflows/inflows with unchanged interest rate elasticities will shift the EE curve to the left (EE_1). Increases in exports, decreases in autonomous imports and autonomous decreases/increases in net capital outflows/inflows with unchanged interest rate elasticities will shift the curve to the right (EE_2).

Figure 9.7: EE curve shifts and changes in exports, imports and capital flows. Decreases in exports, increases in autonomous imports and autonomous increases/decreases in net capital outflows/inflows will tend to increase interest rates and/or reduce income levels and shift the EE curve to the left. Opposite changes will have the opposite effect and shift the curve to the right.

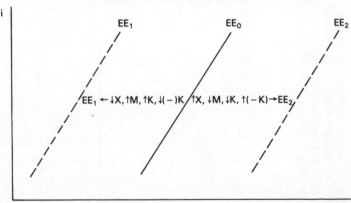

Pivotal shifts (counter-clockwise) will result from increases in induced imports prompted by increases in the marginal propensity to import and from autonomous increases/decreases in net capital outflows/inflows prompted by increases in interest rate inelasticities. Opposite changes will result in opposite (clockwise) pivotal shifts.

Shifts of the EE curve may also be considered in terms of those factors which determine changes in exports, imports and capital flows, of which two are of particular significance to the adjustment process and to the determination of internal and external equilibrium:

(i) Price Changes. Increases in domestic prices (P_D) tend to discourage exports and encourage imports which might be further stimulated by inflation-induced increases in the marginal propensity to import. Price increases might also encourage/discourage capital outflows/inflows at prevailing interest rates. These changes will shift the EE curve to the left and transform external equilibrium into external deficit at prevailing interest rate and income levels. Decreases in domestic prices will have the opposite effect. Notationally:

$$\uparrow P_D \rightarrow\rightarrow \ \downarrow X, \ \uparrow M, \ \uparrow K, \ \downarrow (-)K \rightarrow\rightarrow \text{External Deficit}$$
$$\text{(Leftward shift of EE)}$$
$$\downarrow P_D \rightarrow\rightarrow \ \uparrow X, \ \downarrow M, \ \downarrow K, \ \uparrow (-)K \rightarrow\rightarrow \text{External Surplus}$$
$$\text{(Rightward shift of EE)}$$

Consequently, domestic inflation will, *ceteris paribus*, shift the EE curve to the left, while domestic deflation will shift it to the right.

Foreign price changes may be expected to have the opposite effect on external equilibrium and the EE curve.

(ii) Exchange Rate Changes. The effects of exchange rate changes are similar to those of domestic price changes. Revaluation tends to discourage exports and encourage imports and, through profit-taking in the foreign exchange market, will increase/decrease capital outflows/inflows. These changes will shift the EE curve to the left and transform external surplus into external equilibrium at prevailing interest rate and income levels. Devaluation will have the opposite effect. Notationally:

$\uparrow r \twoheadrightarrow \downarrow X, \uparrow M, \uparrow K, \downarrow(-)K \twoheadrightarrow$ External Equilibrium
(Leftward shift of EE)
$\downarrow r \twoheadrightarrow \uparrow X, \downarrow M, \downarrow K, \uparrow(-)K \twoheadrightarrow$ External Equilibrium
(Rightward shift of EE)

IS-LM-EE curves combined

The intersection of the IS and LM curves along the IE schedule, which combines different interest rates with the full employment level of national income, identifies internal equilibrium. The intersection of the EE curve, which represents external equilibrium, with the IS and LM curves along the IE schedule identifies the interest rate and full employment level of income at which the economy is in **joint** (internal and external) **equilibrium**. This is illustrated by point E in panel (a) of Figure 9.8.

Point E might not be attained, however, since the IS curve (IS_1) and LM curve (LM_1) might, for example, intersect at point F, resulting in internal equilibrium but external deficit. (In joint disequilibrium, the economy is assumed to be located at the intersection of the IS and LM curves.) Alternatively, the IS curve (IS_2) and LM curve (LM_2) might intersect at point I, which represents both internal (unemployment) and external (surplus) disequilibrium. The various combinations of internal and external equilibrium and disequilibrium are illustrated by points A to I, representing hypothetical IS-LM curve intersections, in panel (b) of Figure 9.8. They can be summarised as:

Table 9.1: IS-LM curve intersections.

Point	Internal Condition	External Condition
A	Equilibrium	Surplus
B	Over-full employment	Surplus
C	Over-full employment	Equilibrium
D	Over-full employment	Deficit
E	*Equilibrium*	*Equilibrium*
F	Equilibrium	Deficit
G	Unemployment	Deficit
H	Unemployment	Equilibrium
I	Unemployment	Surplus

Figure 9.8: IS-LM-EE curves combined. The intersection of the EE schedule, which represents external equilibrium, with the IS and LM curves along the IE schedule, identifies the interest rate (i_0) and full employment level of income (Y_F) at which the economy is in joint equilibrium. Points other than E represent various combinations of joint disequilibrium.

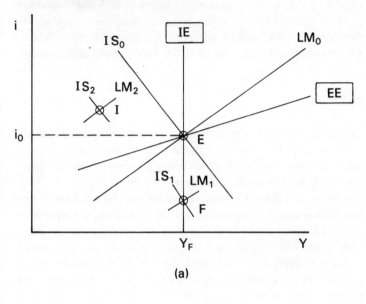

(a)

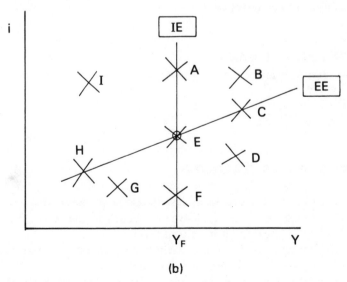

(b)

With three policy targets (interest rates, income levels and external equilibrium) and three policy instruments (monetary policy, fiscal policy and exchange rate policy), there is some combination of policy instruments which will enable joint equilibrium to be established. The object of IS-LM-EE curve analysis, therefore, is to provide an analytical framework within which the adjustment process, incorporating expenditure-adjusting and expenditure-switching policies, may be applied to the determination of internal and external equilibrium under both fixed and floating exchange rates.

SUMMARY

Internal equilibrium can be considered a state of full employment with price stability. It is identified as the point of intersection of the IS and LM curves along the IE schedule which combines different interest rates with the full employment level of national income.

External equilibrium is equality between external autonomous debit and credit transactions on current and capital account. It is represented by the EE curve which identifies different combinations of interest rates and income levels for which the foreign sector is in equilibrium.

Joint equilibrium exists where the EE curve intersects the IE schedule. With three policy targets and three policy instruments, there is some combination of policy instruments which will enable joint equilibrium to be established.

CONCEPTS FOR REVIEW

EE curve	IS curve
External equilibrium	Joint equilibrium
Internal equilibrium	LM curve

QUESTIONS FOR DISCUSSION

1. Use IS-LM curve analysis to show the closed economy effects of: (i) an increase in the speculative or asset demand for money; (ii) an improvement in business confidence.
2. Explain why the IS curve is likely to be more interest inelastic in an open economy than a closed one.
3. Show the effect on the derivation of the EE curve of increases

    in: (i) exports; (ii) the marginal propensity to import; (iii) the interest elasticity of capital flows.

4. Reconcile leftward shifts of the EE curve which lead to external deficit with those which lead to external equilibrium.

5. What is joint equilibrium and how is it established?

10

Internal and External Equilibrium with Fixed Exchange Rates

ECONOMIC DISTURBANCES AND JOINT DISEQUILIBRIUM

Destabilising economic disturbances can originate in both product and money markets and may be internally or externally induced. Figure 10.1 shows the impact of such disturbances on an economy originally in joint equilibrium at point E, with interest rate i_0 and income level Y_F.

LM curve disturbances

Panel (a) of Figure 10.1 shows the effect of shifts of the LM curve caused, for example, by changes in the speculative demand for money. Increases in demand shift the curve up to the left (LM_1) and result in higher interest rates (i_1), unemployment (Y_U) and an external surplus at point A. Decreases in demand shift the curve down to the right (LM_2) and result in opposite changes. Other factors which might account for shifts in the LM curve include changes in the transactions demand for money — caused, for example, by institutional factors — and decreases in the real money supply, caused, for example, by cost-push inflation. Changes in the nominal money supply are not considered a disturbance because the money supply is initially assumed to be exogenously determined by the monetary authorities and is thus a policy variable.

IS curve disturbances

Panels (b) and (c) of Figure 10.1 show the effect of shifts of the IS

182

Figure 10.1: Economic disturbances and joint disequilibrium.
Destabilising economic disturbances may originate in both product
or money markets and may be internally or externally induced. They
move the economy away from joint equilibrium at point E with
interest rate i_0 and income level Y_F.

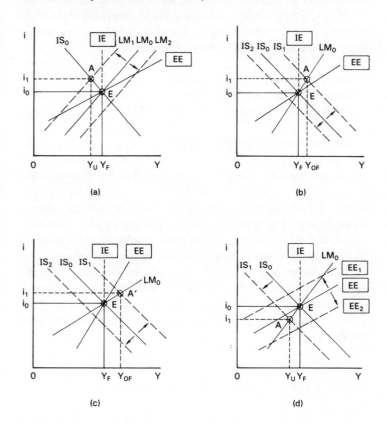

(a)

(b)

(c)

(d)

curve caused, for example, by changes in autonomous investment.
Increases in investment shift the curve up to the right (IS_1) and
result in higher interest rates (i_1) and over-full employment (Y_{OF})
which is potentially inflationary (points A and A'). Decreases in
investment shift the curve down to the left (IS_2) with opposite
results. The external impact of shifts in the IS curve depends on the
relative slopes of the LM and EE curves. If the LM curve is more
steeply inclined than the EE curve (panel [b]), an upward shift in the
IS curve will generate an external surplus (point A) since the
increase in interest rates discourages capital outflows/encourages

183

capital inflows which are more than sufficient to compensate for the income-induced increase in imports. If the LM curve is less steeply inclined than the EE curve (panel [c]), decreases in capital outflows/increases in capital inflows will not compensate for the income-induced increase in imports and external deficit will result (point A'). Corresponding changes apply to downward shifts of the IS curve, whose external impact will also depend on the relative slopes of the LM and EE curves. Notationally:

LM more steeply inclined than EE

Expansionary IS curve shift $\;\to\to\;$ $\downarrow K >$ $\uparrow M$ $\to\to$ External surplus
Contractionary IS curve shift $\;\to\to\;$ $\uparrow K >$ $\downarrow M$ $\to\to$ External deficit

LM less steeply inclined than EE

Expansionary IS curve shift $\;\to\to\;$ $\downarrow K <$ $\uparrow M$ $\to\to$ External deficit
Contractionary IS curve shift $\;\to\to\;$ $\uparrow K <$ $\downarrow M$ $\to\to$ External surplus

Since international capital flows may be expected to reflect a generally high degree of interest-rate elasticity under conditions of imperfect capital mobility, the LM curve in subsequent analyses will be assumed to be more steeply inclined than the EE curve.

Other factors which shift the IS curve are changes in exports, autonomous imports and autonomous consumption. Changes in government expenditure and taxes are specifically excluded, however, since these are policy variables and are not considered disturbances.

EE curve disturbances

Panel (d) of Figure 10.1 shows the effect of shifts of the EE curve caused, for example, by autonomous changes in capital flows. Increases in capital outflows/decreases in capital inflows shift the curve up to the left (EE_1) and create external deficit at the original interest rate (i_0) and income level (Y_F). Opposite changes shift the curve down to the right (EE_2) and result in external surplus. (Since fixed exchange rates are intended to insulate the domestic economy against external disturbances, it can be assumed that the monetary authorities initially sterilise the contractionary/expansionary impact of capital outflows/inflows on the domestic money supply, so that the LM curve does not shift to the left/right in response to these flows.)

Changes in exports and autonomous imports will also shift the EE curve, but in this case the IS curve will also have to shift since injections and leakages will have changed. A decrease in exports, for example, which shifts the EE curve up to EE_1, will also shift the IS curve down to IS_1 and create unemployment (Y_U) and external deficit at point A. Changes in exports and imports might result, for example, from changes in foreign prices, but exchange rate realignments are specifically excluded as a factor since, under a system of fixed exchange rates, they represent deliberate policy options and are not considered disturbances.

STABILISATION POLICIES AND THE ESTABLISHMENT OF JOINT EQUILIBRIUM

Fixed exchange rates are intended to insulate the economy against transitory economic disturbances whose destabilising impact is absorbed by changes in official reserves. If these disturbances are not readily reversed, however, the economy might experience protracted joint disequilibrium, and stabilisation measures, designed to counteract the destabilising impact of the disturbances, will be required to restore joint equilibrium.

Stabilisation measures consist of monetary policy, fiscal policy and, ultimately, exchange rate policy, and may be applied in various combinations depending on the nature and severity of the economic disturbances. The application of these policies to three examples of joint disequilibrium is illustrated in Figure 10.2. The examples are represented by points A, B and C which are illustrated in relation to each other and in relation to hypothetical IE and EE curves in panel (a).

Point A in panel (a) represents internal equilibrium and external surplus. The impact of stabilisation policies is illustrated in panel (b) (i), which shows that an expansionary monetary policy (LM_1), which reduces the rate of interest, encourages capital outflows/discourages capital inflows and reduces the external surplus. The expansionary impact of lower interest rates is counteracted by a contractionary fiscal policy (IS_1). Joint equilibrium is established at point E with a lower interest rate (i_E) and an unchanged level of income (Y_F). Alternatively, joint equilibrium could be established through an exchange rate revaluation. Panel (b) (ii) shows that, by encouraging imports and discouraging exports, revaluation shifts the EE curve up to the left

Figure 10.2: Stabilisation policies and joint equilibrium. Monetary, fiscal and exchange rate policies can be applied in various combinations to establish joint equilibrium.

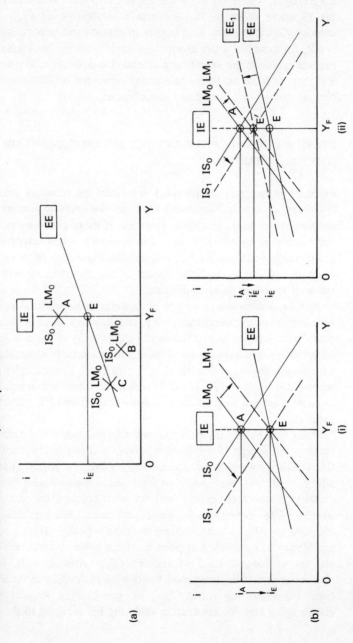

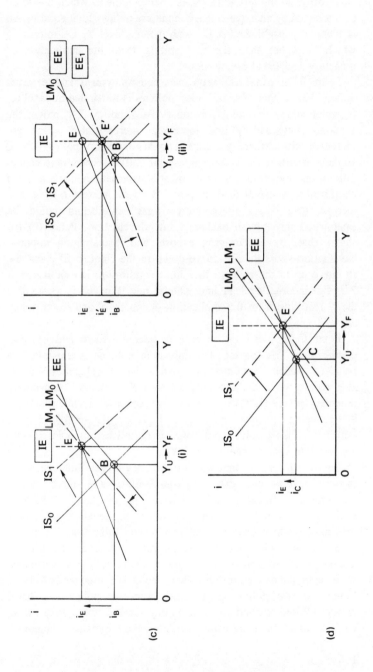

to EE_1 and takes the economy closer to external equilibrium. The increase in imports and decrease in exports, however, shifts the IS curve down to the left and creates unemployment, which has to be counteracted by an expansionary monetary policy. Joint equilibrium is eventually established at E', with income level Y_F and interest i'_E which is higher than the i_E resulting from the application of monetary and fiscal policy alone.

Point B in panel (a) represents unemployment and external deficit. The impact of stabilisation policies is illustrated in panel (c) (i) which shows that an expansionary fiscal policy (IS_1) moves the economy towards Y_F and increases interest rates which are increased still further by a contractionary monetary policy (LM_1). Higher interest rates discourage capital outflows/encourage capital inflows and move the economy towards external equilibrium. Joint equilibrium is established at point E, with interest rate i_E and income level Y_F. Alternatively, joint equilibrium could be established through an exchange rate devaluation. Panel (c) (ii) shows that, by encouraging exports and discouraging imports, devaluation shifts the EE curve down to the right to EE_1 and the IS curve up to the right to IS_1. Joint equilibrium is established at E', with income level Y_F and interest rate i'_E which is lower than the i_E resulting from the application of monetary and fiscal policy alone.

Point C in panel (a) represents unemployment and external equilibrium. The impact of stabilisation policies is illustrated in panel (d) which shows that an expansionary fiscal policy (IS_1) is required to move the economy towards Y_F, but an expansionary monetary policy (LM_1) is required to contain the incipient surplus by reducing interest rates and increasing/decreasing capital outflows/inflows. Joint equilibrium is established at point E with interest rate i_E and income level Y_F.

Figure 10.2 shows that with three policy targets (interest rates, income levels and external equilibrium) and three policy instruments (monetary policy, fiscal policy and, ultimately, exchange rate policy), there is some combination of policy instruments which enables joint equilibrium to be established.

Economies with fixed exchange rates, however, cannot use exchange rate realignments as a policy instrument except in cases of fundamental disequilibrium. Their choice is consequently initially limited to two policy instruments (monetary policy and fiscal policy). When applied to three policy targets, these may create conflicts as attempts are made to achieve the targets simultaneously and establish joint equilibrium.

These potential policy conflicts can be examined in terms of individual IS-LM-EE curve shifts which reflect both economic disturbances and responses in general and policy options and conflicts in particular, under conditions of imperfect and perfect capital mobility. (Adjustment under perfect capital immobility essentially involves previously considered current account absorption changes.)

The analysis incorporates the following simplifying assumptions:

In the absence of specified alternative policies, the expansionary or contractionary impact of international capital flows on the domestic money supply is sterilised to eliminate externally-induced shifts of the LM curve.

Prices are stable to avoid price-induced shifts of the IS-LM-EE curves. Such shifts may be incorporated into the analysis by, for example, shifting the LM curve up to the left in response to price increases, the impact of which is illustrated in the appendix to this chapter.

IS-LM-EE curve shifts are independent and are analysed on a 'net' or non-iterative basis.

Time is sufficient to allow all adjustments to be completed.

The economy moves directly to its projected point of joint equilibrium/disequilibrium.

The effects of growth are abstracted from.

All markets clear efficiently.

ECONOMIC DISTURBANCES AND IMPERFECT CAPITAL MOBILITY

Case 1: Domestic money market shock

The impact of a domestic money market shock is illustrated in Figure 10.3. An increase in the transactions demand for money, caused perhaps by institutional factors, shifts the LM curve up to the left to LM_1.

The economy consequently moves to point A. This represents internal disequilibrium (unemployment Y_U at interest rate i_1) and external surplus which results from the income-induced decline in imports and the interest rate increase which encourages capital

Figure 10.3: Domestic money market disturbances and joint disequilibrium. An upward shift of the LM curve (LM_1) creates joint disequilibrium (unemployment and external surplus) at point A. Joint equilibrium can be restored at point E with an expansionary monetary policy or automatically through capital inflows and the accumulation of foreign exchange reserves. Both possibilities shift the LM curve back to LM_0.

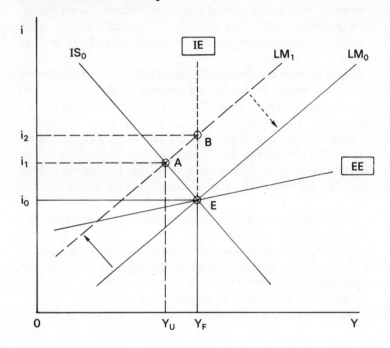

inflows/discourages capital outflows. Joint disequilibrium is thus established at point A.

Conflict: internal and external disequilibrium

Policy options

1. Non-sterilisation. The external surplus necessitates official intervention in the foreign exchange market to stabilise exchange rates through purchases of foreign currency and sales of domestic currency. The former augments foreign exchange reserves and the latter increases domestic liquidity. If this increase is not sterilised

190

by, for example, open market operations, the LM curve will shift back down to LM_0 and joint equilibrium will be restored at point E.

Potential policy conflict: Excess reserve augmentation

2. *Sterilisation.* The expansionary impact of the external surplus on domestic liquidity is sterilised. This maintains the LM curve at LM_1 and the economy in internal disequilibrium (unemployment Y_U) and external surplus at point A. This improbable option might be adopted if greater priority were accorded to reserve augmentation than to full employment.

Policy conflict: Internal and external disequilibrium

3. *Stabilising monetary policy.* The increase in the transactions demand for money is accommodated by an expansionary monetary policy which retains the LM curve at LM_0. Joint equilibrium is thus maintained at point E.

Policy conflict: None (self-equilibrating)

4. *Sterilisation and fiscal policy.* The sterilisation measures which maintain the LM curve at LM_1 are combined with an expansionary fiscal policy which shifts the IS curve up to the right to intersect LM_1 at point B. This restores internal equilibrium but with a higher interest rate (i_2) and a larger external surplus.

Policy conflict: Internal equilibrium but external disequilibrium

Summary

Fixed exchange rates can insulate the economy against domestic monetary shocks. The increased transactions demand for money and resulting external surplus can be accommodated through increases in domestic liquidity and foreign exchange reserves respectively, and joint equilibrium can be restored at point E. An expansionary monetary policy alone will restore joint equilibrium, without reserve augmentation. Fiscal policy cannot restore joint equilibrium.

Case 2: Domestic product market shock

The impact of a domestic product market shock is illustrated in Figure 10.4, where an increase in autonomous investment caused, perhaps, by an improvement in business confidence, shifts the IS curve up to the right to IS_1.

The economy consequently moves from point E to point A. This

Figure 10.4: Domestic product market disturbances and joint disequilibrium. An upward shift of the IS curve (IS_1) creates joint disequilibrium (over-full employment and external surplus) at point A. Joint equilibrium can be restored at point E with a stabilising contractionary fiscal policy which shifts the IS curve back to IS_0.

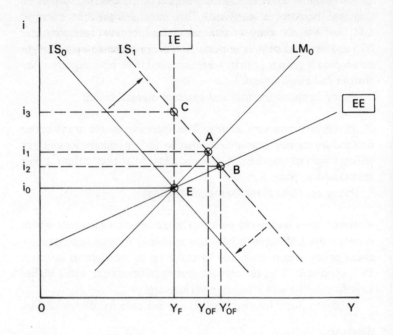

results in internal disequilibrium at interest rate i_1 and income level Y_{OF} (over-full employment) and in external surplus since the income-induced increase in imports is insufficient to offset the interest rate-induced increase in capital inflows/decrease in capital outflows. Joint disequilibrium is thus established at point A.

Conflict: internal and external disequilibrium

Policy options

1. Non-sterilisation. The non-sterilisation of the expansionary impact of the external surplus on domestic liquidity shifts the LM curve down to the right until it intersects the EE and IS_1 curves at point B. This establishes external equilibrium with a lower interest rate (i_2) but with increased over-full employment (Y'_{OF}).

Policy conflict: External equilibrium but internal disequilibrium

2. Sterilisation. The sterilisation of the expansionary monetary impact of the external surplus leaves the LM curve unchanged at LM_0 and the economy at point A in internal disequilibrium (over-full employment) and external surplus. The level of over-full employment at point A, however, is lower than that at point B (Y_{OF} compared to Y'_{OF}).

Policy conflict: Internal and external disequilibrium

3. Contractionary monetary policy. A contractionary monetary policy implemented to reduce over-full employment will shift the LM curve upwards until it intersects the IS_1 curve at point C. This restores internal equilibrium but at a higher interest rate (i_3) and with a larger external surplus.

Policy conflict: Internal equilibrium but external disequilibrium

4. Stabilising fiscal policy. The expansionary impact of the increase in investment is counteracted by a contractionary fiscal policy which shifts the IS curve back to IS_0. Joint equilibrium is restored at point E.

Policy conflict: None (self-equilibrating)

Summary

Fixed exchange rates cannot insulate the economy against domestic product market shocks (points A and B), although sterilisation measures will mitigate the impact of these shocks (point A). A contractionary fiscal policy alone is sufficient to restore joint equilibrium at point E. Monetary policy is incapable of restoring joint equilibrium.

Case 3: External product market shock

The impact of an external product market shock is illustrated in Figure 10.5. A decrease in exports, caused perhaps by a decline in foreign incomes, shifts the EE curve up to the left to EE_1 and the IS curve down to IS_1. (The impact of an increase in autonomous imports would be similar.)

The effect of reduced exports is external deficit, shown in the leftward shift of the EE curve (EE_1), and reduced national income,

Figure 10.5: External product market disturbances and joint disequilibrium. An upward shift of the EE curve (EE$_1$) and a downward shift of the IS curve (IS$_1$) caused by decreased exports creates joint disequilibrium (unemployment and deficit) at point A. Joint equilibrium can be restored at point C, with partial sterilisation and an expansionary fiscal policy, or potentially at point E with a successful devaluation policy.

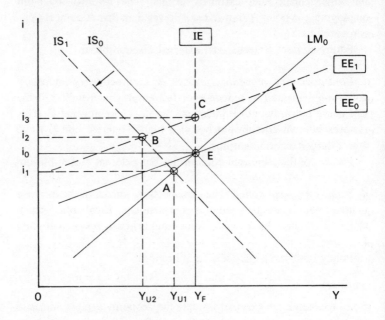

reflected in the leftward shift of the IS curve (IS$_1$). This creates internal disequilibrium (unemployment Y_{U1} at interest rate i_1) and external deficit at point A.

Conflict: Internal and external disequilibrium

Policy options

1. Non-sterilisation. Financing the external deficit reduces domestic liquidity and shifts the LM curve up to the left to intersect the IS$_1$ and EE$_1$ curves at point B. This increases interest rates to i_2 which increases/decreases capital inflows/outflows and, through lower incomes, reduces induced imports. This establishes external equilibrium at point B but with a higher interest rate (i_2) and unemployment (Y_{U2}).

Policy conflict: External equilibrium but internal disequilibrium

2. Sterilisation. Sterilisation maintains the LM curve at LM_0 which, together with the export-induced shift in the IS curve to IS_1, leaves the economy at point A. This represents internal disequilibrium (interest rate i_1 and unemployment Y_{U1}) and external deficit.

Policy conflict: Internal and external disequilibrium

3. Sterilisation and expansionary fiscal policy. The combined effect of sterilisation and an expansionary fiscal policy which shifts the IS_1 curve back up to the right to IS_0 is the restoration of internal equilibrium at point E but with external deficit.

Policy conflict: Internal equilibrium but external disequilibrium

4. Partial sterilisation and expansionary fiscal policy. Partial sterilisation allows the LM curve to shift up only as far as point C on EE_1. This is combined with an expansionary fiscal policy which shifts the IS curve up to the right to intersect the EE_1 curve and upward shifted LM curve at point C. Joint equilibrium is restored at point C with interest rate i_3.

Policy conflict: Joint equilibrium but with higher interest rates

5. Import controls. Introducing import controls, which reduce imports by an amount equivalent to the original decrease in exports, and successfully diverting demand and resources to import substitutes will return all three curves to their original positions and restore joint equilibrium at point E.

Policy conflict: Protectionist and potentially ineffective because of imperfect factor mobility

6. Devaluation. Devaluation might be resorted to if the Marshall-Lerner condition is satisfied and if the decrease in exports is perceived to be permanent (fundamental disequilibrium). A successful devaluation policy, which increases exports and decreases imports such that injections and leakages revert to their original levels, will return all three curves to their original positions and restore joint equilibrium at point E with interest rate i_0 and income level Y_F.

Policy conflict: Potentially ineffective if import demand

elasticities are low and potentially inconsistent with fixed exchange rates

Summary

Fixed exchange rates cannot insulate the economy against external product market shocks (points A and B), although sterilisation will mitigate their impact (point A). Joint equilibrium with only two policy instruments (monetary and fiscal policy) can only be restored with higher interest rates through partial sterilisation and an expansionary fiscal policy. Import controls, which are protectionist and potentially ineffective, are inconsistent with a market-determined adjustment process. Devaluation increases the number of policy instruments to three and, if successful, will restore joint equilibrium at point E.

Case 4: External money market shock

The impact of an external monetary shock is illustrated in Figure 10.6. Autonomous increases in capital outflows/decreases in capital inflows prompted, for example, by a loss of foreign investor confidence in the domestic economy or by an increase in foreign interest rates, will shift the EE curve up to the left to EE_1.

The economy remains at point E, which now represents internal equilibrium (interest rate i_0 and full employment Y_F) but external deficit.

Conflict: Internal equilibrium but external disequilibrium

Policy options

1. Non-sterilisation. Financing the external deficit reduces domestic liquidity and shifts the LM curve up to the left to intersect the IS_0 and EE_1 curves at point A. The increase in the interest rate to i_1 encourages capital inflows/discourages capital outflows and, through reduced income, reduces induced imports. This establishes external equilibrium at point A but with a higher interest rate (i_1) and unemployment (Y_U).

Policy conflict: External equilibrium but internal disequilibrium

2. Sterilisation. The contractionary impact of decreased domestic

Figure 10.6: External money market disturbances and joint disequilibrium. An upward shift of the EE curve (EE$_1$) caused by autonomous increases in capital outflows/decreases in capital inflows creates joint disequilibrium (full employment and external deficit) at point E. Joint equilibrium can be restored at point B with partial sterilisation and an expansionary fiscal policy.

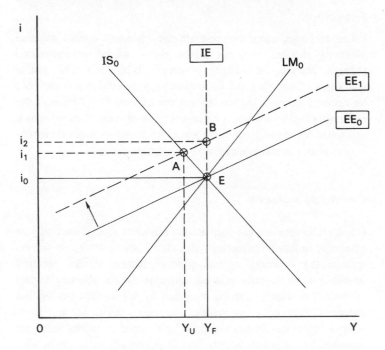

liquidity is sterilised. This leaves the LM curve unchanged at LM$_0$ and the economy at point E in internal equilibrium (with unchanged interest rate i$_0$ and unchanged income level Y$_F$) but external deficit. This policy option might be adopted if the original outflow were considered temporary and likely to be reversed when confidence was restored or foreign interest rates declined.

Policy conflict: Internal equilibrium but external disequilibrium

3. Partial sterilisation and expansionary fiscal policy. Partial sterilisation will shift the LM curve only up to point B. In addition, an expansionary fiscal policy shifts the IS curve up to the right to intersect the EE$_1$ curve and upward-shifted LM curve at point B. Joint equilibrium is restored at point B with interest rate i$_2$.

Policy conflict: Joint equilibrium but with higher interest rates

197

4. Exchange controls. Destabilising capital flows may be curbed through the introduction of capital controls. These are inconsistent with a market-determined adjustment process, however, and may prove both technically and allocatively inefficient.

Policy conflict: Potential resource misallocation

Summary

Fixed exchange rates can insulate the economy against external monetary shocks, since net capital flows can be accommodated through changes in official reserves. With only two policy instruments (monetary and fiscal policy), joint equilibrium can only be restored through higher interest rates (point B) or through the reversal of the foreign confidence/interest rate factors which accounted for the original disturbance. Exchange controls are inconsistent with a market-determined adjustment process.

Concluding summary

Fixed exchange rates can insulate the economy against internally or externally-induced monetary shocks. They cannot, however, insulate the economy against product market shocks, whether internally- or externally-induced, although the destabilising impact of these disturbances can be mitigated by appropriate sterilisation measures. With only two policy instruments (monetary and fiscal policy), joint equilibrium can only be restored if interest rates are abandoned as a policy target. This is potentially inconsistent with long-term economic growth. Exchange rate realignment is undertaken only in cases of fundamental disequilibrium.

The assignment solution

The successful application of monetary and fiscal stabilisation policies depends on the ability to correctly identify and quantify the destabilising impact of economic disturbances. Since this is not always possible, policy ambiguities might arise involving incorrect policy assignments and further destabilisation.

The problem of policy ambiguities can be resolved by recourse to the **Mundell Assignment Solution**, by which:

Fiscal policy is assigned to the attainment of internal equilibrium; Monetary policy is assigned to the attainment of external equilibrium.

These assignments reflect the comparative advantage of fiscal policy in attaining internal equilibrium and of monetary policy in attaining external equilibrium.

Fiscal policy changes income and interest rates in the *same* direction. Since induced imports and capital outflows (K) are directly related to income and inversely related to interest rate changes respectively, the impact of fiscal policy on external equilibrium is limited by *counteracting* changes in induced imports and capital flows.

Monetary policy, in contrast, changes income and interest rates in *opposite* directions and so generates *reinforcing* changes in induced imports and capital flows. The impact of monetary policy on external equilibrium, therefore, is comparatively greater.

The comparative impact of fiscal and monetary policies can be expressed notationally (for increases in income) as:

Expansionary fiscal policy
$$\left.\begin{array}{l} \uparrow Y \rightarrow\rightarrow \uparrow M \\ \uparrow i \rightarrow\rightarrow \downarrow K \end{array}\right\} \rightarrow\rightarrow (\uparrow M + \downarrow K)$$

Expansionary monetary policy
$$\left.\begin{array}{l} \uparrow Y \rightarrow\rightarrow \uparrow M \\ \downarrow i \rightarrow\rightarrow \uparrow K \end{array}\right\} \rightarrow\rightarrow (\uparrow M + \uparrow K)$$

Expansionary monetary policy will therefore exert greater impact on external equilibrium than expansionary fiscal policy, since:

$$\uparrow M + \downarrow K < \uparrow M + \uparrow K.$$

The assignment solution can be summarised as in Table 10.1.

Assigning fiscal policy to internal equilibrium and monetary policy to external equilibrium may thus be expected to eliminate policy ambiguities and establish joint equilibrium provided that these policies are applied smoothly and without lags.

Table 10.1: The assignment solution summarised.

Disequilibrium condition		Stabilisation policy	
Internal	*External*	*Fiscal*	*Monetary*
Over-full employment	Surplus	Contractionary	Expansionary
Over-full employment	Deficit	Contractionary	Contractionary
Unemployment	Surplus	Expansionary	Expansionary
Unemployment	Deficit	Expansionary	Contractionary

ECONOMIC DISTURBANCES AND PERFECT CAPITAL MOBILITY

Perfect international capital mobility might apply to a small country which faces a perfectly elastic supply of international capital at prevailing international interest rates. The EE curve becomes horizontal at this level of interest rates and attempts to raise domestic interest rates above this level will result in large-scale (infinite) capital inflows (surplus), while attempts to lower domestic interest rates below this level will result in large-scale (infinite) capital outflows (deficit). The EE curve cannot shift, therefore, unless international interest rates or exchange rate expectations change.

Case 1: Domestic money market shock

The impact of an increase in the transactions demand for money is illustrated in Figure 10.7 (a), which shows that any tendency for the LM curve to shift to the left will exert upward pressure on domestic interest rates. This will stimulate capital inflows which will increase domestic liquidity and return the LM curve to LM_0. Joint equilibrium will thus be maintained at point E with reserve augmentation.

Alternatively, joint equilibrium could be maintained at point E without reserve augmentation through an expansionary monetary policy which accommodates the increased transactions demand for money. This would relieve pressure on interest rates and preclude capital inflows.

Attempts to sterilise capital inflows and maintain the economy at point A will prove futile because of the infinitely large inflows of capital which will result from any attempt to maintain interest rates above level i_0. With perfect capital mobility, therefore, the LM curve effectively becomes horizontal at the prevailing level of international interest rates (it merges with the EE curve) and the monetary authorities are forced to relinquish control of the domestic money supply.

Case 2: Domestic product market shock

An increase in autonomous investment, shown in Figure 10.7 (b), will shift the IS curve upwards to IS_1, exert upward pressure on interest rates and stimulate capital inflows which shift the LM curve down to the right to LM_1. This restores external equilibrium at point A, but with over-full employment. Attempts to restore internal equilibrium through contractionary monetary policy will prove futile, since decreases in domestic liquidity will be counteracted by interest rate-induced inflows of capital which will return the LM curve to LM_1. Joint equilibrium can thus only be restored with a contractionary fiscal policy which shifts the IS curve back to IS_0.

Case 3: External product market shock

The impact of a decrease in exports is illustrated in Figure 10.7 (c). The IS curve shifts down to the left to IS_1 since net injections have decreased, but there is no corresponding upward shift in the EE curve, since capital flows always adjust to maintain the economy in external equilibrium on the EE curve at interest rate i_0. The downward pressure on interest rates exerted by the shift in the IS curve stimulates capital outflows which shift the LM curve up to the left to LM_1. This restores external equilibrium at point A, but with unemployment. Any attempt to restore internal equilibrium through an expansionary monetary policy will prove futile since increases in domestic liquidity will be counteracted by interest rate-induced capital outflows which will return the LM curve to LM_1. Joint equilibrium at point E can only be restored with an expansionary fiscal policy which shifts the IS curve back to IS_0.

Case 4: External money market shock

Figure 10.7 (d) shows that an increase in international interest rates to i_1 will generate capital outflows and create external deficit at all

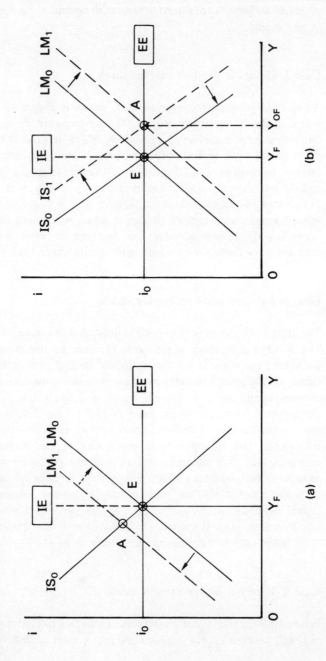

Figure 10.7: Economic disturbances and perfect capital mobility. Perfect capital mobility ensures that the EE curve is horizontal at prevailing international interest rates.

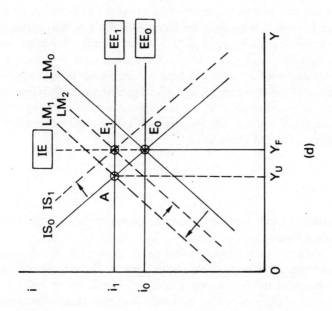

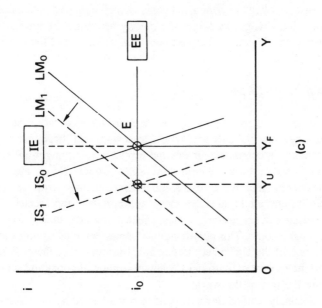

(c)

(d)

interest rates below i_1. These outflows will reduce domestic liquidity and shift the LM curve up to the left to LM_1 until external equilibrium with unemployment (point A) is established at interest rate i_1, which determines the location of the new EE_1 curve. An expansionary monetary policy will be unable to restore joint equilibrium, since any tendency for interest rates to weaken will generate capital outflows and these will counteract the expansionary impact of the monetary policy. Joint equilibrium can therefore only be established at point E_1 by an expansionary fiscal policy which shifts the IS curve to IS_1 and, through interest rate-induced capital inflows, the LM curve to LM_2.

Summary

Perfect capital mobility changes monetary and fiscal policy assignments.

Monetary policy becomes ineffective as an active policy instrument because attempts to expand or contract domestic liquidity will be counteracted by interest rate-induced outflows or inflows of capital. Applied passively, however, it retains some effectiveness and may be used to accommodate changes in the domestic demand for money.

Fiscal policy, in contrast, becomes very effective, since capital flows and changes in domestic liquidity neutralise the interest rate change which would otherwise constrain the impact of fiscal policy.

QUALIFICATIONS

Attempts to establish joint equilibrium through monetary, fiscal and exchange rate policies are subject to several qualifications:

Firstly, a combined current and capital account might not represent 'true' external equilibrium since capital flows might be considered merely a financing/accommodating item. External equilibrium might thus be more appropriately represented by a balanced current account which equates domestic absorption with national income. This qualification assumes potential significance in the case of the US, where large capital inflows have financed large current account deficits and US net absorption of goods and services from the rest of the world.

Secondly, capital flows respond to risk-adjusted, and not absolute, interest rate differentials. Consequently, the increased risk with which the financing of successive current account deficits might be perceived, might reduce the interest rate responsiveness (elasticity) of capital flows, so that the EE curve might eventually become vertical at income levels below full employment. Stabilisation policies which operate through interest rate-induced changes in capital flows will then be unable to achieve joint equilibrium which will be restorable only with direct measures such as import or exchange controls or exchange rate realignments.

Thirdly, continued recourse to capital inflows to achieve external equilibrium will increase foreign indebtedness. Financing this might exacerbate external disequilibrium and so necessitate recourse to further capital inflows. This problem has proved painfully familiar to many debtor nations, in particular the LDCs.

Finally, the achievement of joint equilibrium assumes that stabilisation policies are applied smoothly and without lags. Each policy instrument, however, is subject to potentially serious short-comings: fiscal policy may require legislative approval whose potential delay might seriously undermine the effectiveness of this instrument; monetary policy might be subject to indeterminate lags which might aggravate rather than alleviate disequilibrium; and finally, exchange rate realignments are subject to the constraints of import demand inelasticities, counteracting income changes and domestic supply constraints.

SUMMARY

IS-LM-EE curves provide a framework within which the impact of economic disturbances on joint equilibrium, and also the adjustment process required to restore joint equilibrium, can be analysed. Both the impact and the adjustment process are influenced by the degree of capital mobility.

When capital is imperfectly mobile, fixed exchange rates can insulate the economy against internally- or externally-induced monetary shocks. They cannot, however, insulate the economy against product market shocks, whether internally or externally induced, although the destabilising impact of these disturbances may be mitigated with appropriate sterilisation measures. Joint equilibrium is restored after an internal monetary shock with monetary policy and after an internal product market shock with fiscal policy. Joint equilibrium with only two policy instruments (monetary and fiscal policy) can only be restored after an external shock (money or product market) if interest rates are abandoned as a policy target, in which case monetary policy should be assigned to external equilibrium and fiscal policy to internal equilibrium. Recourse to exchange rate realignments is confined to fundamental disequilibria.

When capital becomes perfectly mobile, fixed exchange rates are only able to insulate the economy from internal monetary shocks. Monetary and fiscal policy assignments change, so that monetary policy becomes ineffective while fiscal policy becomes very effective.

Attempts to establish joint equilibrium through monetary, fiscal and exchange rate policies are qualified by: the appropriate representation of external equilibrium; the appropriateness of financing current account deficits; and the operational efficiency of policy instruments.

APPENDIX: PRICE-INDUCED LM CURVE SHIFTS

Changes in the general level of prices affect the real value of the money stock and hence the location of the LM curve. Economic disturbances and stabilisation policies which affect the general price level will thus change the position of the LM curve. Price increases shift the LM curve to the left; price decreases shift the LM curve to the right.

Price-induced LM curve shifts are illustrated in Figure 10A.1, which shows the impact of an exchange rate devaluation implemented to counteract a deflationary external product market shock (decrease in exports). The EE curve shifts up to EE_1 and the IS curve shifts down to IS_1, thereby taking the economy to point A with sterilisation. Devaluation might not succeed in restoring joint equilibrium at point E, however, since the devaluation-induced increase in import prices might, through cost-push pressures, generate a general increase in domestic prices. This will shift the LM curve to the left (LM') and, through a price-induced curtailment of exports, arrest the upward shift of the IS curve at IS' and the downward shift of the EE curve at EE'. This establishes joint disequilibrium at point B and thus necessitates further stabilisation policies, such as expansionary fiscal and monetary policies, to restore joint equilibrium at, for example, point E'.

Figure 10A.1: Price-induced LM curve shifts and external product market disturbances. An exchange rate devaluation, implemented to restore joint equilibrium from point A, might increase domestic prices through cost-push pressures. This will shift the LM curve to LM' and establish joint disequilibrium at point B. Further stabilisation measures will be required to restore joint equilibrium at, for example, point E'.

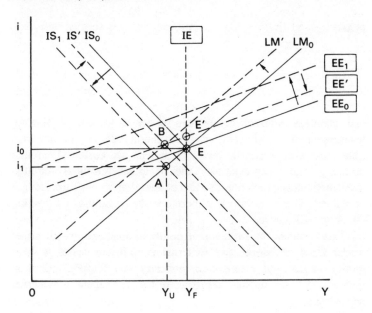

QUESTIONS FOR DISCUSSION

1. Explain why the external impact of an expansionary IS curve shift is potentially indeterminate.
2. Assess the impact of an exogenous increase in exports and the means by which joint equilibrium might be restored under conditions of imperfect capital mobility.
3. What is 'the assignment problem'? How is it resolved?
4. What is 'sterilisation policy'? How are sterilisation and monetary policies affected by perfect capital mobility?
5. Assess the implications for joint equilibrium and the adjustment process of an EE curve which becomes vertical at a less than full employment level of income.

207

11

Internal and External Equilibrium
with Floating Exchange Rates

To maintain external equilibrium under a system of floating exchange rates, in which official intervention is absent, the exchange rate must always adjust. Incipient deficits are corrected through exchange rate depreciations and incipient surpluses through exchange rate appreciations, so that neither deficits nor surpluses are sustained. The economy must therefore always adjust to a position along the EE curve.

This resolves the problem of policy assignments which arises under fixed exchange rates (external equilibrium ceases to be a policy target) and means that monetary and fiscal stabilisation policies can be applied directly to the attainment of internal equilibrium.

The operation of floating exchange rates and the impact of economic disturbances and stabilisation policies may again be examined within the framework of IS-LM-EE curves. The same economic disturbances which were considered under fixed exchange rates will be employed for comparative purposes. The same simplifying assumptions will also be made, with the added assumption that the Marshall-Lerner condition is satisfied, so that exchange rate depreciations increase exports/decrease imports and shift the EE and IS curves downwards and upwards to the right respectively, while exchange rate appreciations have the opposite effect. Notationally:

$\downarrow r \rightarrowtail \uparrow X, \downarrow M \rightarrowtail \downarrow$ EE Curve and $\uparrow$ IS Curve
$\uparrow r \rightarrowtail \downarrow X, \uparrow M \rightarrowtail \uparrow$ EE Curve and $\downarrow$ IS Curve

ECONOMIC DISTURBANCES AND IMPERFECT CAPITAL MOBILITY

Case 1: Domestic money market shock

The impact of an increase in the transactions demand for money is illustrated in Figure 11.1 (a), which shows that the LM curve shifts up to the left to LM_1. In the absence of an accommodating expansionary monetary policy which would restore joint equilibrium at point E, the economy moves to point A which represents unemployment (Y_{U1}) and temporary external surplus since interest rates have increased to i_1 and induced capital inflows. This surplus cannot be sustained, however, because the excess demand for foreign exchange will cause the exchange rate to appreciate, and this will encourage imports/discourage exports and shift the EE curve up to the left to EE_1. The increase in imports and decrease in exports represent an increase in net leakages which shift the IS curve down to the left to IS_1. External equilibrium with internal disequilibrium (interest rate i_2 and unemployment Y_{U2}) will be established at point B.

Point B may be contrasted with point E without sterilisation which could be attained under fixed exchange rates as interest rate-induced capital inflows increased domestic liquidity and shifted the LM curve back to LM_0. With floating exchange rates, there is no official intervention in the foreign exchange market, so that capital flows have no impact on domestic liquidity and the LM curve, which shifts only when domestic liquidity changes, remains unchanged.

Domestic money market shocks are thus more disruptive under floating (point B) than fixed (point E) exchange rates.

Policy options

Fiscal policy can restore joint equilibrium but with relatively high interest rates. An expansionary fiscal policy shifts the IS_1 curve up along the LM_1 curve and increases interest rates. This causes the exchange rate to appreciate and this encourages imports/discourages exports and shifts the EE_1 curve further up to the left. Joint equilibrium may eventually be established at point C with interest rate i_3 and full employment Y_F.

Monetary policy, in contrast, is able to restore joint equilibrium at point E. An expansionary monetary policy shifts the LM_1 curve down to the right and, through lower interest rates, induces capital outflows. The resulting exchange rate depreciation encourages

Figure 11.1: Economic disturbances and imperfect capital mobility. Floating exchange rates ensure that the economy always adjusts to a position along the EE curve, so that stabilisation policies are applied to the restoration of internal equilibrium.

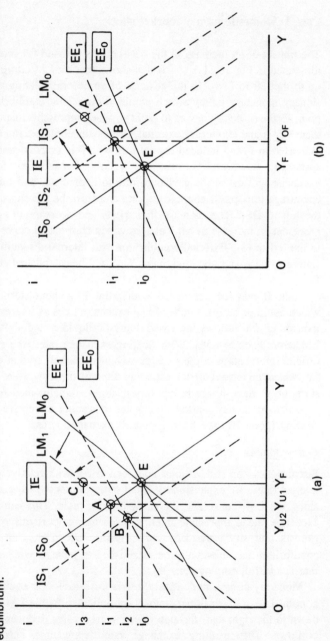

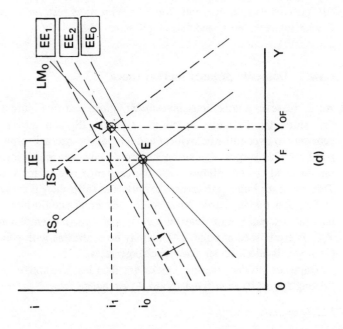

(d)

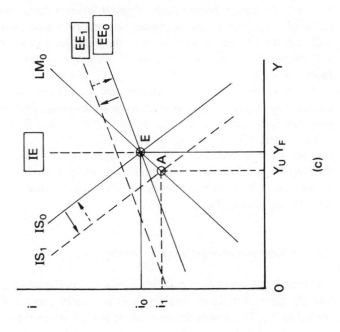

(c)

exports/discourages imports and shifts the IS_1 curve up, and the EE_1 curve down, to the right. Joint equilibrium is restored at point E with interest rate i_0 and full employment Y_F.

Case 2: Domestic product market shock

An increase in autonomous investment, illustrated in Figure 11.1 (b), shifts the IS curve up to the right to IS_1 and moves the economy to over-full employment and temporary external surplus at point A. This surplus cannot be sustained, however, since interest rate-induced capital inflows cause the exchange rate to appreciate. This increases imports/decreases exports and shifts the EE curve up to EE_1 and the IS_1 curve down to IS_2. External equilibrium with internal disequilibrium (interest rate i_1 and over-full employment Y_{OF}) is established at point B. This may be contrasted with point A (with sterilisation) under fixed exchange rates.

Domestic product market shocks are thus less disruptive under floating (point B) than fixed (point A) exchange rates.

Policy options

A contractionary fiscal policy will shift the IS_2 curve down to the left and, through a combination of lower interest rates, capital outflows, depreciation and increased exports/decreased imports, will shift the EE_1 curve back down to the right. Joint equilibrium will eventually be restored at point E with interest rate i_0 and income level Y_F.

Monetary policy can also restore joint equilibrium but with interest rates higher than i_0. A contractionary monetary policy will shift the LM_0 curve to the left along IS_2 and, through higher interest rates, will induce capital inflows. The resulting exchange rate appreciation will encourage imports/discourage exports and shift the IS_2 curve down to, and the EE_1 curve up to the left. Joint equilibrium will eventually be restored along the IE schedule at an interest rate greater than i_0.

Case 3: External product market shock

The impact of a decrease in exports is illustrated in Figure 11.1 (c). The EE curve shifts up to the left to EE_1 and the IS curve down to the left to IS_1. This moves the economy to point A which represents internal disequilibrium (interest rate i_1 and unemployment Y_U) and temporary external deficit which, however, is unsustainable, since interest rate-induced capital outflows will cause the exchange rate to depreciate. This increases exports/decreases imports and shifts the EE_1 curve down, and the IS_1 curve up to the right until joint equilibrium is restored at point E with interest rate i_0 and income level Y_F. This may be contrasted with point A (with sterilisation) under fixed exchange rates.

Floating exchange rates thus insulate the economy against external product market shocks, which are less disruptive under floating exchange rates (point E) than under fixed exchange rates (point A) with sterilisation.

Policy options

None are required, since the system self-equilibrates at joint equilibrium.

Case 4: External money market shock

The impact of an increase in capital outflows prompted, for example, by a loss of foreign investor confidence in the domestic economy or by an increase in foreign interest rates, is illustrated in Figure 11.1 (d). This shows that the EE curve shifts up to the left to EE_1 and that a temporary deficit is created at point E. This deficit cannot be sustained, however, since capital outflows cause the exchange rate to depreciate. This increases exports/decreases imports and shifts the EE_1 curve down to the right to EE_2 and the IS curve up to the right to IS_1 until external equilibrium with internal disequilibrium (interest rate i_1 and over-full employment Y_{OF}) is established at point A. This may be contrasted with point E (with sterilisation) under fixed exchange rates.

External money market shocks are thus more disruptive under floating (point A) than fixed (point E) exchange rates.

Policy options

The impact of the capital outflow can be accommodated in either the money market or the product market.

Accommodation in the money market necessitates higher interest rates which may be effected through a contractionary monetary policy. This shifts the LM curve up to the left along IS_1 and, through higher interest rates, induces capital inflows. This creates

213

an unsustainable surplus which, through exchange rate appreciation, increases imports/decreases exports. This in turn shifts the EE_2 curve up to the left and the IS_1 curve down to the left. Joint equilibrium will eventually be restored along the IE schedule at an interest rate greater than i_0.

Accommodation in the product market necessitates a contractionary fiscal policy which shifts the IS_1 curve down to the left beyond point E. This reduces interest rates and, through a capital outflow-induced exchange rate depreciation, increases exports and decreases imports. This shifts the IS_1 curve up and the EE_2 curve down to the right until joint equilibrium might eventually be restored at point E.

Summary

Floating exchange rates are better able to insulate the economy against product market shocks than fixed exchange rates which, in turn, are better able to insulate the economy against money market disturbances. Both monetary and fiscal policy are able to restore joint equilibrium.

ECONOMIC DISTURBANCES AND PERFECT CAPITAL MOBILITY

Perfect capital mobility applies equally to both floating and fixed exchange rates. The EE curve, which represents a perfectly elastic supply of international capital, becomes horizontal at prevailing international interest rates and shifts only when these or exchange rate expectations change. Attempts to maintain domestic interest rates above international levels results in capital inflows and an exchange rate appreciation, while attempts to maintain domestic interest rates below international levels result in capital outflows and an exchange rate depreciation. Imports, exports and international capital flows consequently combine to establish external equilibrium at the prevailing level of international interest rates.

Case 1: Domestic money market shock

The impact of an increase in the transactions demand for money is illustrated in Figure 11.2 (a). The LM curve shifts up to the left to LM_1 and subjects interest rates to upward pressure at point A'. Through interest rate-induced capital inflows, this results in an appreciation of the exchange rate, which increases imports/ decreases exports and shifts the IS curve down to the left to IS_1. External equilibrium with internal disequilibrium (interest rate i_0 and unemployment Y_U) is established at point A. This may be contrasted with point E (without sterilisation) under fixed exchange rates.

Domestic money market shocks are thus more disruptive under floating (point A) than fixed (point E) exchange rates.

Policy options

Fiscal policy cannot restore joint equilibrium. An expansionary fiscal policy, which attempts to shift the IS_1 curve back to the right to IS_0, will intensify interest rate pressures and, through induced capital inflows, this will cause the exchange rate to appreciate. This will increase imports/decrease exports and return the IS curve to IS_1. Fiscal policy, therefore, is unable to move the economy from point A.

Monetary policy, in contrast, is extremely effective. An expansionary monetary policy shifts the LM_1 curve to LM_0 and depresses interest rates which, through induced capital outflows, cause the exchange rate to depreciate. This increases exports/decreases imports and shifts the IS_1 curve back up to the right to IS_0. Joint equilibrium is restored at point E with interest rate i_0 and income level Y_F.

Case 2: Domestic product market shock

An increase in autonomous investment, shown in Figure 11.2 (b), shifts the IS curve up to the right to IS_1. This subjects interest rates to upward pressure at point A and this, through induced capital inflows, causes the exchange rate to appreciate. This increases imports/decreases exports and returns the IS_1 curve to IS_0. Joint equilibrium is maintained at point E with interest rate i_0 and income level Y_F. This may be contrasted with point A' (without sterilisation) under fixed exchange rates.

Floating exchange rates thus insulate the economy from domestic product market shocks which are consequently less disruptive under floating (point E) than fixed (point A') exchange rates.

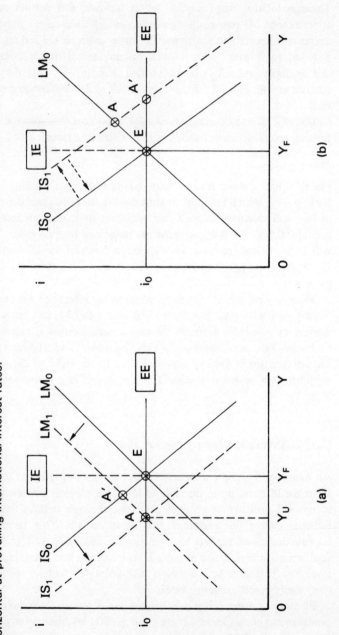

Figure 11.2: Economic disturbances and perfect capital mobility. Perfect capital mobility ensures that the EE curve is horizontal at prevailing international interest rates.

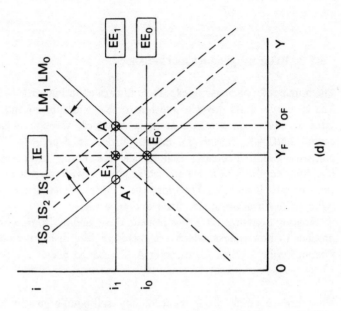

(c)

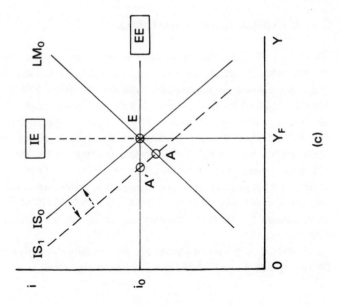

(d)

Policy options

None are required, since the economy self-equilibrates at joint equilibrium.

Case 3: External product market shock

The impact of a decrease in exports is illustrated in Figure 11.2 (c). The IS curve shifts down to the left to IS_1, and subjects interest rates to downward pressure at point A which, through induced capital outflows, causes the exchange rate to depreciate. This increases exports/decreases imports and returns the IS_1 curve to IS_0. Joint equilibrium is maintained at point E with interest rate i_0 and income level Y_F. This may be contrasted with point A' (without sterilisation) under fixed exchange rates.

Floating exchange rates thus insulate the economy from external product market shocks which are therefore less disruptive under floating (point E) than fixed (point A') exchange rates.

Policy options

None are required, since the economy self-equilibrates at joint equilibrium.

Case 4: External money market shock

Figure 11.2 (d) shows that an increase in capital outflows prompted, for example, by an increase in international interest rates to i_1, shifts the EE curve horizontally upwards to EE_1. The capital outflows induced by the unchanged domestic interest rate i_0 cause the exchange rate to depreciate. This increases exports/decreases imports and shifts the IS curve up to the right to IS_1. External equilibrium with internal disequilibrium (interest rate i_1 and over-full employment Y_{OF}) is established at point A. This may be contrasted with point A' (without sterilisation) under fixed exchange rates, which would be established through a leftward shift of the LM curve caused by the contractionary impact of capital outflows on domestic liquidity.

External money market shocks are thus equally disruptive under floating (point A) and fixed (point A') exchange rates.

218

Policy options

Fiscal policy is unable to restore joint equilibrium. A contractionary fiscal policy shifts the IS_1 curve down to the left, but interest rate-induced capital outflows will cause the exchange rate to depreciate and, through increased exports/decreased imports, shift the IS curve back up to the right.

Monetary policy, however, can restore joint equilibrium. A contractionary monetary policy shifts the LM curve up to the left to LM_1. This exerts upward pressure on interest rates which, through induced capital inflows, causes the exchange rate to appreciate and imports to increase/exports to decrease. This shifts the IS_1 curve down to the left to IS_2 and restores joint equilibrium at point E_1 with interest rate i_1 and income level Y_F. Joint equilibrium can only be restored along the new EE_1 curve whose location is determined by the prevailing level of international interest rates i_1.

Summary

Floating exchange rates with perfect capital mobility insulate the economy better than, or as well as, fixed exchange rates for all disturbances except domestic money market shocks.

Stabilisation policies are not required for internal or external product market shocks since floating exchange rates fully insulate the economy, which self-equilibrates at joint equilibrium. Fiscal policy is ineffective as a stabilising response to internal or external money market disturbances. Monetary policy, in contrast, is very effective.

QUALIFICATIONS

The qualifications relating to adjustment under floating exchange rates are similar to those which apply under fixed exchange rates:

Firstly, financing current account deficits with capital inflows might necessitate progressively higher interest rates to compensate for the increased interest rate inelasticity of capital flows. The EE curve might thus eventually become vertical, at which point capital flows will no longer constitute part of the adjustment process which will be shifted entirely to the current account.

Secondly, continued recourse to capital account financing increases foreign indebtedness and corresponding future servicing commitments.

219

Thirdly, the problems associated with the smooth and flexible application of stabilisation policies apply to floating as well as to fixed exchange rates.

Finally, floating exchange rates do not resolve the problem of whether a combined current and capital account adequately represents external equilibrium. To the extent, however, that capital flows reflect the preferences of wealth-holders expressed within a framework of freely, as opposed to administratively determined exchange rates, it might be contended that a combined current and capital account more adequately represents external equilibrium under a system of floating than fixed exchange rates.

SUMMARY

Floating exchange rates are better able to insulate the economy from product market shocks (internal and external), while fixed exchange rates are better able to insulate the economy from money market shocks (internal and external). Consequently, countries which are susceptible to product market shocks might choose to adopt floating exchange rates, while countries which are susceptible to money market shocks might adopt fixed exchange rates.

With floating exchange rates and imperfect capital mobility, either monetary or fiscal policy can be used to restore joint equilibrium, depending on the nature of the economic disturbance. When capital becomes perfectly mobile, monetary policy becomes very effective and fiscal policy ineffective.

The qualifications relating to adjustment under floating exchange rates are similar to those which apply under fixed exchange rates and include: the appropriateness of financing current account deficits, the operational efficiency of policy instruments and the appropriate representation of external equilibrium.

APPENDIX: PRICE-INDUCED LM CURVE SHIFTS

Changes in the general level of prices affect the real value of the money stock and hence the location of the LM curve. Economic disturbances and stabilisation policies which affect the general price level will thus change the position of the LM curve. Price increases shift the LM curve to the left; price decreases shift the LM curve to the right.

Figure 11A.1: Price-induced LM curve shifts and external product market disturbances. An exchange rate depreciation, prompted by an export-induced incipient deficit at point A, might increase domestic prices through cost-push pressures. This will shift the LM curve to LM' and establish joint disequilibrium at point B. Further stabilisation measures will be required to restore joint equilibrium along the IE schedule.

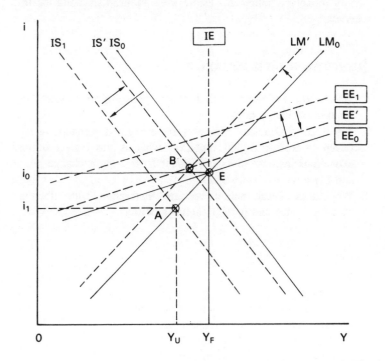

Price-induced LM curve shifts are illustrated in Figure 11A.1, which shows the impact of an external product market shock (decrease in exports). The EE curve shifts up to the left to EE_1 and the IS curve down to the left to IS_1. This moves the economy to point A which represents internal disequilibrium (interest rate i_1 and unemployment Y_U) and temporary external deficit. This cannot be sustained, however, since interest rate-induced capital outflows will cause the exchange rate to depreciate and consequently to increase exports/decrease imports and shift the EE_1 curve down, and the IS_1 curve up, to the right.

Depreciation, however, might not succeed in restoring joint equilibrium at point E, since the depreciation-induced increase in

221

import prices might, through cost-push pressures, generate a general increase in domestic prices. This will shift the LM curve up to the left (LM') and, through a price-induced curtailment of exports, arrest the upward shift of the IS curve at IS' and the downward shift of the EE curve at EE'. This establishes joint disequilibrium at point B and so necessitates further stabilisation policies, such as an expansionary monetary policy, to restore joint equilibrium along the IE schedule.

QUESTIONS FOR DISCUSSION

1. Why is the assignment solution not applicable to a system of floating exchange rates?
2. Are floating exchange rates preferable to fixed exchange rates?
3. Given imperfect capital mobility, what is the impact of an exogenous increase in exports under (i) floating exchange rates and (ii) fixed exchange rates?
4. Why does fiscal policy become ineffective with floating exchange rates and perfect capital mobility?

12

The Monetary Approach
to External Equilibrium

The monetary approach to external equilibrium is essentially a post-war development which evolved in response to the IMF's search for a monetary framework within which balance of payments policies could be evaluated. The search was prompted by the difficulties of applying conventional elasticities/income/absorption policies to LDCs, which lacked the detailed national income accounting data necessary for these policies to be applied. The reliance of these countries, moreover, on monetary policies which operated in conjunction with relatively unsophisticated financial markets suggested that a monetary approach to the balance of payments might better provide a framework within which balance of payments policies could not only be more easily applied, but also more easily evaluated.

The monetary approach to external equilibrium, or international monetarism as it is otherwise known, gained momentum in the 1970s and enjoys considerable support in the 1980s as a monetary explanation of balance of payments disequilibria. But it remains controversial, its policy implications potentially conflicting with those of the conventional non-monetary approach to external equilibrium.

CHARACTERISTICS

The monetary approach to external equilibrium has three basic characteristics:

Firstly, it considers external disequilibrium to be a monetary phenomenon resulting from stock imbalances between the demand for and supply of money.

Secondly, it postulates that, in the absence of official intervention, balance of payments imbalances will restore equality
between the demand for and supply of money. External disequilibria
are thus transitory and will self-equilibrate in the long run.

Thirdly, it applies equally to fixed and floating exchange rates,
although the adjustment process for each system is different.

ADJUSTMENT WITH FIXED EXCHANGE RATES

The non-monetary approach to external equilibrium focuses on
autonomous international *flows* of goods, services and capital, so
that balance of payments disequilibrium results from inequality
between autonomous credit and debit transactions.

The monetary approach, in contrast, does not distinguish between
autonomous and accommodating transactions but focuses, instead,
on the official reserves balance. An imbalance in this account
constitutes external disequilibrium, which may also be expressed as:

A net change in the stock of official reserve assets.

The monetary approach thus makes no distinction between the
various components of balance of payments accounts and makes no
attempt to explain disequilibrium in terms of these components.

The critical determinant of external disequilibrium is internal
monetary disequilibrium, which is *stock* imbalances between the
demand for and supply of money. This is because, in the absence of
official intervention (the monetary authorities being either unable or
unwilling to implement sterilisation measures), internal monetary
disequilibrium will be corrected through external monetary flows.
Internal money stock disequilibrium in the form, for example, of an
excess money stock (relative to demand) will generate outflows to
the foreign sector as attempts are made to reduce excess balances
and restore equality between the demand for and supply of money.
These outflows will continue until equality is restored. The
monetary counterpart of the net increase in imports and foreign
assets induced by these outflows is a decrease in official reserve
assets, which is equivalent to a reduction in the domestic money
stock and which, therefore, completes the adjustment process.
Import-demand elasticities play no direct role in this process.

Since internal monetary equilibrium is restored through net external monetary flows, the monetary adjustment process can be

examined in terms of equality between the stock demand for and supply of money.

Demand for money

The demand for money may be expressed as:

$$M_D = f(Y,i)P \qquad\qquad (12\text{-}1)$$

where:

M_D represents the demand for nominal money balances
Y   represents real income
i   represents the rate of interest
P   represents the price level

The demand for money is directly related to real income, inversely related to the rate of interest and proportional to the price level. Increases in income or decreases in interest rates increase the demand for nominal balances which also increase in proportion to increases in prices. Changes in any of these variables will change the demand for money and so contribute to the monetary adjustment process.

Supply of money

The supply of money, which consists of an internal and an external component, may be expressed as:

$$M_S = m(R_I + R_E) \qquad\qquad (12\text{-}2)$$

where:

M_S represents the supply of nominal money balances
R_I represents the internal component of the domestic monetary base
R_E represents the external component of the domestic monetary base
m   represents the money multiplier

225

The internal component of the domestic monetary base (R_I) is a source of commercial bank reserves. When multiplied by the money multiplier (m) (which in its simplest form is the reciprocal of the banks' reserve ratio and which may be assumed to be constant), it determines the domestic component of the money supply. Since the volume of reserves is controlled by the monetary authorities, who thus control part of the money supply, the domestic component of the money supply is exogenously determined.

The external component of the domestic monetary base (R_E), which represents the country's reserve assets and corresponds to the R_D of the official reserves balance, is the second source of commercial bank reserves. Currency inflows, for example, which threaten to lead to an appreciation of the exchange rate, must be accommodated through official intervention in the form of domestic currency sales/foreign currency purchases. The resulting increase in the country's stock of international reserve assets will correspond to an increase in the stock of commercial bank reserves. Through the action of the money multiplier, this will increase the money supply. Balance of payments surpluses, operating through currency inflows and increases in reserve assets, thus increase the domestic money supply while deficits have the opposite effect. The foreign component of the domestic money supply, in the absence of sterilisation measures, is thus beyond the control of the monetary authorities and the domestic money supply consequently becomes an endogenous variable.

Money market equilibrium

Equilibrium in the money market is expressed as:

$$M_D = M_S.$$

Substituting for M_S from equation 12-2 gives:

$$M_D = m(R_I + R_E) \tag{12-3}$$

or

$$M_D = mR_I + mR_E. \tag{12-4}$$

If the domestic component of the money supply (mR_I) is expressed as M_I and the external component (mR_E) as M_E, equation 12-4 may be rewritten as:

$$M_D = M_I + M_E \tag{12-5}$$

which may be expressed as:

$$M_D - M_I = M_E. \tag{12-6}$$

Equation 12-6 expresses the essence of the monetary approach to external equilibrium. It indicates that, with a stable demand for nominal balances (M_D), changes in the domestic component of money as a *stock* variable (M_I) will be accommodated by changes in the external component of the money stock (M_E), which in turn will correspond to balance of payments disequilibria. Internal monetary disequilibria are consequently the source of external payments disequilibria which are transitory in the long run and which will persist only for as long as it takes to restore internal monetary equilibrium.

To the extent that the economy may be considered self-stabilising, and to the extent that there is an attainable alternative to the 'natural rate' of unemployment with price stability, internal monetary equilibrium can be equated with internal equilibrium. The monetary approach to external equilibrium is therefore consistent with the attainment of joint (internal and external) equilibrium.

Policy implications

The policy implications of internal monetary disequilibrium are also contained in equation 12-6.

An excess stock demand for money, which will be accommodated by an increase in external assets and hence an increase in the external component of the money supply, will result in a balance of payments surplus. This will persist only until the excess demand is satisfied and internal monetary equilibrium is restored. Notationally:

$$M_D > M_I \rightarrowtail \ \uparrow M_E \qquad \text{(Surplus)}$$

An excess stock supply of money, which will be accommodated by a decrease in reserve assets and hence a decrease in the external component of the money supply, will result in a balance of payments deficit. This will persist only until the excess supply is disbursed overseas and internal monetary equilibrium is restored. Notationally:

$$M_D < M_I \quad \rightarrow\rightarrow \quad \downarrow M_E \qquad \text{(Deficit)}$$

External disequilibrium persists only for as long as internal monetary disequilibrium persists. In the long run, therefore, and in the absence of sterilisation measures, external disequilibria will be self-correcting. This implies that stabilisation measures are redundant except, perhaps, to ensure equality between the stock demand for and supply of domestic money.

ADJUSTMENT WITH FLOATING EXCHANGE RATES

The monetary approach to external equilibrium also applies to floating exchange rates, although the adjustment process differs. Since the exchange rate adjusts to maintain external equilibrium, the official reserves balance must remain in continuous equilibrium and there can be no change in reserve assets. The equilibrium condition contained in equation 12-6 may thus be expressed as:

$$M_D = M_I. \qquad (12\text{-}7)$$

Equation 12-7 has important implications for the establishment and maintenance of monetary equilibrium and, by extension, external equilibrium:

Firstly, the money supply, now divested of its external component, becomes an exogenous variable under the direct control of the monetary authorities. It therefore becomes a policy instrument.

Secondly, reserve assets can no longer adjust to restore internal monetary equilibrium since the domestic money supply is insulated against external monetary flows.

Thirdly, internal monetary disequilibrium will manifest itself as exchange rate fluctuations. An excess stock demand for money, which would be accommodated by an increase in reserve assets and a balance of payments surplus under fixed exchange rates, will result in an exchange rate appreciation. Notationally:

$$M_D > M_I \rightarrow\rightarrow \quad \uparrow r \qquad \text{(Appreciation)}$$

An excess stock supply of money, which would be accommodated by a decrease in reserve assets and a balance of payments deficit under fixed exchange rates, will result in an exchange rate depreciation. Notationally:

$$M_D < M_I \rightarrow \rightarrow \ \downarrow r \qquad \text{(Depreciation)}$$

Finally, internal monetary equilibrium is restored through exchange rate changes which, operating through domestic price changes, change the value of the nominal money stock. An excess stock demand for money results in an exchange rate appreciation which reduces domestic prices. This increases the real value of nominal balances and thus restores equality between the stock demand for and supply of money. Similarly, an excess stock supply of money results in an exchange rate depreciation which increases domestic prices. This reduces the real value of nominal balances and again restores equality between the stock demand for and supply of money.

Policy implications

Floating exchange rates maintain continuous external equilibrium through exchange rate fluctuations and establish internal monetary equilibrium through domestic price changes. The policy implications of this adjustment process are:

Firstly, no policy measures, other than non-intervention, are required to correct external disequilibrium, which will prove self-correcting;

Secondly, potential external disequilibrium may be avoided by maintaining internal monetary equilibrium;

Finally, since external equilibrium can be attained by maintaining internal monetary equilibrium, fixed exchange rates may be preferred to floating exchange rates. This is because external equilibrium avoids the potential disadvantages conventionally associated with fixed exchange rates, such as the instability of discrete parity adjustments, while conferring the advantages of an optimal currency area such as the production economies of unified product markets. This preference for fixed exchange rates may be used as a basis for contrasting the monetary and non-monetary approaches to external equilibrium:

229

MONETARY AND NON-MONETARY APPROACHES CONTRASTED

The monetary and non-monetary approaches to external equilibrium generate policy implications which appear to be mutually inconsistent and hence non-interchangeable.

Income changes

Income changes generate policy implications which appear to be diametrically opposed. Income increases, for example, generate external *surpluses* through excess money stock demand under the monetary approach and external *deficits* through induced imports under the non-monetary approach.

Monetary Approach:

$$\uparrow Y \rightarrow\rightarrow\ \uparrow M_D \rightarrow\rightarrow M_D > M_I \rightarrow\rightarrow\ \uparrow M_E \quad \text{(External Surplus)}$$

Non-monetary Approach:

$$\uparrow Y \rightarrow\rightarrow\ \uparrow M \rightarrow\rightarrow\ \downarrow(X - M) \quad \text{(Current Account Deficit)}$$

Reconciliation

The apparent conflict may be reconciled by the inclusion of capital flows in the non-monetary approach since, with an LM curve more steeply inclined than the EE curve, an autonomous investment-induced increase in income, for example, will induce more capital inflows than imports and thus generate a balance of payments surplus.

Price changes

Domestic price changes generate policy implications which also appear mutually inconsistent. Price increases, for example, create external *surpluses* under the monetary approach (price increases not financed by the monetary authorities reduce the value of nominal balances and create excess money stock demand) and external *deficits* under the non-monetary approach.

Monetary Approach:

$$\uparrow P \rightarrow\rightarrow M_D > M_I \rightarrow\rightarrow \uparrow M_E \qquad \text{(External Surplus)}$$

Non-monetary Approach:

$$\uparrow P \rightarrow\rightarrow \downarrow X, \ \uparrow M \rightarrow\rightarrow \downarrow (X - M) \ \text{(Current Account Deficit)}$$

Reconciliation

The apparent conflict may again be reconciled by the inclusion of capital flows in the non-monetary approach. A price-induced decrease in the stock of real balances, which increases interest rates, might induce more capital inflows than the decrease in exports/ increase in imports and thus generate a balance of payments surplus.

Exchange rate changes

Exchange rate changes may lead to comparable, although temporally different results. An exchange rate devaluation, for example, might produce comparable results under both approaches, but the effect under the monetary approach will be only temporary, while under the non-monetary approach it might prove permanent. (Devaluation might even be considered unnecessary in the monetary case, since external equilibrium is automatically restored in the long run.)

Monetary Approach:

$$\downarrow r \rightarrow\rightarrow \uparrow P \rightarrow\rightarrow M_I > M_I \rightarrow\rightarrow \uparrow M_E \ \text{(External Improvement)}$$

Non-monetary Approach:

$$\downarrow r \rightarrow\rightarrow \uparrow X, \ \downarrow M \rightarrow\rightarrow \uparrow (X - M) \qquad \text{(Current Account Improvement)}$$

Reconciliation

The apparent conflict between the optional nature of devaluation under the two approaches and also temporal variations in the results may be reconciled through the monetary model's propensity to self-equilibrate which, in the absence of official intervention, ensures the establishment of external equilibrium and internal monetary equilibrium. Devaluation merely *accelerates* this process and is consequently unable to exert any permanent impact. The non-monetary model, in contrast, might not automatically tend towards external equilibrium (even with capital inflows), in which case devaluation might succeed in effecting a permanent improvement in the balance of payments.

QUALIFICATIONS

The monetary approach to external equilibrium is subject to two important qualifications:

Firstly, the approach makes no attempt to specify the temporal framework within which balance of payments adjustments will occur, other than to postulate a long-run adjustment process. This detracts from the practical application of the approach to external disequilibrium which generally invites more clearly delineated short-run policy responses (stabilisation measures).

Secondly, the approach fails to distinguish between current and capital account flows whose macroeconomic effects may generate different welfare consequences.

SUMMARY

External disequilibrium is considered a monetary phenomenon resulting from stock imbalances between the demand for and supply of money. With fixed exchange rates, external equilibrium is restored through external monetary flows which persist until internal monetary equilibrium is re-established. With floating exchange rates, external equilibrium is continuously maintained with exchange rate fluctuations which, through domestic price changes, restore internal monetary equilibrium. The monetary approach to external equilibrium thus postulates that, in the long run and in the absence of official intervention, external equilibrium and internal monetary equilibrium will be established under both fixed and floating exchange rates.

The approach is constrained, however, by the failure to specify a temporal framework within which adjustment will occur and by the failure to distinguish between the current and capital account components of external disequilibrium.

QUESTIONS FOR DISCUSSION

1. Contrast the monetary adjustment processes under fixed and floating exchange rates.
2. Might stabilisation policies be expected to play an active role in the monetary approach to external equilibrium?
3. The monetary approach predicts that price increases will result in external surpluses. Does this imply that inflationary monetary policies might be pursued to generate external surpluses?

Part Four

The Post-war International Financial System

Since the end of the Second World War, the international financial system has undergone numerous changes and faced a number of crises which have been significantly influenced by the level of international liquidity and the nature of the international adjustment process.

The immediate post-war period was characterised by deficient international liquidity which was rapidly transformed into excess dollar liquidity with the advent of US balance of payments deficits. This excess liquidity contributed to two gold crises and created considerable international adjustment problems. These were eventually resolved in the course of two dollar crises and with the adoption of floating exchange rates.

Further adjustment problems emerged with the advent of the 1973/74 and 1979/80 oil crises. These resulted in the unprecedented transfer of purchasing power from petroleum importers to petroleum exporters and the creation of liquidity imbalances which were largely accommodated by the international banking system. The adjustment problems created by these flows contributed to the international debt crisis which emerged as the dominant feature of the early 1980s.

These issues and developments are examined chronologically but briefly in Chapter 13.

One of the single most important developments of the post-war period has been the establishment and growth of the Euro-currency markets. These markets for foreign currency deposits, which have become a permanent feature of the international monetary scene, are the subject of Chapter 14.

Finally, Chapter 15 considers the characteristics and operation of some of the newer markets in international financial transactions — the markets in currency futures and options.

13

Post-war Issues and Developments

POST-WAR RECONSTRUCTION AND THE IMF

Reconstruction of the international monetary system began even before the end of the Second World War. Draft proposals submitted by Harry Dexter White of the US Treasury and John Maynard Keynes of the UK Treasury culminated in the Bretton Woods conference of 1944 which ushered in a new era of international monetary co-operation and led to the establishment of the International Monetary Fund.

These attempts to improve international monetary co-operation formally recognised that countries are financially interdependent and that there was an urgent need to harmonise national economic policies. They represented an important step towards avoiding the exchange rate chaos which had characterised the 1930s and which, through competitive devaluations and the export of unemployment, had served to spread economic instability internationally.

The IMF, which was to oversee the operation of the proposed system of fixed exchange rates, was conceived as an international fund, although subsequently it came to function as a world central bank. Its major provisions, which were to provide a framework for almost 30 years of comparative economic stability, were to: (i) promote international monetary co-operation and development; (ii) facilitate the growth of international trade; (iii) promote exchange rate stability; (iv) reduce the magnitude and duration of payments imbalances.

These provisions were to be effected by:

(i) the establishment of par values and the maintenance of individual currencies within 1 per cent of declared par values

— requirements which, in practice, evolved into the 'gold exchange standard';

(ii) fund approval for any exchange rate realignments which cumulatively exceeded 10 per cent of declared par values but which were necessary to correct fundamental balance of payments disequilibrium;

(iii) the provision of gold and convertible currencies to finance transitory or cyclical current account deficits.

The immediate task facing the international community in 1945, however, was post-war reconstruction and development. The war had destroyed much of Europe's economic fabric and had left European countries dependent on the US for imports but without the means to pay for them. Rapid European recovery, therefore, seemed unlikely without US assistance.

The Marshall Plan, announced in 1947 and named after the then US Secretary of State, supplied Europe with the physical resources and financial transfers necessary to alleviate the chronic dollar shortage which might otherwise have aborted economic recovery. A subsequent series of European currency devaluations, initiated by a 30 per cent devaluation of sterling from £1 = $4.03 to £1 = $2.80 in 1949, accelerated recovery and contributed to a further alleviation of the international dollar shortage. By the early 1950s, it had all but disappeared.

THE DOLLAR SURPLUS

The transformation of the post-war dollar shortage into a dollar surplus was a gradual and almost imperceptible process which, in the early 1950s, gave little cause for concern. Rapid European economic recovery and the growth of international trade necessitated increases in liquidity which the limited supplies of newly-mined gold were unable to provide. The rest of the world was thus more than willing to accumulate dollars, which had become an international reserve currency and the principal source of international liquidity.

Confidence in the dollar and in its continued convertibility into gold at the official price of $35 per ounce (established in 1934) was underpinned by US gold stocks, which had amounted to approximately 60 per cent of total world gold reserves at the end of the Second World War. The emergence of US deficits in the 1950s and the attendant growth of US foreign liabilities, however, began to focus attention on the emerging dollar surplus and on the reserve/liquidity dilemma which this surplus could create. The dilemma reflected the dollar's role as both an international reserve asset and a US foreign liability. The world was dependent on US dollars as a source of international liquidity (reserves) since the growth of gold reserves was insufficient to finance international trade and development. The growth of dollar liquidity, however, depended on US deficits which, if allowed to continue unabated, would generate US dollar liabilities which might eventually absorb the entire stock of US reserve assets and raise doubts about the dollar's continued gold convertibility.

Implicit in these doubts was the possibility of a gold crisis, which duly manifested itself at the turn of the decade. US liabilities to official foreigners had increased and US gold stocks had decreased throughout the 1950s, until the former amounted to just under and the latter to just over $20 billion by the end of 1959. The reversal of these positions in 1960, together with uncertainty concerning the likely outcome of the November US presidential election and the economic policies which might ensue, intensified gold demand, which reached crisis proportions in the final quarter of the year. This drove the price of gold above the official level of $35 per ounce and weakened the dollar on the foreign exchange markets. The crisis was eventually contained through substantial sales of official gold and a reassurance from presidential candidate Senator John F. Kennedy that, if elected, he would not devalue the dollar.

The 1960 gold crisis was a clear indication of the potentially destabilising consequences of a growing dollar surplus. These became even more apparent in the following year, when dollar selling pressure contributed to a 5 per cent revaluation of the Deutsche Mark and guilder and contributed to the establishment of the US Federal Reserve Swap Network which was intended to stabilise exchange rates through the provision of short-term (reversible) inter-central bank foreign exchange assistance. These currency swaps, however, only proved a palliative and not a cure for the burgeoning US balance of payments deficits which were essentially caused by US capital outflows. (The balance on goods and services account remained in surplus throughout the 1960s.) Measures to curb these outflows were consequently introduced in 1963 with the Interest Equalisation Tax (IET), which proposed a tax on US purchases of foreign securities. This measure was supplemented by the 1965 Voluntary Foreign Credit Restraint Program (VFCRP), which imposed further 'voluntary' restrictions on capital outflows,

Table 13.1: US balance of payments data, 1960–83. ($ billions)

	60	61	62	63	64	65	66	67	68	69	70	71
Current account balance	2.8	3.8	3.4	4.4	6.8	5.4	3.0	2.6	0.6	0.4	2.3	-1.4
Foreign official assets in US* (Increase +)	1.3	0.7	1.1	1.6	1.4	0.1	-0.8	3.4	-0.8	-1.6	7.4	27.4
US official reserve assets (Increase -)	2.1	0.6	1.5	0.4	0.2	1.2	0.6	0.1	-0.9	-1.2	2.5	2.3

	72	73	74	75	76	77	78	79	80	81	82	83
Current account balance	-5.8	7.1	2.0	18.1	4.2	-14.5	-15.4	-1.0	1.9	6.3	-9.2	-41.6
Foreign official assets in US* (Increase +)	10.3	5.1	10.2	5.5	13.1	35.4	31.2	-13.6	14.9	5.3	2.9	5.1
US official reserve assets (Increase -)	—	0.2	-1.5	-0.8	-2.6	-0.4	0.7	-1.1	-8.2	-5.2	-5.0	-1.2

* Excludes government liabilities such as those associated with military sales contracts
Source: *Survey of Current Business*

and reinforced by the 1968 Foreign Direct Investment Program (FDIP), which imposed mandatory restrictions on capital outflows.

Although these measures might have eventually succeeded in reducing capital outflows towards the end of the decade (net capital inflows were recorded in 1968 and 1969), they initially failed to contain the growth of dollar liquidity and the erosion of international confidence. By 1968, these had culminated in a second, more severe gold crisis.

THE GOLD CRISIS

The weakness of the dollar was paralleled by the weakness of sterling, which became the focus of a succession of speculative attacks in the mid-1960s. These were prompted by persistent balance of payments deficits (a cumulative net deficit of £1.6 billion on combined current and capital account was recorded between 1960 and 1966) and by the growing realisation that, since sterling had become overvalued, the existing exchange rate could not be sustained indefinitely.

At first, these speculative attacks were contained through internationally financed official support operations. The US proved a particularly important source of support, since it feared that a sterling devalution might undermine confidence in the dollar and, by extension, the entire monetary system, leading to a collapse of the system and consequent return to the exchange rate chaos of the 1930s.

These fears were partly justified when the dollar became the focus of speculative attacks in the wake of sterling's eventual devaluation in November 1967 from £1 = $2.80 to £1 = $2.40. The attacks were prompted by the dollar's liquidity-induced international weakness and were manifested in increases in the demand for gold. Speculators presumed that a dollar realignment would take the form of an increase in the dollar price of gold and that, since European currencies would probably follow the dollar's devaluation, there was little point in converting dollars into European currencies.

The sustained private demand for gold which developed in the last quarter of 1967 abated in early 1968 but re-emerged in March of that year. The US, fearful that increases in the price of gold might lead to the escalation of conversions of officially held dollars into gold and the eventual suspension of dollar convertibility, attempted to stabilise the price of gold through substantial sales of gold

241

Table 13.2: UK balance of payments data, 1960–9. (£ millions)

	1960	1961	1962	1963	1964	1965	1966	1967	1968	1969
Current account balance	−228	47	155	125	−358	−30	130	−269	−244	505
Capital flows	521	−386	37	−183	−337	−323	−721	−402	−1166	182
Total	293	−339	192	−58	−695	−353	−591	−671	−1410	687

Source: *CSO Economic Trends Annual Supplement 1983*

reserves on the open market. These sales increased in intensity in early March in response to the increase in private speculative purchases, which were essentially a 'one-way bet' with little risk of a downward slide in price. Sales were channelled through the London gold market which was eventually closed by the Bank of England after gold sales reached $400 million on Thursday, 14 March. When the market reopened on 1 April, it was in the form of a two-tier gold market in which official and private gold transactions were separated. The former continued to be transacted at the official price of $35 per ounce, while the latter were conducted in a free market with no attempts to stabilise the price at the official level, through either official purchases or, more likely, sales of gold.

The two-tier market initially succeeded in stabilising the price of gold (although the price subsequently reached an historic peak of $850 per ounce on 21 January 1980) and in preserving a semblance of official gold convertibility. This prevailed until the suspension of official gold convertibility in August 1971, even though in practice little gold was transacted at the official price of $35 per ounce. But the problems were not over. Although the crisis cost the US more than $2 billion in gold reserves, and dollar liabilities were reduced by an equivalent amount, international dollar liquidity continued to grow.

THE DOLLAR CRISES

The political reluctance to devalue sterling in the mid-1960s and the economic instability which this engendered were prominent features of the currency instability which characterised the dollar and, to a lesser extent, European currencies in the late 1960s and early 1970s.

The emergence of French social unrest in 1968 was accompanied by the weakening of the French franc which President de Gaulle refused to devalue. The weakness of the franc was mirrored by the strength of the Deutsche Mark, which the German authorities similarly refused to revalue. This continued until 1969 when, acceding to the inevitable, France devalued the franc by 11.1 per cent and Germany revalued the Mark by 9.3 per cent. While these realignments served to provide a measure of international stability, they failed to resolve the problem of an increasingly misaligned (overvalued) dollar.

US monetary policy in the late 1960s had been contractionary and the resulting increase in US interest rates had succeeded in persuading private holders of dollars to continue holding their assets in dollars, rather than other currencies. By late 1969, however, US monetary policy had begun to be relaxed and this induced substantial US capital outflows which were intensified by European monetary restraint, most notably in Germany where short-term interest rates reached a peak in the second quarter of 1970. The emergence of covered interest differentials in favour of Deutsche Marks prompted large-scale dollar inflows into Germany, whose dollar reserves increased by more than $7 billion in 1970.

Confidence in the dollar was further undermined by a deterioration in the US official settlements deficit to $6 billion in the first quarter of 1971 and by a recommendation from German research institutes that the Deutsche Mark be revalued. This precipitated a dollar/Deutsche Mark crisis which culminated on 5 May in the Bundesbank's purchasing $1 billion in the first hour of trading and the foreign exchange markets being closed. When the markets reopened on 10 May, the Deutsche Mark and the Dutch guilder were floating and the Austrian schilling and Swiss franc had been revalued by 5.05 per cent and 7.07 per cent respectively.

Further evidence that the international monetary system was facing insupportable strains was provided by the proliferation and intensification of European capital controls in the first half of 1971 to prevent dollar inflows and so protect European currencies from speculative (revaluationary) attacks. Despite these strains, however, the US authorities were reluctant to implement appropriate corrective measures. On the one hand the US administration refused to entertain the possibility of a dollar devaluation — both for political reasons and because of the reserve status of the dollar (the dollar was immutable, as sterling had been in the mid-1960s) — while on the other hand, there were few attempts to restore external equilibrium through conventional domestic measures. It can be said that a policy of 'benign neglect' was pursued, which allowed the situation to deteriorate and international dollar liquidity to increase.

Consequently, despite the currency realignments which followed the Deutsche Mark crisis and the intensification of measures to curb destabilising capital flows, an atmosphere of uncertainty pervaded international currency markets in the summer of 1971. The US merchandise trade balance swung from a surplus of $160 million in March to a deficit of $365 million in June, while the seasonally adjusted deficit on current and long-term capital account deteriorated from $1.7 billion to $3.2 billion between the first and second quarters of the year. These flows contributed to an official settlements deficit of $12.1 billion in the first half of 1971 and further undermined confidence in the dollar, which was traded at a spot discount against virtually every major trading currency.

With little prospect of an improvement in the US balance of payments through 'conventional' remedies, some form of discrete adjustment became increasingly inevitable. This was further prompted by a US congressional sub-committee report (the Reuss report), which cautioned that conventional measures could be expected to prove of limited success in restoring payments equilibrium and that consequently, in the absence of a general currency realignment, there might be no option but to suspend convertibility of the dollar. Following the report's publication, there was a flight from the dollar which steadily gained momentum. During the week commencing Monday 9 August, international dollar reserves increased by $3.7 billion ($1.7 billion of which was accounted for by Switzerland), while stabilisation measures resulted in a $1.2 billion decline in US reserve assets. By the end of the week it had become apparent that the situation was untenable and, on Sunday 15 August, President Nixon announced the suspension of dollar convertibility and the imposition of a 10 per cent import surcharge. 'Bretton Woods', in all but name, had collapsed.

When the foreign exchange markets reopened on Monday 23 August, virtually every major industrial currency, except the Japanese Yen, was floating. Four months later, on 18 December 1971, the Smithsonian Agreement concluded a 7.9 per cent devaluation of the dollar, equivalent to the raising of the official price of gold from $35 to $38 per ounce.

This belated attempt to restore international monetary equilibrium could not contain the cumulative effects of an over-valued dollar and the excessive growth of international dollar liquidity. On 1 May 1972, sterling joined the Snake in the Tunnel and less than two months later, following heavy speculative attacks, it was forced to abandon the Snake and float. This was followed by renewed speculative attacks on the dollar, which necessitated substantial intervention by European and Japanese central banks.

It came as no surprise, therefore, when a new crisis developed. It began in early 1973 with the announcement, on 22 January, of the establishment of a dual foreign exchange market in which the commercial lira would be maintained within fixed margins and the financial lira would be free to float. This announcement, however, failed to deter lira outflows and strengthen the currency. Continued sales of dollars, meanwhile, brought the Swiss franc to its upper intervention point against the dollar and on 23 January, following heavy and sustained support measures, the Swiss authorities withdrew from the market and the Swiss franc was allowed to float. These developments were interpreted as reflecting increased willingness to resort to exchange rate flexibility to counter unwanted capital flows, and consequently subjected the dollar to further pressure which assumed crisis proportions following the disclosure of an increase in the US current account deficit for 1972 to a provisional $9.7 billion. Between Thursday 1 February and the official closure of the foreign exchange markets on Friday 9 February, approximately $8–$10 billion was purchased in support operations, with Germany accounting for approximately $6 billion. Dollar purchases on Friday alone amounted to $2 billion, with Germany's share amounting to some $1.7 billion.

In contrast to the delay which had characterised the 1971 crisis, the announcement on Monday 12 February that the US President would request Congress to authorise a 10 per cent devaluation of the dollar represented a concerted attempt to effect a rapid solution to the crisis. It had limited success, however, for the dollar began to weaken again from Wednesday 21 February and, following the purchase of $2.7 billion by the Bundesbank on Thursday 1 March, the foreign exchange markets were closed. When the markets were eventually reopened on Monday 19 March, the major trading currencies were floating against the dollar. The era of floating exchange rates had arrived.

Thus the 1973 dollar crisis was significant not only because it occurred just twelve months after the Smithsonian Agreement's fundamental realignment of international exchange rates, but also because it marked the end of the post-war period of fixed exchange rates which had become increasingly characterised by structural disequilibrium and excess liquidity. These had been caused by an overvalued dollar whose non-realignment prevented the adjustment mechanism from acting to restore international equilibrium. This, in turn, generated capital flows which the Bretton Woods system was eventually unable to contain. A combination of misaligned exchange rates, excess liquidity and large-scale capital flows ultimately imposed their own 'external' adjustment on the international monetary system.

If floating exchange rates were expected to provide a more flexible adjustment process which would avoid the distortions and imbalances of fixed exchange rates, then these expectations were not realised, for the emergence of two international oil crises subjected the international monetary system to disequilibria which were to prove as severe as those encountered under fixed exchange rates.

THE OIL CRISES

In 1973/74 and 1979/80, oil prices were increased by members of the OPEC oil cartel. The impact of this was similar to that of a sales tax which had to be financed domestically but whose revenues were paid overseas. It precipitated an unprecedented transfer of wealth from petroleum-importing countries to petroleum-exporting countries and confronted the international monetary system in general and western economies in particular with both an ultimate adjustment problem and an interim financing problem.

The ultimate adjustment problem arose from the need to transfer real resources from petroleum importers to exporters and was resolved through conventional income and absorption changes.

The interim financing problem arose from the need to effect these changes as smoothly as possible and with minimal domestic deflation.

It might have been initially expected that, through exchange rate realignments, the advent of floating exchange rates would have resolved the problem of resource transfers. The currencies of those countries experiencing oil-induced balance of payments deficits would have depreciated, while the currencies of those countries experiencing oil-induced surpluses would have appreciated. This would have encouraged exports/discouraged imports in the deficit country and encouraged imports/discouraged exports in the surplus country, leading to resource transfers from the former to the latter. These transfers are illustrated in terms of an external product market shock under floating exchange rates in Figure 13.1, which shows that an increase in autonomous imports shifts the EE_0 curve to EE_1 and the IS_0 curve to IS_1. This creates a temporary deficit (point A) which is eliminated through a depreciation-induced increase in exports/decrease in imports, which restores joint equilibrium at point E.

But such an analysis might only be expected to apply to an individual country whose currency is able to depreciate against those of its trading partners to restore external equilibrium. The oil crisis affected all petroleum-importing countries and they were unable to collectively depreciate their currencies since there were few, if any major currencies to depreciate against. Depreciation in the initial stages of the crisis, moreover, might have exacerbated petroleum importers' deficits, since OPEC was characterised by deficient rather than excessive real resource absorption capacity.

In other words, the financing problem was similar to that resulting from an external product market shock under fixed, rather than floating, exchange rates. Figure 13.1 shows that the EE_0 and IS_0 curves shift to EE_1 and IS_1 respectively and that the economy moves into quasi-permanent external deficit at point A if the deficit is financed out of official reserves and the contractionary impact of the deficit on domestic liquidity is sterilised. This minimises the domestic deflationary impact of the deficit by confining unemployment to Y_U rather than Y'_U, which would have prevailed in the absence of sterilisation and in the presence of attempts to eliminate the deficit through domestic deflation. (In both cases, however, the level of unemployment would have been exacerbated by the inflationary consequences of higher oil prices.)

The interim financing problem was consequently one of securing adequate reserves to finance deficits and of providing importing nations with sufficient time to restructure their economies in order to generate the income and resources necessary to correct these deficits. The problem was resolved by recycling balance of payments surpluses from exporters to importers through the international banking system.

The recycling mechanism

The international banking system was instrumental in accommodating oil-induced balance of payments disequilibria and in containing international instability. The banks performed this role through the recycling mechanism, which involved the international borrowing and lending of foreign exchange (dollar) reserves. Petroleum importers' deficits were initially financed with official dollar reserves which exporters received and deposited with banks located in international financial centres such as London and New York. These deposits were then lent to borrowers who used them to finance further oil purchases from exporters who in turn redeposited the receipts with banks in London and New York. This circular flow of deposits from importers to exporters financed the former's deficits and accommodated the latter's surpluses which, after the first oil price rise, increased by a cumulative $227 billion by the end of the decade.

Figure 13.1: Joint disequilibrium and the impact of an external oil price shock. The increased cost of petroleum imports results in a balance of payments deficit which shifts the EE_0 curve up to EE_1 and the IS_0 curve down to IS_1. This might result in individual oil-importing countries allowing their currencies to depreciate, which might eliminate the deficit and return the EE and IS curves to their original positions. This would restore joint equilibrium at point E. The currencies of oil-importing countries, however, cannot collectively depreciate and the countries are thus in a 'fixed exchange rate' position in which their deficits are either financed out of reserves (point A) or eliminated through domestic deflation (point B). (For both floating and fixed exchange rates, moreover, the inflationary effects of higher oil prices are likely to shift the LM curve up to the left and create higher levels of unemployment than those indicated by points A and B.)

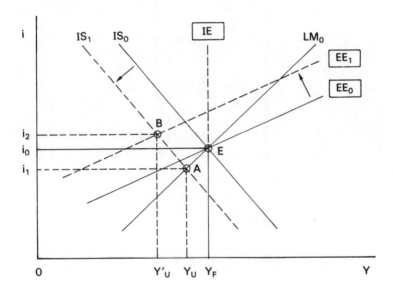

The financial counterparts of the imbalances channelled through the banking system were bank liabilities to exporters and bank claims on importers. The former acted as a temporary store for domestic absorption while the latter enabled importing nations to generate or assign the income required to provide the goods and services necessary to satisfy the increase in absorption by exporting countries. The success of the recycling process was such that just prior to the second oil price increase, exporters' annual financial

Table 13.3: Identified deployment of petroleum-exporting countries' surpluses, 1974–83. ($ billions)

Deployment of surpluses* in:	1974	1975	1976	1977	1978	1979	1980	1981	1982	1983
UK	21.0	4.3	4.4	4.0	-6.8	17.8	18.1	9.3	-8.5	-5.4
US	11.5	8.0	11.2	7.3	0.5	7.0	15.1	15.4	10.7	-9.4
Other countries	20.7	24.2	19.9	21.9	19.2	30.9	54.0	24.0	-0.1	-4.8
TOTAL	53.2	36.5	35.5	33.2	12.9	55.7	87.2	48.7	2.1	-19.6

*Surpluses are those of the 13 members of OPEC and of Trinidad and Tobago, Bahrain, Brunei and Oman
Source: Bank of England.

surpluses had almost disappeared, having declined to less than $13 billion in 1978 from approximately $53 billion in 1974.

The two alternatives to recycling were neither practical nor feasible:

The first would have involved exchange rate realignments (depreciation), but the magnitude of importers' deficits was such that exchange rate alignments could not collectively have eliminated these imbalances. While individual depreciations might have succeeded in restoring external equilibrium for individual countries, such equilibria could only have been achieved at the expense of larger deficits for other oil-importing nations. In contrast to the exporting of unemployment through competitive devaluations which occurred in the 1930s, the exporting of oil deficits through competitive depreciations in the 1970s was not actively pursued.

A second possible method of eliminating importers' deficits would have been through domestic deflation. This is illustrated in Figure 13.1 by allowing the contractionary impact of the deficit on domestic liquidity to shift the LM curve up to the left until it intersects the IS_1 curve at point B. This option would have involved such drastic deflation, however (Y'_U compared to Y_U), that it was politically and socially unacceptable.

The recycling mechanism consequently made both exporters and importers 'captives' of the nominal wealth which the oil price increases had created. Exporters were dependent on importers directly or indirectly to absorb their newly acquired financial claims, since few alternative investment outlets existed. Importers, in turn, were dependent on exporters to provide the financial claims necessary to finance their balance of payments deficits. The international banking community provided the means by which these claims could effectively be recycled.

In this respect, the banks were helped by the rapid dismantling of the intricate network of international capital controls which had been assembled in the early 1970s in increasingly futile attempts to prevent unwanted capital (dollar) inflows. These controls were replaced by policies of capital mobility which were expected to stimulate capital flows and provide the resources necessary to finance prospective balance of payments deficits.

Changes in European capital controls were designed to promote capital inflows and minimise the emergence of deflationary pressures. Changes in US capital controls, in contrast, were designed to promote dollar outflows. The US administration announced, on 26 December 1973, that a significant easing of capital controls would take effect from 1 January 1974. The changes subsequently announced on 29 January, however, were the most significant since the introduction of the IET for, with immediate effect: the IET was reduced to zero; FDIP controls were abolished and the VFCRP was terminated. These controls were removed to permit the smooth recycling of exporters' surpluses and, because of the expected demand for dollar investments, to avoid any excessive appreciation of the dollar which would have eroded the benefits of the devaluations of 1971 and 1973. The impact on US capital outflows for 1974 as a whole was dramatic: US direct investment abroad increased by $9.1 billion; foreign bond issues in the US almost doubled to $2.4 billion and US banks' foreign claims more than tripled to $19.5 billion. At a stroke, the barriers which had impeded the free outflow of US capital in the 1960s and 1970s had been dismantled.

It might have been expected that the surpluses generated by the second oil price increase of 1979/80 would also have been successfully recycled, but the situation which confronted the international banking system in the late 1970s was very different to that which had prevailed in the mid-1970s. It was this differing situation which was to contribute to the emergence of yet another international financial crisis.

THE INTERNATIONAL DEBT CRISIS

The emergence of an international debt crisis in 1982, and the debt rescheduling which followed it, can be attributed to a combination of general factors and a succession of specific developments.

The general factors contributing to the crisis were changes in international macroeconomic conditions and, paradoxically, the success with which the immediate post-1974 oil surpluses had been recycled:

Firstly, banks were required to continue recycling further and even larger exporter surpluses than those which had been recycled in the mid-1970s and which had already substantially increased the volume of banks' loans and deposits. For example, US banks' foreign branches, which featured prominently in the recycling process, increased their assets from $150 billion in 1974 to $460 billion in 1981.

Secondly, the growth of banks' assets was not matched by corresponding increases in banks' capital bases, and these were

Figure 13.2: Claims of nine largest US banks as percentage of primary capital.

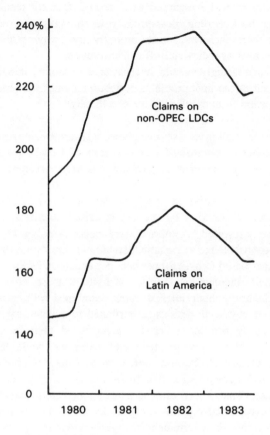

Source: *World Financial Markets*, Oct/Nov 1984

consequently able to absorb only a diminished proportion of potential loan defaults.

Thirdly, the problem of declining capital/asset ratios was compounded by the commercial and political risks arising from the geo-political concentration of deposits among a small number of high output/low absorption exporters and of loans among a small number of less-developed countries. Bank credits to Mexico, for example, which is one of the largest Latin American debtors, amounted to approximately 50 per cent of the capital of the nine largest US banks at the time of the crisis.

Fourthly, the temporary nature of international balance of payments financing through short-term bank deposits and long-term bank loans came to be regarded as a quasi-permanent feature of international bank lending, despite the risks to banks of providing such large-scale facilities, more properly the responsibility of longer-term debt agencies and official institutions.

Fifthly, increasingly hostile international economic conditions exacerbated the economic problems of debtor nations in general and LDC borrowers in particular. More specifically:

The second oil price rise precipitated a severe world recession which reduced the demand for exports from LDCs whose balance of payments and debt-servicing capabilities were correspondingly impaired.

The world recession was accompanied by increasing intolerance of inflation by the industrialised countries, which increasingly resorted to contractionary monetary policies to curb it. This contributed to a dramatic increase in interest rates (the US prime rate soared to over 20 per cent per annum in 1980), which substantially increased the burden of LDC debt financing.

Unrelentingly high interest rates, combined with growing balance of payments deficits, contributed to a deterioration in debt maturity profiles as creditors translated their increased perceptions of risk into shorter credit maturities, while debtors renewed maturing debt on a short-term basis to avoid high-cost long-term financing and to benefit from 'imminent' lower long-term rates. That lower rates did not immediately materialise proved exceptionally painful, especially for countries such as Mexico, whose short-term debt (repayable within one year) came to exceed 30 per cent of its total external debt by 1982.

The combined effect of these general factors was to undermine the confidence with which surpluses had been recycled from exporters to importers. Confidence was further undermined by the nature of sovereign debt which, unlike conventional debt, which is secured against specific or tangible collateral, is only secured against the goodwill of the borrowing government. The possibility of foreclosing on governments and the problems which this might engender had not been seriously contemplated until it was realised that the original sovereign borrower might no longer be relied upon, nor even be vested with the authority to continue guaranteeing outstanding principals and interest repayments.

Figure 13.3: US short- and long-term interest rates (% p.a.), 1979–82.

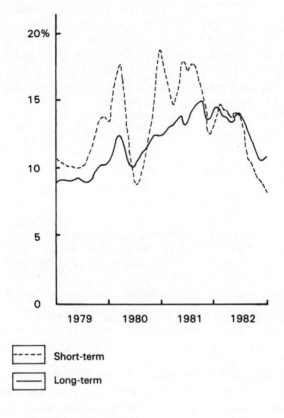

Source: *IMF Annual Report 1983*

There was consequently latent instability. The sequence of events which conspired to transform this instability into a crisis was brief but rapid.

The continuing deterioration in social and political stability in Poland in 1981 rekindled fears of possible debt default. This, in conjunction with Western sanctions, could have developed into a more generalised debt default by Eastern European states.

The Falklands conflict in early 1982 between Argentina and Britain threw into sharp relief not only the risks of large-scale long-distance lending, but also the risks associated with the imposition of exchange controls and the blocking of non-resident accounts.

Table 13.4: Gross external debt of sixteen major LDC borrowers, 1982–3. ($ billions)

	1982	1983
Latin America		
Argentina	41.7	43.4
Brazil	85.3	93.6
Chile	18.0	18.6
Colombia	10.6	11.2
Ecuador	6.3	6.9
Mexico	87.1	90.6
Peru	11.6	12.8
Venezuela	35.6	34.9
Subtotal	296.2	312.0
Other		
Indonesia	24.8	29.2
Korea	37.3	40.1
Malaysia	11.5	14.8
Nigeria	13.8	18.2
Philippines	24.5	26.5
Taiwan	9.7	10.0
Thailand	11.7	12.6
Turkey	22.3	23.9
Subtotal	155.6	175.3
TOTAL	451.8	487.3

Source: *World Financial Markets*, October/November 1984

Finally, Mexico's announcement in August 1982 of a moratorium on its $85 billion debt raised the spectre of a sequential banking collapse involving not just Latin America, within which Brazil, Argentina and Mexico collectively owed in excess of $200 billion, but, conceivably, the entire international banking system. This possibility was reinforced by a spate of rescheduling requests, foremost amongst which were those from Argentina and Brazil.

The crisis was initially contained by official financial assistance channelled through the offices of monetary organisations such as the IMF. General confidence was subsequently restored through a succession of support measures which included debt rescheduling, debt restructuring, conditional additional financing and domestic macroeconomic adjustment (deflation).

It was also helped, somewhat paradoxically, by the near collapse in 1984 of the eighth largest bank in the US, which had undertaken imprudent domestic lending. The Continental Illinois Bank of Chicago was rescued by US government agency purchases of $4.5

billion of the bank's 'problematic' loans. The rescue package, which was the largest in US history, showed that the US monetary authorities were both unwilling and unable to allow a domestic bank of this size to fail. This was also interpreted to apply, by extension, to externally-induced failures, since the nine largest US banks had made loans to four countries (Argentina, Brazil, Mexico and Venezuela) which exceeded their entire equity base. That such assistance might be forthcoming was interpreted as an international lender of last resort facility, which consequently provided the international banking community with the additional support measures and confidence required.

The international debt crisis was a further sign of the liquidity problems which have beset the post-war international monetary system and which have corresponded to an inadequate international adjustment mechanism. From an immediate post-war liquidity deficiency prompted by a dollar shortage, through the liquidity surfeit prompted by a dollar glut, to the oil-price-induced liquidity difficulties of debtor nations, the international adjustment mechanism has been unable to cope effectively with the structural imbalances which have caused these liqiuidity problems. It remains to be seen, therefore, whether a combination of floating exchange rates and relatively stable oil prices will be able to provide the international monetary system with the degree of stability which it requires.

SUMMARY

Post-war financial reconstruction, which formally recognised that countries were financially interdependent, resulted in the establishment of a system of fixed exchange rates and the creation of the IMF.

The growth of US deficits transformed an immediate post-war dollar shortage into a dollar surplus, so that US liabilities to official foreigners eventually exceeded US gold stocks in 1960 and contributed to a gold crisis in that year.

The introduction of US capital controls in the mid-1960s failed to contain the growth of dollar liquidity and the erosion of international confidence which culminated in a second gold crisis in 1968. This resulted in a two-tier gold market in which official and private gold transactions were separated.

Although this succeeded in stabilising the price of gold, it failed to resolve the problems of excessive dollar liquidity and the dollar's increasing overvaluation, neither of which the US administration was prepared to address. The combination of misaligned exchange rates, excess liquidity and large-scale capital flows eventually imposed adjustment on the international monetary system in the form of the 1971 dollar crisis, which resulted in a 7.9 per cent devaluation of the dollar, and the 1973 dollar crisis, which resulted in the abandonment of the 'Bretton Woods' system of fixed exchange rates and the adoption of floating exchange rates.

The oil crisis of the mid- and late 1970s transferred wealth from petroleum importers to petroleum exporters and confronted the international monetary system with adjustment and financing problems. These were resolved through the international banking system which recycled surpluses from petroleum exporters to importers.

The very success of this recycling, together with changes in international macroeconomic conditions, contributed to an international debt crisis in 1982 which was contained through a combination of official assistance and private financing.

QUESTIONS FOR DISCUSSION

1. What might explain the rapid transition from post-war dollar shortage to surplus?
2. What were the causes of the 1960 gold crisis?
3. Was the collapse of 'Bretton Woods' inevitable?
4. Why was the 'recycling mechanism' necessary and how did it operate?
5. Is responsibility for the 1982 debt crisis attributable to borrowers or lenders?

14

The Euro-currency Markets

CHARACTERISTICS

Euro-currency activity is:

The transacting of foreign currency deposits.

The markets in which foreign currency deposits are transacted are **Euro-currency markets**, the largest of which is the **Euro-dollar market**. Euro-markets also exist for the Deutsche Mark, Swiss franc, Japanese Yen, pound sterling and other European currencies of lesser trading importance.

The distinguishing feature of Euro-currency activity is that deposits are denominated in currencies other than that of the country in which the deposits are transacted. Thus 'Euro-dollar deposits' refers to US dollar deposits transacted outside the US. Similarly, 'Euro-Deutsche Mark deposits' refers to Deutsche Mark deposits transacted outside Germany. The term 'Euro', however, has increasingly widened as Euro-currency activities are now conducted in financial centres located throughout the world, in fact, wherever and whenever the demand arises to transact foreign currency deposits. The term 'Euro' thus extends to embrace activities conducted in non-traditional (off-shore) centres such as Singapore and Bahrain, as well as traditional European centres such as London and Paris. Since December 1981, moreover, it includes activities conducted by **International Banking Facilities** (IBFs), which are separate accounting units of US-located banks authorised to engage in activities with US non-residents on the same terms as banks located in Euro-centres.

Banks located in Euro-centres intermediate (channel) deposits between sources and uses, either of which might consist of other banks (the inter-bank market) or non-banks such as governments, corporations and private individuals. Deposits might be intermediated in the inter-bank market several times between their original source and their final use. This intermediation might be confined to one centre or might involve several geographically separate centres. The interest rate at which banks accept deposits, whose minimum value is generally US $25,000 or equivalent, is the **bid rate** and the maturities for which banks regularly accept deposits range from call (repayable on demand) to five years. The interest rate at which banks lend deposits to other banks is the **offer rate**. The rate at which banks lend deposits to prime-name banks in the London inter-bank market is the **London Inter-Bank Offer Rate** (LIBOR), which acts as an international reference rate for loans (credits) to non-bank borrowers who have to pay a spread or premium over LIBOR to reflect the increased risk of such lending. The maturities of these credits may extend to 15 years or more and may involve interest rates which are fixed or variable. In the former case, the interest rate is fixed over the life of the credit. In the latter case, the credit consists of a short-term credit which is rolled-over or renewed, for example every six months, over the proposed life of the loan. The interest rate reflects the size of the spread over LIBOR and the level of LIBOR prevailing at the beginning of each roll-over period and fluctuates in response to changing market conditions over the life of the credit. These credits are referred to as **roll-over credits** and form the basis of medium-term Euro-currency lending.

Medium-term Euro-currency credits are used for a variety of purposes such as the financing of trade, investment projects and balance of payments deficits, and may be extended by banks individually or collectively (syndicated). They are attractive to borrowers not only because of their competitive interest rates and management fees, but also because of the confidentiality, speed and general ease with which they may be secured.

Depositors are similarly attracted by the competitive interest rates paid on deposits and by the speed and ease of transactions. They are also attracted by the anonymity with which transactions are conducted, a factor which contributed significantly to the establishment of the Euro-currency markets.

THE CREATION OF EURO-CURRENCY DEPOSITS

Euro-currency creation in theory

Euro-currency deposits, such as Euro-dollar deposits, may be created in three ways:

Primary Euro-dollar creation

Primary Euro-dollar creation arises when dollar deposits are transferred from US banks to banks located outside the US and are deposited at Euro-dollar rates of interest.

The original deposit may have been held in a variety of forms, such as private resident or non-resident claims on the US or acquired in a variety of ways, for example, purchased in the foreign exchange market. In either case the dollars must have been maintained in the US, since the withdrawal and redepositing of existing Euro-dollar deposits merely entails a change in deposit ownership with no change in the net value of deposits outstanding.

The transfer of deposits may also be undertaken for a variety of reasons, such as the exploitation of interest rate differentials or for safe refuge purposes but, regardless of the reasons, the transfer must involve the depositing of funds at Euro-dollar rates of interest, since this serves to distinguish Euro-dollars from other international financial flows such as foreign exchange transactions.

The process of primary Euro-dollar creation is illustrated in Table 14.1, in which the US bank and the Euro-bank represent the US banking system and the Euro-dollar market respectively. The process might begin when a US resident converts a time deposit, upon its maturity, into a demand deposit (position 2), and transfers this demand deposit from the US bank to a Euro-bank. In the accounts of the US bank, the deposit liability to the resident now becomes a deposit liability to the Euro-bank (position 3), indicating that the latter now holds liquid claims on the US banking system amounting to $10. This is shown in the Euro-bank's balance sheet (position 1) as a $10 demand deposit claim on the US bank, the contra entry to which is a $10 time deposit liability to the US resident. The transfer of $10 by a US resident from a US to a Euro-bank has thus produced no change in total outstanding US liabilities, but has increased Euro-dollar assets and Euro-dollar liabilities by $10 each. If the Euro-bank now loans the $10 to a second US resident, the transaction will be recorded in the accounts of the Euro-bank as a $10 decrease in demand deposit claims on the US bank and a $10

261

Table 14.1: Primary Euro-dollar creation.

Assets	$	Liabilities	$
		US bank	
Position 1			
Various	10	Time deposit US resident	10
Position 2			
Various	10	Time deposit US resident	− 10
		Demand deposit US resident	+ 10
Net change	0	Net change	0
Position 3			
Various	10	Demand deposit US resident	− 10
		Demand deposit Euro-bank	+ 10
Net change	0	Net change	0
Position 4			
Various	10	Demand deposit Euro-bank	− 10
		Demand deposit US resident	+ 10
Net change	0	Net change	0
		Euro-bank	
Position 1			
Demand deposit with US bank	+ 10	Time deposit US resident	+ 10
Net change	+ 10	Net change	+ 10
Position 2			
Demand deposit with US bank	− 10	Time deposit US resident	10
Loan to US resident	+ 10		
Net change	0	Net change	0

Total Net Changes

	Assets $	Liabilities $
US bank	—	—
Euro-bank	+ 10	+ 10
TOTAL PRIMARY EURO-DOLLAR CREATION	+ 10	+ 10

increase in loans (non-deposit claims) to US residents (position 2), while in the accounts of the US bank the demand deposit liability to the Euro-bank will be converted into a demand deposit liability to the US resident (position 4).

The process of converting US residents' claims on the US banking system into Euro-dollar deposits and thence into Euro-dollar credits to other US residents has thus increased Euro-dollar assets and liabilities by $10 each but has generated no net changes in either the assets or liabilities of the US banking system.

Pyramided Euro-dollar creation

Pyramided Euro-dollar creation arises when Euro-dollar deposits are intermediated by one or more banks before eventually being loaned to final use bank or non-bank borrowers. Pyramided deposit creation results in increases in Euro-dollar deposit liabilities to and Euro-dollar deposit claims on other Euro-banks.

The process is illustrated in Table 14.2. It might begin when a US resident transfers $10 to Euro-bank A. Instead of loaning this $10 to a second US resident, Euro-bank A deposits it with a second Euro-bank (B). The $10 therefore remains within the Euro-dollar market. This results in the creation of a further $10 of Euro-dollar liabilities and $10 of Euro-dollar claims on other Euro-banks involving the redistribution of deposit claims on the US from Euro-bank A to Euro-bank B. If these $10 are then deposited with Euro-bank C which loans them to a Swiss firm, and if this firm uses the $10 to purchase goods from a US corporation which deposits them with a US bank, the Euro-dollar deposit will leave the market and the pyramiding process will cease.

The final result (shown at the foot of Table 14.2) will be a zero net change in US reported assets and liabilities and the provision of $10 of final use credit. An additional $20 of assets and liabilities will have been created, however, reflecting not the purchase of goods and services but merely the trail of statistical images as Euro-dollars are intermediated from banks A to C. It is this intermediation which is the essence of pyramided deposit creation.

Endogenous Euro-dollar creation

Endogenous Euro-dollar creation arises when the market creates its own endogenous supply of final use credits, additional to those arising from the market's intermediation of deposits from the US to Europe. These credits increase international purchasing power and hence exert a real, not just a statistical, effect.

Table 14.2: Pyramided Euro-dollar creation.

Assets	$	Liabilities	$
		US Bank	
Position 1			
Various	10	Time deposit US resident	– 10
		Demand deposit Euro-bank A	+ 10
Net change	0	Net change	0
Position 2			
Various	10	Demand deposit Euro-bank A	– 10
		Demand deposit Euro-bank B	+ 10
Net change	0	Net change	0
Position 3			
Various	10	Demand deposit Euro-bank B	– 10
		Demand deposit Euro-bank C	+ 10
Net change	0	Net change	0
Position 4			
Various	10	Demand deposit Euro-bank C	– 10
		Demand deposit Swiss firm	+ 10
Net change	0	Net change	0
Position 5			
Various	10	Demand deposit Swiss firm	– 10
		Demand deposit US corporation	+ 10
Net change	0	Net change	0

Assets	$	Liabilities	$
		Euro-bank A	
Position 1			
Demand deposit with US bank	+ 10	Time deposit US resident	+ 10
Net change	+ 10	Net change	+ 10
Position 2			
Demand deposit with US bank	− 10	Time deposit US resident	10
Claim on Euro-bank B	+ 10		
Net change	0	Net change	0
		Euro-bank B	
Position 1			
Demand deposit with US bank	+ 10	Time deposit Euro-bank A	+ 10
Net change	+ 10	Net change	+ 10
Position 2			
Demand deposit with US bank	− 10	Time deposit Euro-bank A	10
Claim on Euro-bank C	+ 10		
Net change	0	Net change	0
		Euro-bank C	
Position 1			
Demand deposit with US bank	+ 10	Time deposit Euro-bank B	+ 10
Net change	+ 10	Net change	+ 10
Position 2			
Demand deposit with US bank	− 10	Time deposit Euro-bank B	10
Loan to Swiss firm	+ 10		
Net change	0	Net change	0

Total Net Changes

	Assets $	Liabilities $
US bank	—	—
Euro-bank A	+ 10	+ 10
Euro-bank B	+ 10	+ 10
Euro-bank C	+ 10	+ 10
TOTAL PRIMARY EURO-DOLLAR CREATION	+ 10	+ 10
TOTAL PYRAMIDED EURO-DOLLAR CREATION	+ 20	+ 20

The process of endogenous Euro-dollar creation is illustrated in Table 14.3 and begins at the point reached in Table 14.2, when the Swiss firm pays the $10 Euro-dollar credit to the US corporation. On this occasion, the US corporation deposits the receipts with Euro-bank A rather than with the US bank. Bank A now incurs a $10 deposit liability to the US corporation and holds a $10 deposit claim on the US bank (position 2). Two basic possibilities now arise:

Euro-bank A might lend the $10 to a second US corporation which utilises the funds for purely domestic purposes, in which case the deposit leaves the market and the process of endogenous deposit creation ceases. An additional $10 of international purchasing power (in effect a second final use credit) will have been created through endogenous deposit creation. (Primary and pyramided deposits — assets plus liabilities — will remain unchanged at $20 and $40 respectively.)

Alternatively, Euro-bank A might redeposit the funds with Euro-bank B. This might arise, for example, if bank A specialised in deposit intermediation and eschewed the higher risks and returns of final use lending for the lower risks and returns of inter-bank intermediation, preferring to leave such lending to more risk-oriented banks. The final outcome would depend on whether the deposit was further intermediated or whether it was extended as a final use credit, in which case either it might leave the market, thereby precluding further direct Euro-dollar activity, or it might be redeposited, thereby precipitating a further round of endogenous deposit creation.

A special form of endogenous deposit creation, involving increases in both Euro-dollar deposits and foreign exchange reserves, arises when central banks deposit dollar reserves in the Euro-dollar market and the reserves, now in deposit form, are loaned to borrowers who use them to purchase domestic currencies either from those central banks with whom the reserves originated or from other central banks. If the central banks supplying the domestic currencies redeposit their newly acquired reserves in the Euro-dollar market, this will result in a further increase in both Euro-dollar assets and liabilities and the statistical inflation of foreign exchange reserves.

Euro-currency creation in practice

The practical creation of Euro-currency deposits in general, and of

Table 14.3: Endogenous Euro-dollar creation.

Assets	$	Liabilities	$
	US bank		
Position 1			
Various	10	Demand deposit Euro-bank C	10
Position 2			
Various	10	Demand deposit Euro-bank C	− 10
		Demand deposit Swiss firm	+ 10
Net change	0	Net change	0
Position 3			
Various	10	Demand deposit Swiss firm	− 10
		Demand deposit US corporation	+ 10
Net change	0	Net change	0
Position 4			
Various	10	Demand deposit US corporation	− 10
		Demand deposit Euro-bank A	+ 10
Net change	0	Net change	0
	Euro-bank A		
Position 1			
Claim on Euro-bank B	10	Time deposit US resident	10
Position 2			
Demand deposit with US bank	+ 10	Time deposit US corporation	+ 10
Net change	+ 10	Net change	+ 10
	Euro-bank B		
Position 1			
Claim on Euro-bank C	10	Time deposit Euro-bank A	10
	Euro-bank C		
Position 1			
Demand deposit with US bank	10	Time deposit Euro-bank B	10
Position 2			
Demand deposit with US bank	− 10	Time deposit Euro-bank B	10
Loan to Swiss firm	+ 10		
Net change	0	Net change	0

Total Net Changes

	Assets $	Liabilities $
US bank	—	—
Euro-bank A	+ 20	+ 20
Euro-bank B	+ 10	+ 10
Euro-bank C	+ 10	+ 10
TOTAL PRIMARY EURO-DOLLAR CREATION	+ 10	+ 10
TOTAL PYRAMIDED EURO-DOLLAR CREATION	+ 20	+ 20
TOTAL ENDOGENOUS EURO-DOLLAR CREATION	+ 10	+ 10

Euro-dollar deposits in particular, has been a contentious issue, focusing principally on whether Euro-dollars are the result of concomitant or cumulative US payments deficits, whether they emanate from US gross capital outflows or whether they are, in fact, the product of endogenous deposit creation.

US payments deficits constitute a prodigious potential source of Euro-dollar deposits, although it is difficult to establish a determinate causal relationship between deficits and the growth of the Euro-dollar market, since deficits merely place dollar claims at the disposal of US non-residents who may or may not transfer them to the Euro-dollar market. In other words, deficits could — but do not necessarily — create deposits, which are entirely consistent with balance of payments equilibria or even with balance of payments surpluses. The $26 billion growth of Euro-Deutsche Mark liabilities between 1971 and 1974, for example, corresponded to a $19 billion accumulated German payments surplus over the same period, which tends to refute the alleged *a priori* link between payments deficits and Euro-currency growth.

A second major potential source of Euro-dollar deposits is US gross capital outflows which are capable of financing increases in Euro-dollar deposits, without corresponding increases in US payments deficits, through the circular flow of dollar claims from the US to Europe. The transfer of demand deposits from the US to Europe, initiated by either US residents or non-residents, will create Euro-dollar deposits whose impact on the US balance of payments will depend on the form and ownership of the original dollar assets and the uses to which these deposits are put. Several flows are consistent with substantial Euro-dollar creation and a zero net change in the US balance of payments, the most prevalent of which arises from the simple transfer to Europe of private US non-resident claims on the US banking system and the maintenance of these claims in private circulation outside the US. This will increase both Euro-dollar assets and liabilities without any corresponding net change in either the US banking system or the US balance of payments. (If these deposits were subsequently used to finance US exports, the transaction would be recorded as a capital inflow which would finance a current account surplus but which would still be consistent with the original creation of Euro-dollar deposits.)

A significant volume of Euro-dollars may thus be created through US gross capital outflows independently of US payments deficits or net changes in US liquid liabilities to foreigners. Given the institutional mechanics of the Euro-dollar market and the substantial

268

increase in net capital outflows (principally errors and omissions) recorded during periods of speculative activity, it seems most likely that US gross capital outflows have proved a significant source of Euro-dollar creation.

Endogenous Euro-dollar deposit creation is a complex issue which involves the extent to which the reserve ratios (if any) maintained by Euro-banks against deposit liabilities reflect the market's credit-creating potential. The way reserve ratios are derived raises serious conceptual and computational problems, such as the selection of an appropriate measure of Euro-dollar reserves and the selective application of this measure to Euro-dollar and non-Euro-dollar transactions. A serious fundamental shortcoming, moreover, arises from the very assumption that there is a quantifiable determinate relationship between market reserve ratios and total Euro-dollar positions. This has invited direct comparisons between the Euro-dollar market and conventional domestic banking systems, with the consequent adoption of the reciprocal of the market's reserve ratio as a statistical measure of the Euro-dollar market's deposit multiplier. Such reasoning is fallacious, however, for any given reserve ratio is consistent with a redeposit ratio of 0 per cent to 100 per cent. It is consequently erroneous to derive a deposit multiplier on the basis of a reserve ratio which is consistent with a potentially low redeposit (high leakages) ratio. This failing is of particular relevance to the late 1960s, when US banks' Euro-dollar borrowing reduced alternative deposit usage (low redeposit ratio) and attendant scope for endogenous deposit creation.

Because of the lack of quantifiable data when measuring the size of the Euro-dollar market's deposit multiplier, the market's endogenous deposit-creating capacity remains a contentious issue.

MARKET QUANTIFICATION

Euro-currency activity was originally confined to European banks' foreign currency positions which represented claims on, and liabilities to, bank and non-bank residents and non-residents. The term 'Euro', however, now extends to embrace activities conducted in non-European centres and, especially since the dismantling of US capital controls in 1974, also incorporates non-resident positions denominated in domestic (predominantly dollar) currencies. Consequently the terms 'Euro-currency activity' and 'international banking activity' are often used interchangeably, even though technically the former constitutes only part of the latter.

The growth of international banking activity is shown in Table 14.4. This shows that the gross external assets of banks reporting to the Bank for International Settlements (BIS), which is the central banks' bank, increased through the early 1980s to reach $1.8 trillion by the end of 1983. (This figure may be contrasted with the negligible sums outstanding at the end of the 1950s when the Euro-currency market was established.) The elimination of double-counting, which reflects pyramided deposit creation, gives a measure of net international bank lending which also increased throughout the early 1980s to reach $1.1 trillion by the end of 1983.

The market shares of reporting banks are also given in Table 14.4 which shows that, at the end of 1983, banks located in Europe accounted for 58 per cent of gross external assets, the UK accounting for the largest single share. Banks located in the US constituted the second largest source (23 per cent) of gross international bank lending.

The currency distribution of gross external assets in Table 14.4 shows the predominance of foreign currency positions in general and dollar-denominated positions in particular.

Care must be taken in interpreting and applying these positions, however, since market data suffer from a number of conceptual and statistical shortcomings:

The most serious conceptual problem at an aggregate level concerns the question of whether the economic impact of financial markets is more accurately rendered by stock or flow meaures of market activity. This assumes particular significance in the case of the Euro-currency markets, whose hybrid role emphasises both capital stock and flow functions. Stock estimates of outstanding Euro-currency claims may constitute an appropriate measure of Euro-currency capital financing but may prove an equally unreliable indicator of capital flows such as those which arise during periods of currency instability. Flow data, on the other hand, may accurately reflect the velocity of Euro-currency conversions but, by including all financial flows, may distort net capital financing patterns. There is unfortunately no way in which these two functions can be satisfactorily reconciled within the existing framework of Euro-currency data.

The statistical shortcomings of market measures result from:

Firstly, the possible inclusion of only assets or liabilities in statistical analyses, since these positions need not necessarily balance. Banks might, for example, build up substantial net foreign

Table 14.4: Selected international banking data, 1980–3. ($ billions and %)

	1980	1981	1982	1983	Outstanding end of 1983
Gross external domestic and foreign currency assets of reporting banks	241	265	176	108	1,754
Less double-counted pyramided deposits	81	100	81	23	669
Net international bank lending	160	165	95	85	1,085
Gross external domestic and foreign currency assets of reporting:					
European located banks	159 (66)	134 (50)	58 (33)	46 (43)	1,027 (58)
US located banks	40 (17)	76 (29)	107 (61)	33 (30)	396 (23)
Japanese located banks	18 (7)	21 (8)	8 (4)	19 (18)	109 (6)
Other banks	24 (10)	34 (13)	3 (2)	10 (9)	222 (13)
TOTAL	241	265	176	108	1,754
Gross external domestic and foreign currency assets of reporting banks denominated in:					
Domestic currency	70 (29)	100 (38)	129 (73)	50 (46)	569 (33)
Foreign currencies (dollars)	126 (52)	118 (44)	20 (12)	33 (31)	902 (51)
Foreign currencies (non-dollar)	45 (19)	47 (18)	27 (15)	25 (23)	283 (16)
TOTAL	241	265	176	108	1,754

Source: *Bank for International Settlements Annual Reports 1983 and 1984*

currency liabilities which are converted into domestic currencies and used to finance domestic currency lending which would not be reflected in foreign currency assets alone.

Secondly, the exclusion of resident inter-bank positions. Since these might not just represent pyramided deposits, excluding them might lead to underestimation of the full economic impact of market activity.

Thirdly, differing definitions and reporting discrepancies, which result in problems of data comparability and statistical accuracy. For example, in 1980, an $83 billion increase in foreign currency assets *vis-à-vis* residents was excluded from increases in reporting banks' total ($241 billion) external assets denominated in domestic and foreign currencies. These assets also excluded an estimated $42 billion increase in external assets accounted for by non-reporting banks.

These definition inconsistencies partly explain the discrepancies between BIS data and other statistical series such as that published by the Morgan Guaranty Trust Company of New York. Based on foreign currency liabilities, Morgan Guaranty estimates the size of the gross Euro-currency market to be $2.3 trillion at the end of 1983; the BIS estimate is $1.7 trillion.

ESTABLISHMENT

The establishment of the Euro-currency markets can be attributed to a combination of political and economic factors.

Perhaps the earliest political factor of significance occurred in the 1950s, with the Soviet fear of seizure or blocking of dollar balances by the US in the event of an outbreak of hostilities. In a desire to avoid such risks, the Soviets transferred their dollar balances to European banks where they were 'camouflaged' and so protected. These banks attempted to deploy the deposits in a more profitable form than traditional US investments by onlending them as dollar-denominated foreign currency deposits. The demand for these deposits was subsequently augmented by the 1957 sterling support measures which imposed restrictions on third-party sterling trade credits and reduced sterling's role as an international financing medium.

The increasingly widespread use of dollar-denominated foreign currency deposits was also fostered by the actions and accommodating attitudes of central monetary authorities. The market was viewed by the Germans, for example, as a convenient channel through which dollar reserves could be reduced, by the Italians as an additional source of dollar financing, by the Swiss as a profitable outlet for the deployment of trustee funds and by the British as a means of benefiting the UK balance of payments and enhancing London's role as an international entrepot centre. The US authorities also encouraged the use of European dollar balances, albeit indirectly, through the inflexible and non-selective use of **Regulation Q**, which prohibited the payment of interest on demand deposits (deposits with maturities of less than 30 days) and limited the payment of interest on all other time deposits. European banks, in contrast, were free to pay market-determined rates on all dollar deposits, regardless of maturity — a competitive advantage which extended to the lending side of the market, since European banks were not party to dollar cartel agreements, did not require compensating loan balances and were not subject to either deposit insurance or statutory reserve requirements on foreign currency liabilities. These advantages of higher returns and greater liquidity, moreover, were not achieved at the expense of greater political or financial risk, since trading tended to be concentrated in politically stable centres such as London and Paris and confined to prime European banks and the overseas branches of prime US banks.

Further factors contributing to the establishment of the Euro-currency markets were US capital outflows and the stability and confidence provided by the existing order of fixed exchange rates. The former placed a substantial volume of dollar deposits at the disposal of US non-residents, while the latter limited exchange rate fluctuations and enabled the risks associated with the accepting, placing and arbitraging of deposits to be evaluated and more effectively hedged.

Thus, by the late 1950s, the Euro-currency markets had become sufficiently well established to command their own interest rate structure, create a further interest rate parity to which forward exchange rates could adjust, possess the capacity to augment international foreign exchange reserves and, in later years, contribute to international balance of payments financing.

DEVELOPMENT

The development of the Euro-currency markets was subsequently fostered by both private and official attempts to exploit domestic financial rigidities.

273

The major determinant of Euro-dollar activity in the early 1960s was the wide US trading margins established by Regulation Q deposit-rate ceilings and prime rate-determined credit-rate floors. The Euro-dollar market, which was not subject to these constraints, effectively exploited these trading margins by offering higher deposit and lower credit rates. Similar cartel restrictions imposed on European financial transactions denominated in domestic currencies were also exploited by the non-dollar Euro-markets.

Euro-currency growth was also promoted by official market intervention in the form of direct and indirect Euro-currency depositing and borrowing. The Italian monetary authorities, for example, used the Euro-currency markets to regulate domestic liquidity by depositing Euro-dollars both directly and indirectly in exchange for domestic currency deposits, while the UK monetary authorities sanctioned local government Euro-dollar borrowing.

The introduction of US capital controls in 1963 (IET) and their intensification in 1965 (VFCRP) provided a further stimulus to Euro-currency activity by encouraging US corporations to resort to Euro-currency borrowing to finance overseas investment and by obliging US non-residents to rechannel their financing needs to European (Euro-currency) markets.

By the mid-1960s, therefore, the Euro-currency markets had become sufficiently well developed to play an active international financing role which was eventually to embrace international balance of payments financing.

ROLE

The Euro-currency markets' active international financing role emerged first in 1966 and again in 1969 in the form of US banks' Euro-dollar borrowing, undertaken to mitigate the contractionary effects of US monetary policy. By borrowing Euro-dollars either from overseas branches or on an overnight basis, US banks were able individually and collectively to achieve net reserve savings. This borrowing exerted a major expansionary impact on the Euro-dollar market, particularly in 1969 when reporting banks' liabilities increased by $19 billion, more than 50 per cent of which was accounted for in the first six months of the year. The borrowing was not without repercussions, however, since US contractionary pressures were transmitted to Europe. When subsequent repatriations amounted to $13.5 billion in the 18 months ending May 1971,

Europe experienced even more serious monetary dislocation in the form of unwanted capital inflows which were to contribute indirectly to the dollar crises of 1971 and 1973.

The Euro-dollar market's role in the financing of the 1971 dollar crisis did not assume significant proportions, since the principal source of speculative financing was US capital outflows effected through conventional rather than specific Euro-dollar channels. The market's role in the 1973 dollar crisis, in contrast, was more significant, as is reflected in changes in aggregate reporting positions and the positions of US banks' foreign branches.

The Euro-currency markets' most active financing role arose in response to the 1973/74 and 1979/80 oil crises, the former of which was the more significant since it was largely unexpected and occurred at a time when official financing channels had not been developed. The three principal channels through which transfers of wealth from oil importers to oil exporters could have been accommodated were: the US banking system, reserve adjustments and the Euro-dollar market.

The US banking sytem was physically capable of accommodating the flows, but its contribution was limited by the political reluctance of exporting nations to deposit revenues directly with a country which was itself the subject of an oil embargo. The use of reserve adjustments, on the other hand, was limited by the quantitative inadequacy of global reserves and by the deflationary consequences of this means of financing for importing nations. The Euro-dollar market, in contrast, was not only politically acceptable but also had the financial capacity to recycle deposits from exporters to importers.

Demand developments

The role of recycling surpluses from exporters to importers was technically no different from that which the markets had performed since the late 1950s, although an increase in the size of individual credits and a lengthening of maturity transformations were necessitated by the crisis. Where a marked disparity between the markets' pre- and post-oil crisis financing roles did emerge, however, was in terms of the strategic economic and political importance with which this latter role came to be regarded. Not only did the markets' recycling of surpluses enable importing nations to finance their deficits and continue pursuing policies of 'full employment' —

thereby avoiding the necessity of adopting deflationary measures — it also contributed to the avoidance of political problems which might have ensued when importing nations were denied access to oil supplies, either because they could not finance these purchases or because exporters would not accept their resources as a medium of payment or as a store of wealth. The strategic importance of this role was clearly demonstrated by a rapid change in the monetary authorities' attitude to the markets. Whereas in the early 1970s they had been hostile, now they not only condoned Euro-dollar borrowing but also made active recourse to Euro-dollars on their own account, an example of which was the $2.5 billion Euro-dollar credit extended to the UK government in 1974.

Supply developments

Just as the large-scale demands for deficit financing by oil-importing nations had threatened to impose a severe burden on the international monetary system, so the existence of highly liquid and volatile payments surpluses threatened to impose similar burdens on the system's capacity to absorb and recycle these funds. The basic problem arose from exporters' inability to spend all, or even a significant proportion of, their newly acquired wealth and from the need to recycle these surpluses to importing nations if global deflation was to be averted. It was a problem compounded, moreover, by the conflicting interests of exporters and importers, with exporters seeking to maintain their reserves in highly liquid and relatively risk-free forms, while importers sought to finance their deficits on a medium- to long-term basis. There was thus a need to both recycle surpluses from exporters to importers and transform them from short-term deposits into long-term credits.

The Euro-currency markets played a major role in this. Of the $53 billion surplus of oil-exporting countries in 1974 and $56 billion in 1979, the London Euro-currency market alone absorbed $14 billion and $15.5 billion respectively.

The successful recycling of exporters' surpluses and the growth of Euro-currency activity continued throughout the 1970s and into the early 1980s, so that by the second half of 1981, the gross external assets of reporting banks were increasing at a record rate of $370 billion a year, $200 billion of which represented net international bank lending. The onset of the international debt crisis in 1982, however, curtailed both market activity in general and individual trading positions in particular.

The most pronounced effect of the crisis was a marked decline in general Euro-currency activity. This was shown in a deceleration in the annual growth of reporting banks' gross external claims from $265 billion in 1981 to $176 billion and $108 billion in 1982 and 1983 respectively. Similar declines were recorded in the annual growth of international bank lending, from $165 billion in 1981 to $95 billion and $85 billion over the same period (Table 14.4). The greater deceleration in gross assets reflected banks' negative re-appraisal of the risks of inter-bank lending and was particularly pronounced in the case of European located banks, whose total market share declined from 66 per cent in 1980 to 33 per cent in 1982 (Table 14.4).

A second repercussion of the crisis was a significant slow-down in the growth of dollar-denominated foreign currency assets, whose market share declined from 52 per cent in 1980 to 12 per cent in 1982 (Table 14.4). This reflected partly the general decline in market activity and partly the increased exposure of US banks, whose lending was primarily denominated in domestic currency (dollars) and whose market share increased from 17 per cent in 1980 to 61 per cent in 1982 (Table 14.4).

The most serious consequence of the crisis was the decline in new credits extended to individual borrowers. Most severely affected were Eastern European and Latin American sovereign borrowers. The former were particularly affected by Poland's debt servicing difficulties, which contributed to a $4.6 billion absolute decline in reporting banks' gross external claims on this area in 1982. The latter were principally affected by the rescheduling problems of the area's major debtor nations (Argentina, Brazil and Mexico), whose problems contributed to a substantial deceleration in the growth of reporting banks' claims on this area from $31 billion per annum in 1981 to less than $1 billion per annum in the latter half of 1982.

Nevertheless, the fact that the Euro-currency markets seem to have survived the international debt crisis is testimony to their depth and resilience. It remains to be seen, however, whether the markets are capable of further development or whether the continued transfer of international banking activity to US-located banks will result in the consolidation or even, perhaps, retrenchment of Euro-currency activity.

ADVANTAGES

Firstly, the Euro-currency markets have contributed to the international integration of national capital markets. This has reduced transaction costs through economies of large-scale transactions and increased both technical (trading) and allocative (capital utilisation) efficiencies.

Secondly, the markets have provided, particularly in the early 1970s, the financial resources to help fuel and thence sustain LDC growth.

Finally, the markets have, especially since the 1974 oil crisis:

contributed substantially to the international financing of balance of payments deficits;

facilitiated the accommodation of global reserve imbalances;

avoided excessive recession by enabling countries which might otherwise have adopted deflationary measures to pursue policies of full employment;

helped governments to avoid the political crises and even military confrontations which might have ensued from a situation in which oil-importing nations were denied access to oil supplies, either because they lacked the resources necessary to finance purchases or because exporters were unwilling to accept these resources as a medium of payment or as a store of wealth.

DISADVANTAGES

Firstly, the markets might undermine national capital controls and exacerbate the problems of monetary management by providing alternative capital sources and uses;

Secondly, they might contribute to monetary and exchange rate instability by providing financial resources which are readily mobilised and easily convertible;

Thirdly, the markets might contribute to the misallocation of resources if these are provided on an 'unconditional' market basis and used to finance consumption rather than investment.

Finally, the unregulated nature of Euro-currency activity might directly, or indirectly through the generation of deregulatory pressures, undermine the stability of national capital markets.

SUMMARY

Euro-currency activity, which is the transacting of foreign currency deposits, is conducted in Euro-currency markets, of which the largest is the Euro-dollar market. Banks intermediate deposits between sources and uses, either of which consists of banks or non-banks. The bid and offer rates are the rates at which banks accept and lend deposits. The London Inter-Bank Offer Rate acts as an international reference rate for non-bank credits which are rolled-over regularly and form the basis of medium-term Euro-currency lending.

Euro-currency deposits, such as Euro-dollar deposits, can be created in three ways. Primary Euro-dollar creation arises when dollar deposits are transferred from US banks to banks located outside the US and deposited at Euro-dollar rates of interest. Pyramided Euro-dollar creation arises when Euro-dollar deposits are intermediated by one or more banks before eventually being loaned to final use borrowers. Endogenous Euro-dollar creation arises when the market creates its own endogenous supply of final use credits, additional to those arising from the market's intermediation of deposits from the US to Europe. In practice, US payments deficits are a sufficient but not necessary source of primary Euro-dollar deposits, while US gross capital outflows are a potentially prodigious source of such deposits. The creation of endogenous Euro-dollar deposits is constrained by a potentially low redeposit (high leakages) ratio.

Euro-currency activity can be quantified in two basic ways: Banks' gross external domestic and foreign currency assets are a measure of overall positions, while the elimination of double-counted pyramided deposits from these positions provides a measure of net international bank lending.

The Euro-currency markets became established in the late 1950s in response to a combination of political and economic factors. Their subsequent development was fostered by both private and official attempts to exploit domestic financial rigidities. The markets' international financing role was fostered by: US banks' Euro-dollar borrowing, the dollar crises of 1971 and 1973 and the oil crises of 1973/74 and 1979/80. In this latter case, the Euro-dollar market played a major role in recycling surpluses from oil exporters to oil importers and in transforming these surpluses from short-term deposits into longer-term credits. The onset of the international debt crisis in 1982, however, curtailed both market activity in general and individual trading positions in particular. While the markets appear to have survived the crisis, it remains to be seen whether they are capable of further development in their present form.

The principal advantage of the Euro-currency markets is that they have contributed to the international integration of national capital markets. The principal disadvantages are that they might undermine national capital controls, exacerbate the problem of monetary management and contribute to monetary and exchange rate instability.

CONCEPTS FOR REVIEW

Bid rate	London Inter-Bank Offer Rate
Endogenous Euro-dollar creation	Offer rate
Euro-currency activity	Primary Euro-dollar creation
Euro-currency markets	Pyramided Euro-dollar creation
Euro-dollar market	Regulation Q
International Banking Facilities	Roll-over credits

QUESTIONS FOR DISCUSSION

1. How are the Euro-currency and foreign exchange markets distinguished?
2. Distinguish between primary, pyramided and endogenous Euro-dollar deposit creation.
3. Is pyramided deposit creation economically meaningful?
4. Assess the strategic importance of the Euro-currency markets' role in absorbing and transforming the surpluses of petroleum-exporting countries.
5. Have the Euro-currency markets helped or hindered international economic development?

15

Currency Futures and Options

Currency futures and options are a recent development, futures having emerged in the early 1970s and options in the early 1980s, each in response to the growth of international trade and the increase in exchange rate volatility. They are two further channels through which hedging, speculation and arbitration can be conducted, and provide the means by which the risks, profits and revenues associated with exchange rate fluctuations may be hedged, exploited and generated.

Currency futures are contracts specifying the *obligation* to buy or sell standard amounts of currencies at a future date at current specified prices.

Currency options are contracts specifying the *right* to buy or sell standard amounts of currencies on (European options) or until (US options) a future date at current specified prices.

In practice, trading in futures and options extends to include contracts on financial instruments such as stock index futures and options on stock index futures.

SIMILARITIES

Contracts are traded in organised markets with specific physical locations. Futures are traded, for example, on the International Money Market (IMM) at the Chicago Mercantile Exchange, and options are principally traded on the Philadelphia Stock Exchange. This is in direct contrast to spot and forward currency markets, which have no specific location but in which currencies are traded amongst banks and brokers by telecommunication links.

Contracts involve standard amounts of specified currencies. The sizes and denominations of IMM futures are £25,000, C$100,000, SwFr 125,000, DM 125,000 and ¥12.5 million. Philadelphia options are one half of these amounts. Spot and forward transactions, in contrast, are not limited to specific quantities or specified currencies.

Contracts have standardised maximum maturities of typically three, six or nine months. Forward contract maturities, in contrast, are not standardised and are subject to individual negotiations.

Contracts are guaranteed by and cleared through a centralised clearing corporation. This eliminates the credit risk involved in forward transactions which are conducted directly between individual trading parties.

DIFFERENCES

The principal distinction between futures and options is that futures *oblige* buyers to buy or sell foreign currencies (unless the contract has been sold prior to maturity), whereas options confer the *right* but not the obligation on buyers to buy or sell foreign currencies.

Futures are fulfilled only on specified maturity dates whereas options (US) may be exercised at any time up to the specified maturity date. Futures buyers thus take receipt or make delivery of currencies at the expiry of the three, six or nine months' maturity date (unless the contract has been resold prior to its maturity), whereas options buyers may take receipt or make delivery of currencies (spot) at any time up to the option's maturity.

Futures attract margin requirements (security deposits), whereas options, which are paid for at the outset of the contract, do not.

Options enable transactions which might not arise (contingencies) to be hedged since, should such contingencies not, in fact, emerge, the option can simply be allowed to expire.

OPERATION

Futures

Futures prices are illustrated in panel (a) of Table 15.1, which shows the dollar prices of Deutsche Marks ($/DM) for contracts of DM125,000 for delivery in September, December, March and June 1985. Columns (i) through (viii) show: the range over the life of the

Table 15.1: Deutsche Mark futures and options prices, 17 September 1984.

Season High (i)	Low (ii)	Maturity (iii)	High (iv)	Day Low (v)	Close (vi)	Change (vii)	Open Interest (viii)
.4037	.3288	SEP	.3266	.3247	.3247	−0.0043	8,518
.4080	.3340	DEC	.3316	.3279	.3283	−0.0058	29,800
.4110	.3388	MAR	.3362	.3322	.3328	−0.0061	1,067
.3733	.3440	JUN	.3410	.3385	.3380	−0.0060	65

Contract size: DM125,000
(a) Deutsche Mark Futures Prices ($/DM) — Chicago Mercantile Exchange

Current spot rate (i)	Strike price (ii)	Call premiums Sep (iii)	Dec (iv)	Mar (v)	Put premiums Sep (vi)	Dec (vii)	Mar (viii)
32.34	32	s	1.55	2.02	s	0.60	r
32.34	33	s	0.85	1.44	s	1.04	1.20
32.34	34	r	0.47	1.02	r	1.79	1.85
32.34	35	r	0.25	0.71	r	r	r
32.34	36	r	0.17	0.46	r	3.32	r
32.34	37	r	0.07	0.29	r	r	4.45
32.34	38	r	r	0.20	r	r	r
32.34	39	r	0.03	0.12	r	r	r

r — Not traded
s — No option offered

Contract size: DM 62,500
(b) Deutsche Mark Options Prices (¢/DM) — Philadelphia Exchange

Source: The *New York Times*, 18 September 1984.

contract (i) and (ii), the maturity date of the contract (iii), the day's trading range (iv) and (v), the closing (settlement) price (vi), the change from the previous day (vii) and the number of contracts outstanding with the exchange (open interest) (viii). The December row, for example, shows that the price of Deutsche Marks for December delivery is $0.3283/DM.

Futures contracts enable market operators to profit from or hedge against exchange rate movements. A speculator, for example, who expects the December price (spot rate) of Deutsche Marks to rise above $0.3283 (Deutsche Mark appreciation), will contract to buy Deutsche Marks for December delivery at $0.3283/DM in anticipation of selling the Deutsche Marks in the spot market at the higher prevailing price. The profit or loss realised will equal the December spot exchange rate less the previously contracted futures price less transaction (brokerage) costs. For example, if the Deutsche Mark appreciates to a spot exchange rate of $0.3583/DM at the expiry of the futures contract, profits will amount to $3,750 ($0.3583/DM − $0.3283/DM × DM 125,000) minus transaction costs. In the same way, a US importer, who expects to make a payment of DM 125,000 in December, might hedge the foreign exchange risk by contracting to buy Deutsche Marks for December delivery at $0.3283/DM. If the December spot rate increases to $0.3583/DM (Deutsche Mark appreciation), the importer avoids the additional exchange rate costs ($3,750) resulting from the purchase of Deutsche Marks in the December spot market. If the December spot rate decreases to $0.2983/DM (Deutsche Mark depreciation), however, the importer forgoes the opportunity of reducing exchange rate costs by $3,750.

Regardless of the exchange rate prevailing in the December spot market, however, both the speculator and the importer are obliged to take delivery of December Deutsche Marks, unless the futures contract has been resold prior to its maturity. The size of the speculator's profits or losses and of the importer's decrease or increase in implicit costs are thus unlimited, being constrained only by the range of future (indeterminate) spot exchange rate movements.

Options

A **call option** confers on option buyers the *right* to buy and on option sellers (option writers) the *obligation* to sell currencies on (European options) or until (US options) a future date at a current specified price. A **put option** confers on option buyers the *right* to sell and on option sellers (option writers) the *obligation* to buy currencies on (European options) or until (US options) a future date at a current specified price. The specified price at which currencies are contracted for receipt or delivery is the **exercise** or **strike price**. The price of the option (call or put) is called the **premium** and is paid by the buyer to the seller. The buyer thus pays for the right to buy/sell currencies, while the seller is compensated for the risk inherent in contracting to sell/buy currencies.

Option prices are illustrated in panel (b) of Table 15.1, which shows the dollar prices ($/DM), at different strike prices, of call and put options for contracts of DM62,500 for delivery in September, December and March 1985. Columns (i) through (viii) show: the current spot rate (i), the strike price (ii), premiums for call options expiring on or before September, December and March (iii, iv and v) and premiums for put options expiring on or before September, December and March (vi, vii and viii). The December call column, for example, shows that the cost of buying spot Deutsche Marks for receipt on or before December is 1.55¢/DM at a strike price of 32¢/DM, while the December put column, for example, shows that the cost of selling spot Deutsche Marks for delivery on or before December is 0.60¢/DM at a strike price of 32¢/DM.

The December call column also shows an inverse relationship between the strike price and the call option premium. This indicates the diminishing probability, reflected in reduced premiums, that the future Deutsche Mark spot rate will rise appreciably above the current spot rate of 32.34¢/DM (Deutsche Mark appreciation). A speculator, for example, who nevertheless expects the spot price of Deutsche Marks to rise above 39¢/DM by December might be willing to pay 0.03¢/DM for the right to *buy* Deutsche Marks at 39¢/DM for subsequent resale in the spot market at an anticipated price (including transactions costs) in excess of 39.03¢/DM. The speculator will exercise the call option if the spot price exceeds this level, but will allow it to expire if it fails to reach this level, in which case the speculator's loss will be confined to 0.03¢/DM. Total loss on DM 62,500 option: $18.75.

Similarly, the December put column shows a direct relationship between the strike price and the put option premium. This indicates the increasing probability, reflected in increased premiums, that the future Deutsche Mark spot rate will remain below successively higher strike prices (close to the spot rate of 32.34¢/DM). A speculator, however, who expects the spot price of Deutsche Marks to fall by December might be willing to pay 3.32¢/DM for the right to *sell*, at 36¢/DM, Deutsche Marks simultaneously purchased in the spot market at a price (including transactions costs) below 32.68¢/DM. The speculator will exercise the put option if the spot price falls below this level but will allow it to expire if it remains above this level, in which case the speculator's loss will be confined to 3.32¢/DM. Total loss on DM62,500 option: $2,075.

The relationship between profit/loss and the strike price is illustrated in Figure 15.1. Panel (a) shows a call option with a strike price of 39¢/DM and a premium of 0.03¢/DM. The cost of the option is $18.75 (0.03¢/DM × DM 62,500). The option buyer incurs a loss (including transactions costs) when the spot price remains below 39.03¢/DM. The buyer will then be 'out of the money' and will allow the option to expire (solid line). The option becomes profitable, on the other hand, when the spot price exceeds 39.03¢/DM, in which case the buyer is said to be 'in the money' and will exercise the option (broken line). The call option buyer's loss is thus confined to the size of the total premium, while his profit is potentially unlimited. The call option seller's (writer's) loss, in contrast, is potentially unlimited, while his profit is confined to the size of the total premium.

Panel (b) of Figure 15.1 illustrates a put option with a strike price of 36¢/DM and a premium of 3.32¢/DM. The cost of the option is $2,075 (3.32¢/DM × DM62,500). The option buyer incurs a loss (including transactions costs) when the spot price remains above 32.68¢/DM. The buyer will then be 'out of the money' and will allow the option to expire (solid line). The option becomes profitable, on the other hand, when the spot price falls below 32.68¢/DM, in which case the buyer is 'in the money' and will exercise the option (broken line). The put option buyer's loss is thus similarly confined to the size of the total premium, while his profit is potentially unlimited. The put option seller's (writer's) loss is again potentially unlimited, while his profit is confined to the size of the total premium.

Option buyers (call and put) benefit from exchange rate volatility, while option sellers (call and put) benefit from exchange rate stability. These benefits may be further exploited through **straddles** which represent the simultaneous purchase of a call and put option with the same strike price and maturity. Straddle buyers benefit from exchange rate fluctuations above and below strike prices, while straddle sellers (writers) benefit from exchange rate stability. Panel

Figure 15.1: Call, put and straddle option purchases. In panel (a), the call option buyer/seller benefits as the spot price rises above/remains below 39.03¢/DM. In panel (b), the put option buyer/seller benefits as the spot price falls below/remains above 32.68¢/DM. In panel (c), the straddle option buyer benefits as the spot price rises above 45¢/DM or falls below 35¢/DM and the seller benefits if the spot price remains within this range.

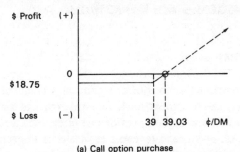

(a) Call option purchase

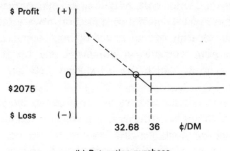

(b) Put option purchase

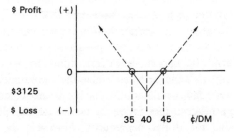

(c) Straddle purchase

287

(c) of Figure 15.1 illustrates a hypothetical straddle with a strike price of 40¢/DM and a combined premium of 5¢/DM. The cost of the straddle is $3,125 (5¢/DM × DM62,500). This determines the loss incurred/profit realised by the straddle buyer/seller, if the spot price remains between 35¢/DM and 45¢/DM (solid line). Correspondingly, the profit realised/loss incurred by the straddle buyer/seller will be determined by the extent to which the spot price rises above 45¢/DM or falls below 35¢/DM.

ADVANTAGES

Currency futures and options offer significant trading advantages, both absolutely and in comparison to forward exchange transactions:

Firstly, futures and options provide two further channels through which the risks, profits and revenues associated with exchange rate volatility may be hedged, exploited and generated.

Secondly, trading in foreign currencies is facilitated by the standardised sizes and maturities of futures and options contracts.

Thirdly, the transaction costs of futures and options may be lower than those for equivalent quantities traded in forward markets.

Fourthly, the clearing of futures and options contracts through a centralised clearing corporation eliminates the credit risks of forward transactions, which are conducted between individual trading parties.

Fifthly, option purchase losses are confined to the size of the purchase premium, while profits are potentially unlimited. This asymmetry enables contingencies (events whose occurrence is uncertain) to be more effectively hedged with options than with futures or forward contracts. A German corporation, for example, might expect to sell a patent for US dollars whose Deutsche Mark value is to be hedged. The purchase of a Deutsche Mark future will expose the corporation to foreign exchange risk if the patent sale fails to materialise and the corporation is consequently required to deliver dollars which it does not possess. The purchase of a Deutsche Mark call option, however, limits the corporation's foreign exchange risk and potential loss to the premium paid for the option. If the sale fails to materialise, or if the sale materialises but the dollar appreciates, the option is not exercised. If the sale materialises and the dollar depreciates, however, the option is exercised.

Sixthly, option purchases are not subject to margin requirements, since purchase premiums are paid in full at the outset of contracts.

Finally, option premiums constitute an additional source of income for option writers.

DISADVANTAGES

Firstly, futures and options lack the flexibility of forward transactions which may be contracted for varying amounts and maturities.

Secondly, futures purchases are subject to margin requirements which may increase in frequency and intensity if exchange rates move against buyers.

Thirdly, futures and options provide considerable trading leverage which may destabilise currency markets.

SUMMARY

Currency futures and options provide two further channels through which hedging, speculation and arbitrage may be conducted. Contracts are traded in organised markets with specific physical locations and in standard amounts. The contracts have standardised maximum maturities and are guaranteed by and cleared through a centralised clearing corporation.

Currency futures are contracts specifying the obligation to buy or sell currencies at a future date at current specified prices.

Currency options are contracts specifying the right to buy or sell currencies on or until a future date at current specified prices. A call option confers on option buyers the right to buy and on option sellers the obligation to sell, while a put option confers on option buyers the right to sell and on option sellers the obligation to buy currencies. The specified price at which currencies are contracted for receipt or delivery is the exercise or strike price. The price of the option (call or put) is called the premium and is paid by the buyer to the seller. Straddles are the simultaneous purchase of a call and put option with the same strike price and maturity.

The principal advantages of futures and options are: improved foreign currency trading facilities, potentially lower transactions costs, reduced credit risks and limited options trading losses. Their major disadvantage is that they are potentially less flexible than forward transactions.

CONCEPTS FOR REVIEW

Call option	Option premium
Currency futures	Put option
Currency options	Straddles
Exercise or strike price	

QUESTIONS FOR DISCUSSION

1. Explain why option buyers are exposed to limited losses and unlimited potential profits while option sellers are exposed to limited profits and unlimited potential losses.
2. Contrast the potential profits/losses which a 'bull' speculator in Deutsche Marks might incur using futures, with profits/losses incurred using options.
3. Why might options enable contingencies to be more effectively hedged than futures?

Selected Further Reading

GENERAL TEXTS

A more advanced text which, despite its years, is still highly recommended, is:
Stern, R.M., *The Balance of Payments: Theory and Economic Policy* (Aldine Publishing Company, New York, 1973).

At a similar level is:
Heller, H.R., *International Monetary Economics* (Prentice-Hall, New Jersey, 1974).

A broader treatment of International Finance is found in:
Levi, M., *International Finance: Financial Management and the International Economy* (McGraw-Hill, New York, 1983).

More general texts, which also include Trade Theory, are:
Chacholiades, M., *Principles of International Economics* (McGraw-Hill, New York, 1981).
Grubel, H.G., *International Economics* (Richard D. Irwin, Illinois, 1981).
Lindert, P.H. and Kindleberger, C.P., *International Economics*, 7th edition (Richard D. Irwin, Illinois, 1982).

More recent, less advanced treatments of International Finance can be found in most macroeconomics texts, including:
Cargill, T.F., *Money, The Financial System and Monetary Policy*, 3rd edition (Prentice-Hall, New Jersey, 1986).
Dornbush, R. and Fischer, S., *Macroeconomics*, 3rd edition (McGraw-Hill, New York, 1984).

Froyen, R.T., *Macro-Economics: Theories and Policies*, 2nd edition (Macmillan, New York, 1986).

Ritter, L.S. and Silber, W.L., *Principles of Money, Banking and Financial Markets*, 5th edition (Basic Books, New York, 1986).

FINANCIAL PUBLICATIONS

Developments in International Finance are frequently and often extensively analysed in financial publications such as:
Bank of England Quarterly Bulletin
Bank for International Settlements Annual Report
Bank for International Settlements Economic Papers
Euromoney
Morgan Guaranty Trust Company of New York: *World Financial Markets*
The Banker
UK Banks: *Reports* and *Reviews*
US Federal Reserve Banks: *Reports* and *Reviews*

Articles on International Finance of topical interest are regularly found in:
Far Eastern Economic Review
Financial Times
The Asian Wall Street Journal
The Economist
The Wall Street Journal

CHAPTER READINGS

Chapter 2: Capital Flows and the Foreign Exchange Market

Chrystal, K.A., 'A Guide to Foreign Exchange Markets', *Federal Reserve Bank of St Louis Review*, Vol. 66 No. 3, March 1984, pp. 5–18.

Levi, M., *International Finance: Financial Management and the International Economy* (McGraw-Hill, New York, 1983), Chapters 2, 3, 7.

Chapter 3: The Balance of Payments

Kindleberger, C.P., 'Measuring Equilibrium in the Balance of Payments', *Journal of Political Economy*, Vol. 77 No. 6, Nov/Dec 1969, pp. 873–891.

Kubarych, R.M., 'Financing the US Current Account Deficit', *Federal Reserve Bank of New York Quarterly Review*, Vol. 9 No. 2, Summer 1984, pp. 24–31.

—— *Survey of Current Business*, US Department of Commerce, various issues.

Chapter 4: The Gold Standard

Argy, V., *The Postwar International Money Crisis — An Analysis* (Allen and Unwin, London, 1981), Chapter 1.

Schwartz, A.J., 'Alternative Monetary Regimes: The Gold Standard', in *Alternative Monetary Regimes*, ed. C.D. Campbell and W.R. Dougan (Johns Hopkins University Press, Baltimore, 1986).

Chapter 5: Fixed Exchange Rates

Batten, D.S. and Ott, M., 'What Can Central Banks Do About the Value of the Dollar?' *Federal Reserve Bank of St Louis Review*, Vol. 66 No. 5, May 1984, pp. 16–26.

Mayer, H. and Taguchi, H., 'Official Intervention in the Exchange Markets: Stabilising or Destabilising?', *BIS Economic Papers No. 6*, March 1983.

Chapter 6: Floating Exchange Rates

Bergstrand, J.H., 'Is Exchange Rate Volatility Excessive?', *Federal Reserve Bank of Boston: New England Economic Review*, Sept/Oct 1983, pp. 5–14.

Carlozzi, N., 'Exchange Rate Volatility: Is Intervention The Answer?', *Federal Reserve Bank of Philadelphia Business Review*, Nov/Dec 1983, pp. 3–10.

Friedman, M., 'The Case for Flexible Exchange Rates', in: M. Friedman, *Essays in Positive Economics* (University of Chicago Press, Chicago, 1953), pp. 157–203.

Mayer, H. 'The Theory and Practice of Floating Exchange Rates and the Role of Official Exchange-Market Intervention', *BIS Economic Papers No. 5*, February 1982.

Chapter 7: Alternative Exchange Rate Systems

Ungerer, H. with Evans, O. and Nyberg, P. *The European Monetary System: The Experience, 1979–82*, Occasional Paper 19, IMF, Washington DC 1983.
——— *World Financial Markets*, Morgan Guaranty Trust Company of New York, August 1985.

Chapter 8: External Disequilibrium and Current Account Adjustment

Heller, H.R. *International Monetary Economics* (Prentice-Hall, New Jersey, 1974), Chapters 6, 7, 8.
Alexander, S.S. 'Effects of a Devaluation on a Trade Balance', reprinted in *Readings in International Economics* (Richard D. Irwin, Illinois, 1968), pp. 359–373.

Chapter 9: Internal and External Equilibrium
Chapter 10: Internal and External Equilibrium with Fixed Exchange Rates
Chapter 11: Internal and External Equilibrium with Floating Exchange Rates

Chacholiades, M., *Principles of International Economics*, (McGraw-Hill, New York, 1981), Chapters 16, 17, 20, 21.
Froyen, R.T. *Macro-economics: Theories and Policies*, 2nd edition (Macmillan, New York, 1986), Chapter 17.
Hakkio, C.S. and Higgins, B., 'Is the United States Too Dependent on Foreign Capital?', *Federal Reserve Bank of Kansas City Economic Review*, June 1985, pp. 23–36.
Stern, R.M., *The Balance of Payments: Theory and Economic Policy* (Aldine Publishing Company, New York, 1973), Chapter 10.
Tanzi, V. and Blejer, M.I., 'Fiscal Deficits and Balance of Payments Disequilibrium in IMF Adjustment Programs', in

Adjustment, Conditionality and International Financing, ed. J. Muns, IMF, Washington DC, 1984, pp. 117–136.

Chapter 12: The Monetary Approach to External Equilibrium

Kreinin, M.E. and Officer, L.H. *The Monetary Approach to the Balance of Payments: A Survey* Princeton Studies in International Finance No. 43, New Jersey, 1978.

Chapter 13: Post-war Issues and Developments

Hakkio, C.S. and Whittaker, J.G., 'The US Dollar — Recent Developments, Outlook and Policy Options', *Federal Reserve Bank of Kansas City Economic Review*, Sept/Oct 1985, pp. 3–15.

Solomon, R., *The International Monetary System, 1945–1981* (Harper and Row, New York, 1982).

Tew, B., *The Evolution of the International Monetary System, 1945–1981* (Hutchinson, London, 1982).

—— *World Financial Markets* Morgan Guaranty Trust Company of New York, Oct/Nov 1984 and Jan 1986.

—— *The US Dollar — Recent Developments, Outlook and Policy Options*, proceedings of a symposium sponsored by the Federal Reserve Bank of Kansas City, Wyoming 1985.

Halm, G.N., *A Guide to International Monetary Reform* (Lexington Books, Massachusetts, 1975).

Chapter 14: The Euro-currency Markets

Chrystal, K.A., 'International Banking Facilities', *Federal Reserve Bank of St Louis Review*, Vol. 66 No. 4, April 1984, pp. 5–11.

Kane, D.R., *The Eurodollar Market and the Years of Crisis* (Croom Helm Ltd, London, 1983).

Chapter 15: Currency Futures and Options

Chrystal, K.A., 'A Guide to Foreign Exchange Markets', *Federal Reserve Bank of St Louis Review*, Vol. 66 No. 3, March 1984, pp. 5–18.

Gendreau, B., 'New Markets in Foreign Currency Options', *Federal Reserve Bank of Philadelphia Business Review*, July/August 1984, pp. 3–12.

—— *Understanding Futures in Foreign Exchange* International Monetary Market of the Chicago Mercantile Exchange, Chicago, 1979.

Index